Walking

e2e

LINDA BRACKENBURY

Published by Linda Brackenbury, 127 Glandon Drive, Cheadle Hulme, Cheadle, Cheshire. SK8 7HD

First edition

Printed by
Deanprint Ltd, Cheadle Heath Works, Stockport Rd, Stockport. SK3 0PR

Whilst every effort has been made to ensure that the information in this book is correct, the author or the publisher can accept no responsibility for errors, loss or injury however caused.

The map sketches in this book are intended as a rough guide only and should not be used for navigational purposes.

Brackwalks

http://www.brackwalks.co.uk

ISBN: 978-0-9931833-0-0
A catalogue record for this book is available from the British Library

CONTENTS

Pre-amble

There are many accounts of end-to-end walks between Land's End and John O'Groats but most are a personal account of how the author fared, accompanied by a summary of the route. This book is a detailed route description, as well as a few personal comments, derived from notes I took during a continuous end-to-end (e2e) walk, designed to be unsupported, between April and June of 2012. It represents what was actually found and followed rather than what can be seen on maps.

Having read many accounts of off-road end-to-end walks, I have been struck by the large amount of mileage most participants do. This usually results from the inclusion of national trails which are usually not particularly direct. Many walkers choose to use the Pennine Way up the spine of England. This ends at Kirk Yetholm on the east side of Scotland and walkers then often cross to the west side to follow the West Highland Way from just north of Glasgow to Fort William. The Great Glen Way to Inverness on the east side of Scotland can then be taken. This means that most walkers will cross Scotland from side to side twice, adding to the mileage. Furthermore, once at Inverness it is difficult to escape the A9 racetrack in getting to John O'Groats, as the A9 follows the coastline and there are few roads and tracks inland. By using the national trails it is not unusual for walkers to clock up a mileage of at least 1,200 miles.

Having done and enjoyed most of the national trails used in getting to John O'Groats and not being a lover of heights, making the south-west coastal path a no-go area, I chose to devise my own off-road route in the belief that an interesting walk using tracks and paths with much less mileage should be possible. The walk described is 1,035 miles with over 101,000ft of ascent split into 71 stages. The distance described is the equivalent of walking four Pennine Ways (4PWs) and this turns out to be a nice way of measuring progress in reaching John O'Groats. The first PW is completed at St Briavels in Gloucestershire, whilst the second is at the halfway point of Carlingill Bridge in the Howgill Fells and the third is on the stage to Dalwhinnie in the Scottish Highlands.

Throughout the whole route I have sought neither to use nor avoid available trails. Official routes often meander as their aim is to demonstrate the best features of an area. Thus I have only used parts of them in those places where they provide a direct line of travel to where I wish to go. As a result, the

1

described end-to-end route may join a trail then come off it to follow some alternative route, which might or might not rejoin the trail at some later point. People claim that the advantage of using the trails is that they are better maintained and marked than other rights of way. This is usually true but not always and a number of routes appear very unloved!

Rules

Every walk has its rules about what's allowed and what's not allowed. My rules are that the feet have to contact solid ground throughout the e2e route. Therefore ferry rides as part of the route are not permitted. However, being picked up to go off-route to accommodation is permissible, provided that on leaving the route some object is tagged (e.g. a gatepost) with the same feature being touched on resuming the route. Bag carrying is allowed and we were fortunate in being able to carry day sacks on 15 stages; we carried all our gear on all the other stages.

Route Overview

After a small coastal section from Land's End to St Just, the route turns inland to cross the Penwith Moors to St Erth. Beyond, the farmland of rural Cornwall is crossed to Tehidy Country Park, close to the north coast. An old mineral tramway, farm tracks and lanes lead on to St Newlyn East. The hilltop of Castle-an-Dinas is incorporated in the route to the farming village of St Wenn and it's then only a few miles into Bodmin, the first sizeable town encountered. Beyond, the route makes for the pleasant old village of Cardinham on the south-west fringe of Bodmin Moor. After crossing the south end of the Moor to the high level village of Minions, it's still another day's walk to the crossing of the River Tamar into Devon over ancient Horsebridge. The inland route through Devon takes in the church atop Brent Tor, Lydford Gorge and Dartmoor before reaching Okehampton. More walking in the Dartmoor National Park follows, before field paths and farm tracks of mid-Devon take over to reach Bickleigh, from where the River Exe is followed into Tiverton. A route through Knightshayes Court leads onto a track across Bampton Down and into Somerset.

Somerset is a county of contrasts, ranging from the Quantock and Mendip hills to the low-lying land of the Levels, with its extensive network of drains.

Cothelstone Hill at the end of the Quantocks is the first objective before the route makes for a crossing of the River Parrett in Bridgwater. This town cannot be described as scenic so a quiet footpath route is taken which avoids its noise, traffic and bustle. From here, the Levels are crossed to Cheddar at the foot of the Mendips. The route ascends to Beacon Batch, the highest point on the Mendips, before descending to Blagdon Lake and continuing northwards across Felton Common to reach the outskirts of Bristol. Here the route crosses the Avon by the Clifton Suspension Bridge and keeps to a green corridor to the west of the city by using its Downs and the Blaise Castle Estate grounds. Farmland paths and tracks are then used to reach the River Severn and the river is followed to the Severn Bridge, which is crossed to reach Chepstow.

Having moved in a predominantly east-northeast direction through the south-west counties, the route now strikes north making a beeline for the Scottish border and this results in a fairly westerly route up England. Between Chepstow and the Manchester Ship Canal, the route traverses Marcher territory, which refers to the boundary area between England and Wales, although the route stays on the English side of the border as it crosses the counties of Gloucestershire, Herefordshire, Shropshire and Cheshire. Gloucestershire is characterised by its steep pull ups and descents. From Chepstow the route first makes for St Briavels village, high above the Wye Valley, before passing through the Forest of Dean to reach the viewpoint over the Wye at Symonds Yat. The route drops to the Wye, entering Herefordshire, and then keeps above the river passing over Chase Hill to reach Ross-on-Wye. Farmland of rural Herefordshire follows, with Hereford approached via the ancient hill fort of Dinedor Hill. It's farming country up to Leominster with the route passing through some of the orchards for which the county is famous. Continuing north after Orleton village, Shropshire is entered and the route crosses Hanway Common and briefly passes through Mortimer Forest to reach Onibury north-west of Ludlow.

From Onibury to beyond Wem the route largely uses the Shropshire Way, with the approach to and departure from Shrewsbury taking to the Marches Way, which I think provides a better walk. After the pleasant but low level walking through Herefordshire, the route takes to the Shropshire hills over Hopesay Common, along the Long Mynd ridge and over Adstone Hill to Bridges. From there, the route leads up the Golden Valley onto the Betchcott

Hills before descending to the Shropshire Plain to reach Shrewsbury. The way is less hilly to Wem being lush farmland. Beyond Wem, there is a section on the Shropshire Union Canal, before rich farm land takes over, as the route enters Cheshire making for Bickerton Hill, where the sandstone ridge is followed over the Peckforton Hills and on to Tarporley. From here the route threads its way through rural Cheshire via Little Budworth Country Park and Arley Park to reach Lymm. This town is a short distance from the Manchester Ship Canal which is crossed on the Warburton toll bridge (free to walkers).

Beyond the bridge, the nature of the walk changes. Before it's very much lush agricultural land with some upland areas. Afterwards, the scenery tends to be more dramatic with moorland, hills and a sense of wide spaces dominating. The animals and people seem much hardier. Between the Warburton bridge and the Scottish border, the route first uses a green passageway which keeps west of the Manchester conurbation to reach the bleak moorland around Winter Hill. After passing over Longridge Fell and through the peat moors of the Forest of Bowland, the route takes to the limestone pothole area and fells to the south of Sedbergh. After a pastoral interlude along the Lune Valley, the e2e takes to the west side of the rounded Howgill Fells. Further north, the route passes through several small and charming villages in the former county of Westmorland as it crosses the Eden valley to reach and follow the western fringes of the Pennine Hills.

As Hadrian's Wall is approached, the route passes through Brampton, which is the last sizeable town encountered until Hawick in the Scottish Borders. The Wall is crossed at Walton. Beyond, as the border with Scotland approaches, there's a paucity of paths and the area appears to be not well walked, with some of the available paths in a bad state. The border is crossed at Kershopefoot, just south of the small town of Newcastleton. An interesting feature of Scottish places is that (just to confuse the outsider) they sometimes have two names. So Newcastleton is also known as Copshaw Holm.

In Scotland the e2e route has been heavily influenced by the old roads, drove tracks and military roads described in the Scottish Rights of Way Society publication, 'Scottish Hill Tracks'. My copy is the third edition published in 1995, although there are newer editions. In choosing tracks from those listed, important factors were the need to keep moving predominantly northwards until at least the Great Glen was reached, whether the route was visible on the ground and so fairly easy to follow, the wish to avoid walking extensively in evergreen forests, and the need to stop for catered accommodation every 15 miles or so. Having selected the historic paths to be used in progressing beyond the border, I used whatever else was shown on the map to link these. Surprisingly, it all mainly worked very well and the scenery encountered was magnificent.

Regardless of where Hadrian's Wall from Carlisle to Newcastle is crossed, it is necessary to go West-of-North to pass west of Edinburgh. This is due to the way the UK 'bends', whereby Edinburgh near the east coast is more westerly than Carlisle near the west coast. Newcastleton makes an excellent entry point into Scotland, being situated in the midst of good scenery in Liddesdale. A fairly direct route is taken to reach the Forth Bridge, starting with great use of much of the disused railway line from Newcastleton to Hawick. Yarrowford can then be reached by the Borders Abbey Way and the Buccleuch County Ride. The old drove route up the Minchmoor Road is used to reach the ridge where the Southern Upland Way is joined into Traquair. From here, there's a further climb to join the ridge drove route down into Peebles. A good drove route is then taken to West Linton and a Roman Road to Carlops, from where there's a crossing of the Pentland Hills past the Bore Stane stones to the south-west outskirts of Edinburgh. Advantage is then taken of Edinburgh's extensive cycle track network to reach and cross the Forth Bridge.

The e2e route now makes for Dollar from where a succession of excellent hill tracks, drove routes and old military roads can be linked to move northwards through the middle of Central Scotland. From Dollar the drove route through Glendevon to Auchterarder is taken. Gentle tracks and paths through the Strathallan Castle Estate and by the River Earn lead to Crieff and on to General Wade's Military Road through narrow Sma' Glen. The military roads were built in the 1730's in response to the Jacobite uprising of 1715. General Wade was responsible both for the building of garrisons and the roads servicing them, enabling English troops to move quickly around the highlands. There are still good examples of the Wade roads that can be walked, although some sections have been incorporated into present day roads.

The route turns west-northwest at Amulree, to pass round the back of Loch Freuchie, and then joins the lonely road over to Kenmore at the eastern end of Loch Tay, where the route turns northwards again. A good drove route over to Kinloch Rannoch from Fortingall ensues, followed by the drove route to Dalnaspidal, south of Dalwhinnie. It's then necessary to use the cycle path parallel to the A9 to reach Dalwhinnie. From here, good tracks are taken down Loch Ericht over to Loch Pattack and then northwards along the River Pattack to Kinloch Laggan. A track along Glen Shirra meets the Wade Military Road from Laggan. The Wade road is then followed over the Corrieyairack Pass to Fort Augustus. It's a wonderful feat of engineering, rising to a height of 2,500 ft. It is the highest point on the e2e and fulfilled my personal ambition to walk it.

Beyond the tourist hot-spot of Fort Augustus, the route wriggles northwards using part of Wade's route over to Glen Moriston, and then a hill track to reach tiny Tomich. Lovely Strathglass, through large touristy Cannich village, leads on to Struy and then a good hill track is taken over to Marybank. Paths and tracks lead on to Contin village and forest tracks are then taken to Garve, with a small detour to view the Rogie Falls. Picturesque Black Water leads onto the drove route over the hills to the old droving inn at Aultguish; the inn lies on the fairly deserted main road from Ullapool to Inverness. From Aultguish, the hill track up Strath Vaich and down into Gleann Mor is taken to Alladale Lodge. From here, there's a direct path down to Croick Church, with its sad history of the forcible eviction of respectable law-abiding families, to make way for more profitable sheep. From Croick, there's a good track along Strath Cuileannach and through Einig Wood to reach Oykel Bridge. This must have been an important point in bygone days as there are hill tracks or roads from it in all directions except north and north-eastwards.

Having travelled predominantly northwards since leaving Chepstow, Oykel Bridge marks a turning point. From here, the route direction is mainly eastwards or north-eastwards as it starts to move towards John O'Groats. Also from Oykel Bridge, the ground is at a much lower height and there are fewer paths and tracks that can be taken so there is more road walking involved, albeit on roads where the sighting of a car is rare. The River Oykel, tracks and lane lead to Rosehall and then road and a path over The Ord hill are taken to the large village of Lairg. This is the last significant settlement until John O'Groats is reached and for this reason has more facilities, (such as a chemist), than would be expected of a village of its size. From Lairg the route turns north again to the isolated old drove inn at Crask before turning east on a spectacular drove route, which descends to enter flow country; this is a large expanse of waterlogged peat referred to as blanket bog. This flattish bog land extends on the e2e route all the way to the coast.

On reaching Kinbrace, the route turns north along Strath Halladale to Forsinain passing through Forsinard, with its hotel which is the only catered accommodation for miles around. Forest tracks take the end-to-ender eastwards and beyond there's virtually no paths or tracks, so very quiet minor roads are taken eastwards to Watten and then north-eastwards to reach the coast at Gills Bay. It's then a short hop eastwards to reach the pier at John O'Groats. As a place it is a major disappointment, lacking both character and quality. However, better awaits, as the e2e continues with a magnificent and memorable coastal walk to the true north-easterly point by the lighthouse at Duncansby Head. The walk then continues for a short distance southwards to the rock arch of Thirle Door and the two large jagged pyramid of rocks just off the coast forming the Stacks of Duncansby, before turning back inland to John O'Groats village. The high sandstone cliffs on this corner of the mainland are awesome, having natural deep inlets and huge clefts, and their ledges provide a sheltered home to hundreds of birds. This truly makes a fitting climax to the e2e walk.

Acknowledgements

Getting lost on your own when it's pouring is not a lot of fun. Getting lost with a companion is less miserable! So if you can find another person to go with then that's much better. Hopefully when one of you feels down, then the other will be around to offer support and encouragement. However, choose carefully as you are going to be in close proximity for a very long time.

I have been blessed with the very best and most cheerful of walking companions on the e2e. Gwen has done a fantastic job, both in navigating us across the country and in providing a wonderful photographic record of our particular adventure. As well as support and encouragement, there was humour and patience in abundance. Given the dreadful weather conditions that came our way, I'm sure that anyone else would have thrown in the towel long before reaching John O'Groats. She, above all, has my particular thanks.

Gwen and I are indebted to the relatives and friends across the country who put us up (or put up with us), dried us off, did our washing, provided meals, sent us on our way with sustenance and provided pick-ups and drop-offs, often involving quite a lot of travel. So a special thank you to Peter & Georgie, Peter & Irene, Sylvia & Gordon, Barbara & Joe, Iris, Lesley & Sandy, and

Richard & Martina.

Our B&Bs turned out to be very good and many of them were outstanding in their helpfulness. We feel it's a pity that the official star system takes no account of the ambience of a place. To us, this is far more important than the other factors contributing to the official ratings.

We issued an open invitation for people to join us in walking stages or part stages. In all we were joined by 41 people on 21 stages, including a party from the East Cheshire branch of the Ramblers' Association. We have a lot of pictures of these people, mainly huddled in their cagoules. Our thanks go to all who joined us and we hope they enjoyed the experience as much as we enjoyed their company.

My drawing skills are on the wrong side of dreadful so I am indebted to my brother John for doing the sketches indicating where we went and assembling this book, and his wife Sarah for proof reading and editing.

Duration & Time of Year

The walk is described in 71 stages and apart from the first and last stage I have aimed for an average of 15 miles a day. This seemed to me to be the optimum choice. A consistently higher mileage results in over-tiredness, whilst a lower mileage results in too little progress towards the final destination, and hence many more stages. Some stages are of course longer and in this case, I have tried to make the following day shorter.

We aimed to set off close to 9am and to arrive at our accommodation close to 4pm. This timing is good as B&Bs generally don't expect or want you to arrive before 4pm. It also gives the feet a good rest before needing to set off the next day. During a day's walk, we normally had a morning break at 11am, lunch at 1pm and an afternoon break if required around 3pm. Naturally we took advantage of any establishment on the way offering refreshments, particularly if it included a pot of tea!

We set off on a continuous journey from Land's End to John O'Groats starting in mid-April and ending towards the end of June, with an additional three rest days and two days for travel built into the schedule. The theory for this directional choice was that starting in the south-west in the spring, the good weather and longer days would move north with us. In addition, the wind and the sun should be behind us. Moreover, the vegetation is normally at a fairly low level since it is near the start of the growing season. Walking through central and northern Scotland in June proved to be a good move as it is before the deer stalking season which starts in July, and it's before the midges really start getting going.

However, if starting in September, there is much to recommend starting from the north. This will allow Scotland to be walked before the real winter sets in, although Scottish folk will tell you that it sometimes snows in June and indeed snow was visible on the tops above 2,500 ft in June on our journey. Furthermore, you will be walking towards the milder south with its longer daylight hours.

Although the walk was done as a continuous journey, it could easily be done in sections as the route passes several places which have or are near to a railway station with a good service. In the southern half, there's Bridgwater, Bristol, Chepstow, Hereford, Leominster, Ludlow, Shrewsbury and Horwich. In the north there are fewer stations. From Brampton, it's easy to get to Carlisle which has a good service, and the centre of Edinburgh is also easy to reach from its outskirts. Quite a bit north of Edinburgh, the route passes through Dalwhinnie which is on the main line to Inverness. There are regular but widely spaced train services beyond Inverness at Garve, Lairg and Forsinard, and the route uses the service between Alnabreac and Forsinard as part of the walk. However, to use these as a starting or finishing point of a longer section would require careful planning.

Maps

Only rudimentary sketches of the route are provided and they are not to scale. Classified roads crossed or walked are indicated with a solid black line; the line width indicates their importance. Where helpful to the description, a track joining or leaving the route is indicated by a dashed line. Unsurfaced white roads, farm accesses and tracks passed are generally not shown and when used as part of the route are indicated with the 'feet' symbol used for such off-road walking. High standard surfaced white roads and estate roads incorporated in the route are normally shown as lanes. In the text, for compactness, the crossing of staggered junctions is often referred to as opposite right or left. Opposite right means turning right briefly and then left, and vice versa for opposite left.

The included diagrams are designed to enable the route to be located on more detailed and accurate maps of the area. Thus details of the Ordnance Survey 1:25000 (Explorer and Outdoor Leisure) maps and the 1:50000 Landranger maps for each stage are given. In England, the use of 1:25000 maps is highly recommended. This map scale equates to 2.5 inches to the mile with paths and bridleways clearly marked. These maps have the advantage of showing field boundaries, although the maps do not always reflect boundary changes (often long standing), such as removing a hedge or installing a new fence. Furthermore, paths are often subject to minor re-routing which may not follow the legal right-of-way. However, these maps do represent the best resource for walkers. In Scotland, the Landranger maps should suffice. These maps equate to a scale of 1.25 inches to the mile and therefore do not display the detail of the Explorer maps. In particular, field boundaries are not shown. However since negotiating a network of fields does not feature highly in Scotland, this is not a problem.

We decided to use 1:25000 maps throughout and took the entire map minus the cover (to save weight) rather than just the strips of our projected route. On the occasions that we found that our planned route was not feasible then we had a sufficient map area to be able to re-route. To complement the maps, a compass is essential and a GPS is highly recommended.

Grid References

The UK is divided into squares of 100 km x 100 km with each square having a unique two-letter name. Squares in the southern half of the country start with the letter 'S' while those in the northern half start with 'N'. In order to define a position within a square, the square can be subdivided into cells and the number of figures used to define the horizontal and vertical position within the square indicates the size of this cell. Usually just three figures are used, indicating the accuracy of manual measurements. This defines the position of a 100 metres x 100 metres cell within the 100 km x 100 km square. In the text, grid references are given as the nearest cell to a particular point. Their inclusion is so that you can see from the map which path or track is being taken and should enable you to get back onto the route if you happen to lose your way.

There are two occasions on the route when features are difficult to locate and in this case, five figure cell readings from my GPS are given to aid navigation.

Apart from those two times, we only needed to use the GPS on four other occasions to check our location.

Units

People of my age still think in terms of the imperial measurements using pounds (lbs) for weight and feet (ft), yards (yd) and miles (m) for height and distance. I know that nowadays metric measurements are taught so that it's kilograms for weight, metres for height and kilometres for distance (although bizarrely road distances are given in miles). I know what a hill of 2,000 ft feels like but I have difficulty conjuring the same vision with 615 metres. This always results in me doing conversions to imperial quantities. So, as this is *my* book, I thought I'd use the units I like. If this bothers you, you can always occupy your time while plodding along in the rain by converting any figures given into metric quantities; in this case you need to know that a mile is 1.6 kilometres, a foot is 0.3 metres and hence a yard is 0.9 metres. For weight, 2.2 lbs is 1 kilogram.

Measurements

The distances given are the flat distance as can be measured on a map. This takes no account of extra mileage due to ups and downs, plus in and out wriggles, which a map cannot show. This will take the overall real distance to more than 1,035 miles. Ascents and descents are even harder to measure accurately as these take no account of the many ups and downs between contour lines. Thus the ascent and descent given should be treated as only a rough guide of how much climbing and descending there is. In the text, an indication of the mileage during a stage is given so that you can measure your progress towards completing the stage.

Rights of Way

Usually when national treasures are referred to, people are talking about some famous person or building. However, to my way of thinking, our national treasures are the footpath and bridleway network, which is freely available for us all to use. In England and Wales, where you are legally allowed to go is defined by the paths, bridleways and byways clearly indicated on the maps. Scotland has very few rights of ways but does have a right to responsible roaming. I understand this to mean that you are allowed to go where you want apart from houses, gardens, growing crops (although field margins are OK), airfields and military bases. The Scottish Access Code expects walkers to take responsibility for their own actions, respect the interests of others (particularly people working the land) and care for the environment.

For people from England, such as myself, who are used to a map defining exactly where you can go, it's initially difficult to get one's head round where one is allowed to go in Scotland. You may have the right to roam but there's a great deal of Scotland that's so rough underfoot and choked with undergrowth or trees that nobody in their right mind would want to do any roaming there! Thus having entered Scotland there was a great deal of uncertainty about where we could really go and whether the paths and tracks shown on the maps were usable. We learnt (the hard way) that paths on the map are not always honoured by the landowner. We found a good number to be blocked by barbed wire, deer or electric fencing, or now covered by an impenetrable plantation or undergrowth (about 50% of those tried). On the other hand, we found quite a number of paths, some of which have clearly been established for some time, that are not shown on the maps. As a good general rule of thumb, a track shown on the map will be present on the ground and do-able. However, paths shown should be regarded as iffy; if the path proves to be viable then this should be regarded as a bonus.

Accommodation

Enjoyment when walking is inversely proportional to the weight you need to carry and the mileage walked. Therefore I cannot summon one iota of interest in or enthusiasm for camping and all that it entails, such as sleeping on the ground plus lugging a wet tent, cooking equipment, sleeping bag and food around. For this reason, we opted for overnight accommodation throughout the walk. Mostly this was in bed & breakfast establishments but also included inns and hotels and the occasional stay in catered and non-catered hostel-type accommodation. We regarded this level of accommodation as an essential part of the support we needed to undertake such a long walk. It has the advantage of enabling a much lighter sack to be carried and we always set off in a dry and good state in the mornings. I have never understood why the national trails usually eschew passing through places of habitation. In my view, towns and villages are as much a part of our wonderful heritage as are the hills and moorlands. Not only are the towns and villages historically interesting in their own right, but they often have accommodation and places to eat in the evening.

In a great leap of faith, we booked all the accommodation needed well in advance. This meant that we were committed to the schedule we had drawn up. Many of the places we stopped in had only one place offering accommodation with just one or two rooms. Thus it is essential in these places to secure the accommodation well in advance. If traversing central and northern Scotland in June, you are competing for accommodation with fishermen, so again booking well in advance is highly desirable.

Logistics

Put simply, if you fail to plan, you plan to fail. Logistics are about tying up all the loose ends and nailing the detail down; this can take a significant amount of time. After route planning, the details of accommodation and any pick-ups/drop-downs required need to be specified. This often proves to be an iterative process. Thought needs to be given to how you are going to access money for your daily needs. Most towns and some large villages have ATM machines. Failing that, there's often a Post Office where money can be withdrawn. You will not want to carry all the maps you need so you will need to organise for the picking up of maps covering the next sections of the walk.

Finally you need to give thought to the weight you will have to carry. This is not a walk where you will be able to have your bag carried. Therefore cutting the kit weight to an absolute minimum by splashing out on lightweight gear is a very worthwhile investment for a walk of this length. We spent a lot of time (and money) obtaining the lightest serviceable items we could find and regularly arrived at shops with a pair of scales! We operated on the basis of a set of clothes for walking and a set for the evening. With a full set of maps for the next ten days, food and a litre of water, the rucksack weighed no more than 16 lbs. Maps no longer required were posted back at every available opportunity, so that the normal bag weight was around a very manageable 14 lbs. Any kit purchased can of course be used on future trips.

Weather

It seemed appropriate to include some mention of the prevailing weather as this featured heavily in our memories of our end-to-end journey. Ideally for walking, cool dry weather is optimum. When we started the walk, drought restrictions were in force in the West Midlands southwards. We walked in 2012 which had the wettest April on record and the wettest summer for 100 years. So the southwest of England mainly yielded torrential rain with accompanying high winds. The Marcher counties and the north of England proved to be drier, although the waterproofs were again much in evidence and it was bitterly cold on some days. Unsurprisingly, drought restrictions were lifted in nineteen counties by mid-May. However the weather changed as the Scottish border was approached and we spent a week being roasted to a turn. Beyond the Scottish Border area, the weather offered largely ideal walking conditions until the last few days when it turned wet and gloomy.

Disclaimer

The description given relates to the conditions we encountered when doing the walk in 2012 and is given in good faith. Things change! A farmer removes a hedge or erects a new fence or a bridge which we crossed is now washed away. In Scotland, a path indicated on the map which was passable may become blocked by the planting of a new section of forest or by the erection of an electric or high deer fence. Therefore be prepared to be flexible in undertaking the walk. Your maps will let you plan an alternative if it's needed. You are responsible for your own health and safety, and for this reason should stay within your comfort zone at all times on the walk.

Stage 0
Land's End to St Just

VIA:	Coast path and the Cot Valley
DISTANCE:	6m [6m]
ASCENT:	960ft DESCENT: 720ft
EXPLORER:	102 (Land's End)
LANDRANGER:	203 (Land's End)

The first stage of only 6 miles is a gentle warm up for what's to follow. Following the coast northwards to St Just enables the Cornish Moors to be crossed in the following stage to St Erth. As there's no accommodation for many miles after St Just, this small town makes an appropriate end to the first stage. Although the distance is relatively small, the path is not level so progress will not be fast. Furthermore, the coastal scenery is delightful and dramatic. You will want to linger and take it in, as well as making a significant photographic record of this stage.

The route uses the South West Coastal Path following the coast closely to reach the Cot Valley. The coast path is straightforward but surprisingly rocky and undulating. When the Cot Valley is reached, the coastal path is left and the stage turns inland through the valley. After passing the Youth Hostel the route turns to cross the valley stream and continues into St Just.

There's a two-hourly bus service to Land's End from Penzance (not Sunday). The journey takes just under an hour and in itself is full of scenic interest as it winds through small settlements, never far from the coast. On arriving at Land's End, prepare to be amazed at the number of people congregating there. Keep right of the buildings to find the signpost marking the start of the journey. You will almost certainly want a photograph against the signpost (costs!) so be prepared to wait in a lengthy queue for this. Having completed the starting formalities, you are now ready to start the e2e.

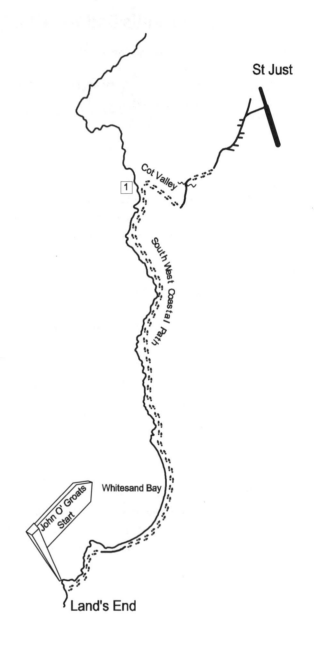

Start: Facing the sea, from the much photographed signpost (SW 342 251) turn right to the whitewashed First & Last House. Inland, behind this building, pick up a signpost to the Coastal Path and follow the well trodden path to the old lookout tower at Pedn-men-du. Here, turn right and descend on a paved track, turning left onto a path to meet a lane. Continue straight across into the car park at Sennen Cove (1m). Turn right through the car park and out onto the promenade. At its end, follow the Coastal Path signpost onto the beach and proceed along the beach edge of wide Whitesand Bay for as long as possible; if the tide is in or if preferred, take to the footpath just above. Eventually, the path rises from the bay and continues close to the coast, but at a modest height above the sea below. Follow the Coastal Path signs and drop to cross a stream. Afterwards the path ascends higher. Ignore a sign off right to the YHA (signed 'via Letcha Farm') and carry on along the coast path, which descends doubling back on itself before continuing northwards.

1: Stay on the coastal path until overlooking a lane (356 308) (4.6m) with car parking space. Don't descend to the lane, but turn right on a gently ascending path up the right side of the Cot Valley. When the path forks, take the higher path, signed to the YHA. This grassy path emerges on a rough track. Go straight ahead (left) and if staying at the YHA look for a grassy path off right. Otherwise continue on the track to meet a lane. Turn left and follow the descending lane across a stream. Very shortly afterwards, when the lane ends, ascend on a stony track which quickly curves right. At the top, it emerges at the end of a lane. Turn left for a quarter of a mile to a T-junction. Turn left through St Just, turning right after a free car park to reach its pleasant village square (371 314) (6m).

Stage 1
St Just to St Erth

VIA: Bosullow Common, Lady Downs and Ninnes Bridge
DISTANCE: 15.9m [21.9m]
ASCENT: 1480ft **DESCENT:** 1850ft
EXPLORER: 102 (Land's End)
LANDRANGER: 203 (Land's End)

This stage is in complete contrast to the coastal scenery of the preceding stage. It stays inland as it crosses the bleak moorland downs which are the dominant feature of the terrain between St Just and the small village of St Erth. This is an area of Neolithic remains in the form of ancient stone circles, settlements and burial places, which date from around 3,000BC. Neolithic burial sites are called 'quoits' and are characterised by hefty standing stones capped by a large stone slab. The other noticeable feature of the landscape is the more recent remnants of the mining for tin and copper over the last two centuries. The route taken contains a generous helping of the major quoits, stone circles and ancient settlements that are within easy reach to enhance the feeling of history during this stage.

This section is difficult to navigate from the map because many paths shown are just not there and many other tracks/paths on the ground, particularly on the open access land or permissive paths linking access land, are not shown. Thus we are most grateful to Peter and Georgie for sharing their knowledge of the paths and tracks in this area, many of which have been incorporated into this stage. Late in the day the route passes the car park for Trencrom Hill so there is the opportunity for an optional detour to its top, from where on a day with good visibility there will be views of both coasts of Cornwall.

This is a sparsely populated region and the only village passed through towards the end of the stage is Canon's Town. In this part of Cornwall, you are never far from either the north or south coast and at many points on this stage there are good views of both coastlines. Towards St Erth there are unusual stiles in the form of stone posts laid horizontally to form separated steps; these function as both a stile and a cattle grid and appear to be unique to the western end of Cornwall.

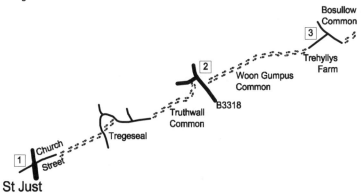

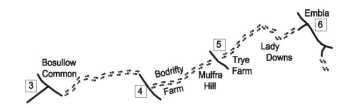

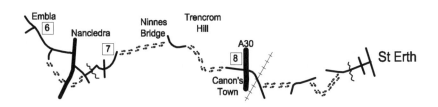

1: Cross St Just's square (SW 371 314) into Church Street and pass to the right of the church into Venton East Square. Take the lane (to the left of the signed footpath) which quickly becomes a steeply descending surfaced path to a road. Turn left for 100 yds then take a behind-houses footpath off right, just before a road off right. At the end of the path, don't cross the footbridge but turn right on the path alongside the stream which becomes a track. When the track meets a lane, turn left to cross the stream and meet a lane. Turn right and ascend gently on the main lane branching right at a T-junction. When the lane ends, take the stony track straight ahead and when this branches turn left to Hailglower Farm (384 322). The track passes left of the farm and is followed for 270 yds to a cross-track. Here, go through the walkers' gate on the right into open-access Truthwall Common. Follow the main track. The track soon passes to the left of a stone circle and shortly afterwards starts to gently ascend making a large sweep around the rocks visible on the hilltop to the left. Keep to the main track until a significant branch is reached. Here, take the right branch heading to the right of the rocks (the left branch heads towards the rocks) and just keep going to reach a walkers' gate which is taken. Follow the grassy track ahead to shortly meet a gravel farm access drive (392 331) and go ahead (left) on this. The farm access soon turns left and heads north to meet a road. Turn right to shortly meet a B-road (393 334) (2.3 m).

2: Cross to the car park opposite and pass through the gate at the back of this small car park onto Woon Gumpus Common. Take the grassy track half right which soon turns left towards the flat stone, Chun Quoit, visible on the hilltop. The track passes the odd waymark and at a track branch, follow the waymarked left branch to shortly reach a gate plus stile. Cross out of open-access land onto a signed permissive path across a field in the same straight-on direction to a stile. Cross to enter the open-access land of Chun Downs and follow the clear gently ascending path which leads directly to Chun Quoit with its standing stones topped by a large flat stone. Pass right of the Quoit and take the good wide path half-right going east to shortly reach the entrance, between two stone pillars, to circular Chun Castle. After inspecting this ancient settlement, exit by the entrance pillars and immediately turn left on a path. This follows the castle boundary to meet a good path. Turn left here on a south-east path which descends to a farm track to the right of Trehyllys Farm (408 337). Turn left to very shortly meet the start of the public road (3.5 m) which is followed north-east for three quarters of a mile to meet a minor road

(418 344) (4.3 m).

3: Turn right for 60 yds then turn left for the footpath signed to Men-an-Tol. Follow the excellent enclosed track, ignoring the footpath off right to Men-an-Tol to remain on the main track. When the track ceases to be enclosed, the track curves gently right and continues near to a right boundary to reach a track junction (430 354). Go left on a grassy track for just a few yards and then turn right through a metal walkers' gate and follow a path north-east then east-ish along the right boundary to another metal walkers' gate. Pass through onto open moor and follow the well-trodden main path ignoring turn-offs right. The path comes close to and follows the open-access boundary on the left, with views of the Nine Maidens stone circle on the horizon to the right. The path leaves the access boundary as it descends to meet a good track. Turn right and when an even better track is met, turn right again. This track becomes a public road and is followed to the entrance to Bodrifty Farm (446 351) (6.3 m).

4: Turn left up the access drive to Bodrifty Farm. At the track junction, turn right towards the farm and immediately right into a field, on a signed path to Mulfra Quoit. In the field go half-left on a trodden path to and through a gate gap (the right of the two gaps). In the field entered continue in the same direction on a trodden path to an electric fence crossing point guarding an awkward stile. Cross and drop briefly onto a path on the other side. Turn left and follow the path to a wooden stile on the right. Cross and follow the path. After crossing a ruined wall, the path turns left before turning right and wriggling its way gently upwards to another wooden stile. Cross and follow the path as it gently ascends all the time to meet a path. Turn right here and follow the path which directly goes to Mulfra Quoit whose top slab has met with an accident! Pass right of the quoit and take the north-east path behind the quoit. This descends to meet a path. Turn left here and follow the path as it descends to the minor road (454 356) (7.1 m) in the Trye Valley. Turn right for just over a quarter mile and then turn off left on the access to Trye Farm.

5: After crossing a stream, ascend to the top of a climb where the access drive turns right to Trye Farm. Turn left here through a gate onto a signed bridleway. Follow the track to a gate at its end and enter a field. Follow the right edge to a stile by a gate. Cross and continue in the same direction across the field to a double gate. Pass through the left hand gate into a large field. Here go parallel to the right fence, veering left before a pile of largish stones, to pass left of a pond. Now make towards a nearby medium size stone ahead in the hedge in order to find a walkers' gate just to the right of this stone. Beyond the gate, go forward on a path to shortly meet a better path. Turn left here and follow the path out onto a stony access track (464 362) (8.3 m). Turn right along this track. After the last house, the track becomes a good path. Continue to a waymarked bridleway fork and take the left branch. Follow the main path which runs close to the right boundary of open-access land. Continue to a waymark post and continue straight ahead on the bridleway and very shortly reach a waymarked fingerpost (472 368). Turn right here along the waymarked footpath across Lady Downs. Follow the trodden path to a gate. Pass through and turn left to descend along a left boundary to a farm track. Turn right along the track to a gate and out onto a surfaced access drive. Turn right and follow this to meet a lane at Embla (483 371) (9.8 m).

6: Turn right and take the first turn off right (signed to Georgia), cross Georgia Bridge, ascend to the first surfaced lane off left which is an unsigned byway (488 365). Follow the lane past The Count House to where the surfacing ends. Beyond, continue on a good, well walked and ridden track, keeping straight on at track junctions; the village below on the left is Nancledra. The track passes the odd dwelling and eventually becomes surfaced again. Pass the residence of Myquest on the left, follow the lane as it bends left and then take a grassy track off left which becomes a well-trodden path leading down past houses to a B-road (495 356) (11.3m). Go straight across onto a good track which descends steeply to a lane junction. Take the lane straight across and descend to cross a stream, then ascend on the lane which soon turns right, still ascending. At a cross-road, go straight on along the major lane. Ignore a signed bridleway off right, which would provide a direct route to Canon's Town, as it is impassable (unless you are keen to wade through muddy water that's literally up to the knees). Instead continue on the lane to Trembethow Farm (508 357) (12.2 m).

7: Just past the farm buildings, take the signed footpath off right, pass through a walkers' gate onto a farm track following this to a stile on the right which is just past a hedge coming in from the right. Cross and go a quarter-right across a field to cross a stile; St Michael's Way from Lelant on the north coast to

Marazion on the south coast is joined here. In the field entered go half-right to a stile just left of a telegraph pole. In the next field go half-left to a stile in the bottom left corner. Now follow the trodden path ahead which curves right following parallel to the course of a stream and reach a stile. Cross and follow the stream closely to a gravel drive which is followed left to a lane at Ninnes Bridge (515 359) (12.7 m). Turn left, ascending to shortly reach a lane branch and fork right to reach the top road. Turn right and shortly pass a car park on the left for Trencrom Hill where St Michael's Way is left. For those wishing to undertake the detour to the hilltop, the walkers' gate straight ahead in the car park leads to a sharp climb to the top. Continue on the road past the car park for another 100 yds to an unsigned byway off right (518 359) (13 m). Take the descending unsurfaced track, ignoring a track off left, and reach a stream which can be crossed by a stone bridge. Across, ascend to meet a track. Turn left and when the major track turns right after a few yards, carry straight on along a bridleway track. This eventually becomes a lane which leads to the main A30 road at Canon's Town (535 353) (14.4 m).

8: Turn left for a few yards and then take a lane off right. As soon as the railway is crossed (535 350), turn off left on a path. This briefly runs parallel to the railway line but then turns right to follow the right then left field edges east to meet Tredrea Lane. Turn left but after 320 yds as the lane curves left, take a bridleway off right (543 350) which is the access drive to Tredrea Manor. At the manor turn off left onto a signed footpath which follows a right boundary and continues as a trodden path east-northeast across a field to rejoin Tredrea Lane. Turn right, cross the River Hayle and go straight ahead to very shortly reach the cross-road in the centre of St Erth village (551 351) (15.9 m).

Stage 2
St Erth to Nance (Illogan)

VIA: **Gwinear, Roseworthy and Tehidy Country Park**
DISTANCE: 12.4m [34.3m]
ASCENT: 1110ft   DESCENT: 910ft
EXPLORER: **102 (Land's End), 104 (Redruth & St Agnes)**
LANDRANGER: **203 (Land's End)**

Today's stage runs parallel to the north coast of Cornwall, with the coast usually just a couple of miles away. The route threads its way through farmland via footpaths, old tracks and quiet roads to the entry to the Tehidy Country Park, just north of Camborne. A delightful section on good tracks through deciduous woodland follows which is the highlight of the stage. The stage finishes at the small hamlet of Nance, on the edge of Illogan, because it has a self-catering Youth Hostel, B&B and hotel accommodation. An evening meal can be had at the pub in nearby Bridge which the route passes through on the following stage. This is all pleasant easy walking but can't be described as dramatic.

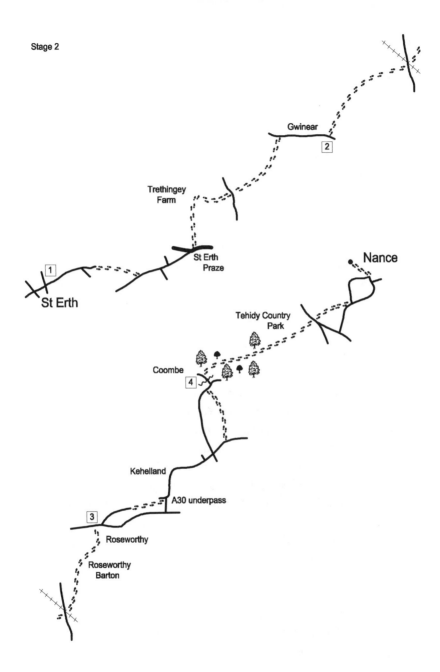

1: From the centre of St Erth (SW 551 351) continue east along the road in St Erth for a short distance and when the road swings right, continue straight on along the 'No Through Road' of Vicarage Gate. This continues as a well-trodden byway into a field. Follow the left hedge in this field and in the next field follow the left boundary to an exit point left onto a track. Turn right briefly to where the track turns right and here go straight on along a field path down the right hedge to emerge on Steppy Downs Road. Turn left and follow the road (ignoring turn-offs) to a B-road at St Erth Praze (1.6m). Turn right briefly and immediately after the Smugglers Inn take an enclosed bridleway off left (576 352) to Trethingey Farm. The bridleway track curves right to the farm. At the farm when the bridleway turns left to go north, take an unsigned path off right which passes through two gates and then follows right boundaries eastwards across two fields to Wheal Alfred Road (582 360). Turn left for a few yards and then turn right on an enclosed byway which runs northeast to Nanpusker Road (593 374). Turn right, pass a church on the right and shortly reach the hamlet of Gwinear (4m).

2: In Gwinear, turn off half-left on a signed track (598 374) which passes houses into a field. Follow the clear path east-northeast across the field to meet an access track. The path continues in the same direction opposite along a crop break to reach a hedge turn. Follow the left boundary in this and the next field to a farm track. Turn left on this and follow it as it curves right to Lanyon Farm. Follow the track as it circles to the left of the house and go past its front looking for a bridleway sign off left which is taken. Follow the bridleway north-east away from the farm. On reaching the next farm, Trevaskis, this is sufficiently large to operate a one-way system(!) and the bridleway is surfaced from here until near the end when a walkers' gate off left leads via a short path to Station Road (613 383) (5.3m). Turn left under the railway line and immediately take an enclosed bridleway right. This soon curves left and is followed to a track junction. Here, turn left, signed 'Deliveries'. The track soon curves right passing the buildings of Roseworthy Barton. Follow the track left and keep straight on northwards at a bridleway fork (615 390). After another 0.4mile, the bridleway meets a track. Turn left past housing and curve right to a minor road at Roseworthy (616 397) (6.3m).

3: Turn right for 140 yds and then take an ascending surfaced lane off left through Merry Meeting. This eventually becomes a rough track which meets a lane (7m). Turn left, immediately pass under the A30 and then immediately meet a minor road (625 404). Turn right and follow the lane to a junction of lanes at Kehelland (626 409). Turn right to follow a lane east and then north-east to a cross-road (633 412) (8m). Go straight across along Puggis Hill descending to just past a sharp right bend sign and turn left (635 415) on a signed enclosed bridleway. The path becomes a good track which later becomes surfaced and emerges on a road (629 423). Turn right for 200 yds before forking left to cross Red River (9m).

4: Very shortly after crossing the river, the road turns sharp left. Leave the road here, just after a white house on the right, for a footpath off right (630 425) signed 'Mineral Tramway Trail'. The path passes the Polcrowjy Tea Room almost immediately and continues as an excellent wide track which follows West Drive through delightful woodland. On reaching a path signed off half-left take this (temporarily leaving the mineral trail) and ascend to meet a track (where the trail is rejoined). Turn left and ascend to a signpost. Follow the trail sign right, signed to East Lodge. Carry on following signs to 'East Lodge' or 'Engine House' until just beyond the golf course on the right when there is a fork. Take the right fork to East Lodge (left takes you to the car park) and emerge on a road (659 439) (11.2m). Turn left briefly and then right along the access to Trengrove Farm, but after a few yards turn right on a signed back-of-houses enclosed path. Maintain the same direction until directed right to meet a track after a brief distance. Now go left to maintain the same overall direction and reach a lane (666 438). Turn left and after 250 yds take the first left into Well Lane. The lane turns right, then passes Aviary Court Hotel and at the next sharp right bend (671 442), turn off left for Nance Farm with its adjoining Youth Hostel (670 444) (12.4m).

Stage 3
Nance to St Newlyn East

VIA: Mawla, Callestick and Zelah
DISTANCE: 15.9m [50.2m]
ASCENT: 1290ft   DESCENT: 1240ft
EXPLORER: 104 (Redruth & St Agnes)
LANDRANGER: 203 (Land's End), 204 (Truro), 200 (Bodmin)

This stage borrows heavily from the suggested route across Cornwall by the British Horse Society at their web site www.bhsaccesscornwall.org.uk. This is a lovely pastoral part of Cornwall, well away from the bustle of the coast. From Bridge, the old mineral tramway to Cambrose, now a footpath, is taken followed by a bridleway to Forge. Quiet lanes through Mawla then lead to a lovely section of tracks leading east-northeast and then north-east to Callestick where there is both a cider and an ice cream farm; we stopped at the latter for a brew (tea!). From there, it's a mixture of paths, tracks and quiet lanes eastwards to the village of Zelah which has the Hawkins Arms.

From Zelah to Newlyn East there is a paucity of linking paths, so the route takes to the very busy and fast main A30 road for half a mile; however, there is a pavement or verge all the way although care needs to be exercised for its two crossings. Beyond the main road section, much quieter roads are taken to the end of the stage at St Newlyn East, which lies about 5 miles south of Newquay. On our journey we were pleased to be joined by a former member of our walking group and although now living in the area, she was amazed by the tracks and paths the route revealed! Zelah marked the start of the torrential rain that was to characterise much of our walk until Shropshire was reached. Despite our saturated state (and our host laughing when he beheld us), we were made to feel very welcome at our B&B, who got our wet gear dried out by the next morning. We ate at the nearby Pheasant Inn in the evening.

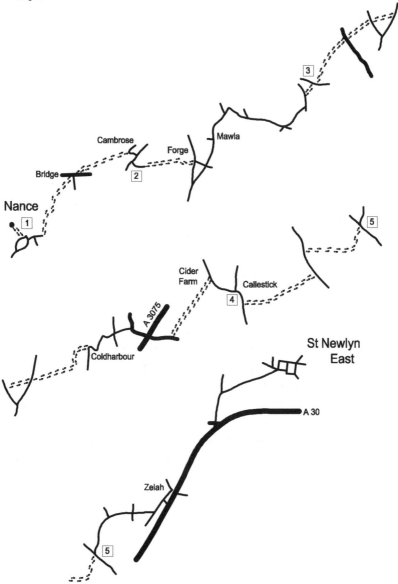

Nance

Bridge

Cambrose

Forge

2

Mawla

3

Cider Farm

Callestick

4

A 3075

Coldharbour

5

St Newlyn East

A 30

Zelah

5

1

1: From Nance Farm (SW 670 444) return southwards down its access drive to the lane and here go straight on (left) to shortly reach a T-junction. Turn left and in a short distance reach another T-junction. Turn left here, pass a telephone box and then very shortly turn off left on a wide grass track (starting between houses) with a hard to spot footpath sign. The path soon enters a field where the right boundary is followed to a stile in the field corner. Cross and follow the left boundary. Cross ahead to the next field and turn right along the right boundary. Partway along the second side, turn right through a walkers' gate and follow the left fence to another walkers' gate. Beyond, maintain the same direction along the tree line (to the right of a sunken track) down to a gate and out onto a lane. Follow this down past a chapel to shortly meet the road at Bridge (674 448) (0.7m). Turn left briefly to meet a B-road. Turn right briefly and look on the left for an ascending doubling-back clear, but unsigned path, off left just before a white house on the left. Follow this onto the disused tramway and turn right. The tramway forks right just afterwards (follow the 'Engine' sign). Follow the excellent track which crosses a lane until the next lane is met. Here, descend half-right to a road at Cambrose (687 453) (1.7m).

2: Turn right briefly then turn left on an enclosed bridleway which starts as a surfaced lane. After crossing a stream, the lane turns left to run eastwards. The bridleway runs past Forge Manor Farm becoming a track which emerges at a lane junction (698 454) (2.5m). Take the lane opposite and shortly reach a cross-road. Turn left, north-east, for the hamlet of Mawla, ignoring a turn-off left onto a more minor lane. In the hamlet keep to the major lane, pass the chapel and continue beyond north-east ignoring turn-offs. A third of a mile beyond Mawla the lane curves distinctly right to run east-southeast and meet the road from Porthtowan (711 461). Turn right for 500 yds then take the first left signed to Mount Hawke. After a few yards, go left again on the lane signed to Mount Hawke. Follow the lane towards Mount Hawke for just over three quarters of a mile to a severe left curve (723 468) with the entrance to Coosewartha Farm on the left. Turn off the lane to the right by going straight on, along a good unsurfaced enclosed track, following it northwards to a minor road (723 470).

3: Turn right for 80 yds and then turn off left (5m) on a good mainly enclosed track which soon turns north-east. The track keeps left of Penhallow Farm and passes under a disused railway line before turning east-northeast to meet a B-road. The track continues opposite left running east-northeast, crosses a lane and continues to a minor road with Silverwell Farm (743 486) (6.5m) opposite. Here go straight across onto the track to the left of the farm buildings, following the track eastwards. A sharp bend left is reached after a quarter mile. Here go straight on along a trodden path which leads to a footbridge across a stream. Beyond follow the track which curves left. Ignore a track off right and continue to meet a track. Here turn right briefly to emerge at a lane corner (752 489). Follow the lane to the left, eastwards, crossing a minor road to reach a B-road. Turn right on this to shortly reach the main A3075 road (760 490) (7.8m). Go opposite left onto the B-road signed to Truro, then take the wide unsigned unsurfaced track off left after 150 yds. Eventually the track passes a cider farm and the track now metalled is followed to a lane. Turn right and follow the lane a short distance into the hamlet of Callestick (775 504) (9.4m).

4: The road curves right in Callestick signed for Truro (left takes you to Callestick Farm). Descend to cross a stream and just afterwards turn left on a signed bridleway (776 503). Initially the bridleway is enclosed and when this ends at a gate, pass through then go half-right up a slope to a grassy track. Follow the sign to the right, descending slightly to a sign on a fence. Turn left along the fence to a waymark on a farm gate. Pass through, immediately turn left on a path which meets a farm track. Turn left into a field. Go straight across the field in an easterly direction to a walkers' gate in the field corner. Cross and follow the right hedge to a serious stone stile leading onto a lane (790 505) (10.4m). Turn left and after a quarter of a mile take the first track off right (788 508). On very shortly meeting a track go right, eastwards, along a byway. Maintain an easterly direction, ignoring turn-offs; in particular ignore a path off left to the engine house chimney, unless of course your day will be incomplete if you don't view it. Eventually the track turns steeply left and after another 240 yds meets a lane (796 511) (11.3m).

5: Turn left for a few yards and then take a lane off right which descends and ascends to tiny Little Callestock. Here take the first turn-off right (signed to Zelah). Continue eastwards to a cross-road (803 516) and go straight across. The lane ascends and descends to meet the road in Zelah (811 518) (12.5m). Turn left. Ignore a turn off right onto the A30 and carry straight on to the end of the pavement and then go through a gap on the right to the A30. Cross to the pavement opposite left and follow it to the left up Zelah Hill. After the pavement ends, continue on the verge for a short distance before crossing to take the B-road opposite signed to Perranporth. Follow this relatively quiet road for a short distance to a cross-road and go straight across onto the minor road signed for St Newlyn East. Follow this road through Fiddlers Green, cross a disused railway and then fork right as signed for St Newlyn East (820 550) (14.8m). Keep going until a cross-road is reached. Turn right, signed Mitchell, following the road to shortly reach the lane round St Newlyn East's church which marks the centre of the village (828 564) (15.9m). The Pheasant Inn is to the left and the village's B&B to the right.

Stage 4
St Newlyn East to St Wenn

VIA: White Cross, Ruthvoes and Castle-an-Dinas
DISTANCE: 13.4m [63.6m]
ASCENT: 1350ft   DESCENT: 1280ft
EXPLORER: 106 (Newquay & Padstow)
LANDRANGER: 200 (Bodmin)

This stage continues the steady progression across inland Cornwall and after the drenching of the previous day, it was a relief to see the sun shining as we left our B&B. Initially, there are no paths resulting in the route from St Newlyn East village to the main road at White Cross being all quiet minor roads. However, it's all pleasant, peaceful lanes amidst pleasant surroundings. The stage passes a caravan park on either side of the main road at White Cross and we stopped for mid-morning coffee in the second of these, Whiteacres Park; this site also had a shop. Beyond the main road, the route gradually improves as paths appear and the terrain becomes hillier. The appearance of a real hill, in the form of the ancient fort atop Castle-an-Dinas at nearly 700ft, is too good to miss and there is a good panoramic view from the top; the 'Cornish Alps' visible east-of-South are evidence of the effect the china clay industry has had on the landscape. I had expected that the hill would be thronged with tourists, but we had it to ourselves and the path down was surprisingly rough indicating it is not well loved which is a shame.

The area around St Wenn is well walked with the county's excellent promoted trail, the Saints Way, from Padstow on the north coast to Fowey on the south coast passing close by. There's no accommodation or eating place in St Wenn village, but Treliver and Tregolls beyond, both offer accommodation and the route passes both B&B's. We stayed and ate at Treliver on our journey and the distance given is measured to there. Tregolls is a further half mile.

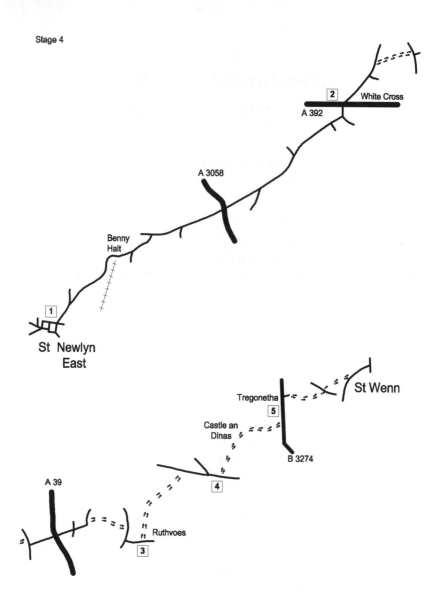

1: From the lane around the church (SW 828 564), turn left and after a few yards at the T-junction (with the Pheasant Inn opposite) turn right to shortly reach a lane fork. Branch left here, signed to the Lappa Valley Railway. Ignore a turn-off left so as to pass Benny Halt (838 573), the terminus of the preserved railway. Shortly afterwards ignore a turn-off right to Mitchell and continue to a T-junction (845 576) (1.5m). Turn right, signed St Columb. Ignoring a turn-off right to Degembris, follow the lane to a main road and take the lane opposite. Keep to the 'major' lane ignoring turn-offs. Eventually the lane passes a caravan park, crosses under the railway and very shortly reaches the main road at White Cross (891 598) (4.8m).

2: Go straight across to the minor road opposite and follow this for 0.5mile (ignoring a lane off right) to the access drive on the right to Trugo Farm. At the farm, when the drive turns right, go straight on along a grassy track. Pass through the farm gate ahead (unsigned) and briefly turn left along the left field boundary to reach and take a gap into the next field. Here, turn right following the right hedge round until a wide gap on the right can be taken onto a lane junction (903 606) (6m). Take the lane opposite which goes east-northeast and then turns east. Shortly afterwards, pass under the A39 road and reach a cross-road. Go straight across, signed Quoit. After a quarter mile, follow the lane as it turns sharp left and 50 yds beyond take a footpath off right, opposite to the signed path off left. Go over the bank (gap) to a stile. Cross the field entered half-left to a stile in the fence. Continue in the same direction (diverging from the fence) to and through a farm gate onto a farm track. Follow the farm track to the farm. Keep going straight ahead over a stile, along the edge of a garden and through a gate onto a drive which leads onto a lane. Turn right for a short distance then turn off left into Ruthvoes village (925 606) (7.5m).

3: In the village pass a 'No Through Road' sign with a postbox on the right and a few yards further on turn off left on a signed delightful track which eventually enters a field. Proceed to the top right corner of the field to find a farm track. Turn right and follow this track until it curves right. At this point go straight on following a path through and beyond a patch of woodland to reach the access drive of Ennisworgey Farm. Turn left along the drive to shortly reach a busy minor road (933 617) (8.6m). Turn right, eastwards, for 0.8mile keeping to the major road and turn left at the Castle-an-Dinas sign (946 617).

4: Take the right of the two tracks. Follow the track up to the direction viewer at the top. After admiring the view, leave just east-of-North to find a walkers' gate. From here follow the fence line down passing through a succession of walkers' gates to reach a farm track. Here turn right and keeping straight ahead, reach a waymarked farm gate. Pass through into a field where the left hedge is followed.to meet a farm track. Turn left on the track for a few yards then turn off left through a gate into the open-access scrubland of Tregonetha Downs. Follow a track, initially close to the left boundary of the downs (heading for Tregonetha village ahead) but when the track turns left, go half-right on a path. Follow the path until a fence is approached and then use a walkers' gate in the fence just to the left to reach a B-road (957 632) (11m). Turn left to the small village of Tregonetha.

5: Towards the far end of the village, turn right on a track after Lowena B&B. Follow the track to a footpath sign off left to St Wenn. In the field entered, follow the left hedge to a waymarked gate ahead. In the next field follow the left hedge briefly to a gate on the left and descend the field entered to a gate. Pass through and immediately cross a stream. Then go half-right across a field to a stone bar stile. Ascend in the same direction to the next stile and in the next field diverge gently from the left hedge to a stone stile onto a lane (963 645) (12m). The path continues opposite. Go half-right to a stile (some distance right of the gate). Cross and now go just left of straight ahead to a stile. In the final field follow the left hedge to another stile onto a lane. Turn left and shortly reach St Wenn. Follow the lane through and beyond the village for 0.6mile to a T-junction (981 655) (13.4m). Treliver is on the corner on the left.

Stage 5
St Wenn to Cardinham

VIA: Camel Trail, Bodmin and Callabarrett Wood
DISTANCE: 11.3m [74.9m]
ASCENT: 1470ft   **DESCENT:** 1310ft
EXPLORER: 106 (Newquay), 109 (Bodmin Moor)
LANDRANGER: 200 (Bodmin)

This stage continues the march across Cornwall, moving eastwards to reach the charming village of Cardinham on the south-western edge of Bodmin Moor. This is an attractive walk with plenty of paths to choose from. After briefly joining the Saints Way, paths and bridleways lead to the multi-user Camel Trail along a disused railway line and a short section of this is taken into Bodmin. This compact town offers a good range of shops and eating places. As there's nowhere to eat at Cardinham, a short detour into Bodmin's centre for a lunchtime meal and something to eat in the evening is a smart move! From Bodmin, good tracks can be taken into and through Callabarrett Wood followed by field paths to Cardinham. There is an excellent B&B at Cardinham and the church is well worth a look with its two Celtic crosses, one of which dates from the eighth century. There is also a B&B further on in Mount if not stopping in Cardinham.

Another noteworthy feature of the day is the fact that the stage has moved from the SW 100 km x 100 km square on the maps into the SX square. Progress indeed!

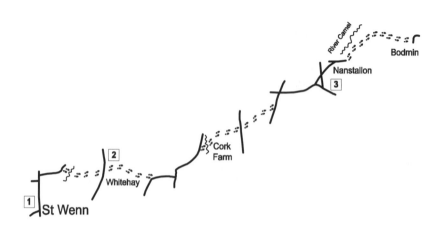

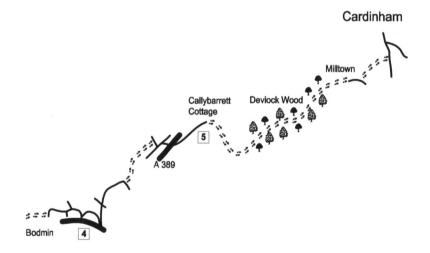

1: From the T-junction at Treliver (SW 981 655) turn left, descend the hill, ignore the turn off left and shortly after take the lane on the right. Pass Tregolls Farm (B&B) and continue for another quarter mile to take an unsigned track off right. Descend to a stream, cross by the substantial footbridge and ascend to Blackhay Farm. Just before the farm, turn left on a track as directed for the Saints Way, which uses a Celtic cross as its sign. When the track shortly bears right, leave the Saints Way to follow the yellow waymark through the farm gate ahead. Cross the field to the gate opposite (the upper of the two), then go parallel to the left hedge to a stile. Cross and go straight on along the right boundary to an unusual 'stile' set in a deep bank. In the field entered go half-left to a stile at a waymarked gate. Beyond, follow the left hedge, then the track straight ahead and continue passing to the right of a house out onto a lane (998 658) (1.6m).

2: Go straight across up the access drive to Whitehay. Pass to the left of the house and its turning waterwheel, then take the waymark left to follow a grassy track to the right. Follow the waymarks down to a stream. Cross and take a short track to a gate into a field. Here follow the right boundary eastwards to a gate onto a farm track and turn right briefly to meet a lane (SX 006 656); note the entry into SX. Turn left and follow the lane to a T-junction. Turn left towards Ruthernbridge. After a third of a mile, take a bridleway track off right marked Cork Farm. Use the walkers' bridge over a significant stream to join the track. Soon after joining it, the track branches. Go straight on (left) here, following the waymark. The clear track meets a lane and continues opposite right, eventually reaching another lane (030 665) (4m). Turn left and follow the lane to a cross-road. Turn right signed for Bodmin. After 0.4 mile, ignore a turn-off right to Bodmin so as to stay on the lane to Nanstallon and after another 300 yds reach a cross-road in this village.

3: Go straight across into Marshall Road. Follow this and having passed the end of the houses, ignore a lane coming in on the left and a few yards beyond this, turn off left on a track signed to Boscarne with a 'No Vehicular Access to the Camel Trail' notice (040 672). Descend on this concrete track to a footpath sign off to the right just before the River Camel is crossed. Take this path along the south bank of the river. Pass under the railway bridge and continue along the river to a slope up which meets a path. Turn right on this to meet the surfaced Camel Trail. Turn right on the trail, soon pass Dunmere Halt and continue on the track towards Bodmin for as far as it goes before joining the road on the left. Turn right into Berrycombe Road. Ignore turn-offs to stay on this, passing the fire station and continuing on until it curves right to meet a main road (070 672) (7m). Turn left, eastwards. To reach the town centre, use the pedestrian crossing, turn left for a few yards then turn right to steeply ascend the 'No Through Road' of Market Street to reach Fore Street, in the centre of Bodmin.

4: Return to the main road via Market Street and continue eastwards. Just after the Westberry Hotel on the left, turn off left up Rhind Street. Ascend to a T-junction, turn right for a few yards and turn left up Roseland Road. Follow this old lane past the speed derestriction sign and continue on the lane for another quarter mile to a severe right turn in the lane. Here (079 676) carry straight on along a track and at its end meet a lane (with the Cornish Lime Company opposite). Turn right on Penbugle Lane and shortly reach a T-junction. Turn left and follow the road as it curves right to meet the slip road for the A30. Cross with care to the 'No Through Road' opposite (085 679) (8.2m). Follow the lane which soon crosses the A30, passes Callybarrett Farm and continues to Callybarrett Cottage on the right, where the lane ends at a track fork (094 683).

5: Take the right branch (signed as a bridleway) and almost immediately pass through the right of two gates onto a farm track beyond. Follow the track along the left boundary across two fields, then enter a field and maintain the same direction through it to a waymark and then a gate into woods. Follow the track through Callabarrett Wood to a track junction and go ahead on a steeply descending track to a forest road. Turn left, cross a stream and on meeting another track turn right to shortly meet another forestry road on the far side of a stream; ancient Ladyvale Bridge (107 677) (10m) is visible to the right. Turn left to follow the forestry road to the right of the stream. Keep to the main track. At a bridleway sign, fork left as directed towards buildings and up to meet a lane at Milltown (116 681) (10.7m). Turn right briefly and at a corner, turn off left on a signed path. On entering a field, go half-left to a stile. Cross and take the trodden path half-left to a wall. Turn right along the wall, go through two gates and then cross a field on an east-northeast path to exit via the farm gate onto a lane at Cardinham (123 685). The village church is to the left but turn right for Cardinham's B&B (124 683) (11.3m) and the e2e route.

Stage 6
Cardinham to Minions

VIA: Goonzion Downs, Draynes Bridge and Common Moor
DISTANCE: 13.5m [88.4m]
ASCENT: 2060ft   **DESCENT:** 1430ft
EXPLORER: 109 (Bodmin Moor)
LANDRANGER: 200 (Bodmin), 201 (Plymouth)

This stage crosses the southern end of Bodmin Moor to reach the small high-up historic village of Minions, close to the moor's south-eastern edge. The paths round Cardinham are rather limited, so quiet lanes and bridleways are used to reach and cross open access Goonzion Downs, with its grazing ponies, into St Neot. St Neot village is large enough to have a shop and the London Inn. The church is next door to the inn and its stained glass windows, dating from the early sixteenth century, are magnificent with their depiction of biblical stories and scenes from the life of St Neot and St George. From St Neot the route ascends to open access Berry Down and from there goes eastwards across the open access land beyond Carpuan Farm to reach the hamlet of Draynes. A very quiet lane leads to Draynes Bridge over the River Fowey.

Here, one is exhorted to visit the Goliath Falls, which requires a detour since it is in the opposite direction to Minions. The biblical Goliath was enormous while his opponent David was relatively small. Having made the detour, we can report that the falls are more 'David' than 'Goliath' although there had been significant rain before and on the day; thus this detour, taking about 40 minutes, is not recommended! From Draynes Bridge, the route uses paths across open access Bulland Downs to reach the village of Common Moor. Beyond, paths lead onto the open moor surrounding Minions. The directions beyond Draynes Bridge look complex, but the path is actually quite straightforward and partly uses the route of the Copper Trail circuit round Bodmin Moor. Minions is very small and is considered to be the highest village in Cornwall at 980 ft. It is a tourist destination because of its position, its industrial remains and the superb surrounding moorland for those wishing to explore on foot and by bike. Its visitors are well catered for with a tea room, general shop and inn.

The stage mileage includes a two-mile circuit from Minions to visit the Bronze Age stone circles called the Hurlers, and to then climb up to the Cheesewring, named because its large granite plates resemble a cheese press. The view from the Cheesewring is panoramic and a memory highlight. However, it's an exposed spot and although mid-April when we were there, it was bitterly cold with rain clouds (yet again) sweeping in.

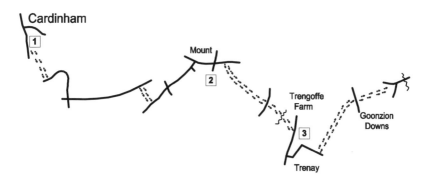

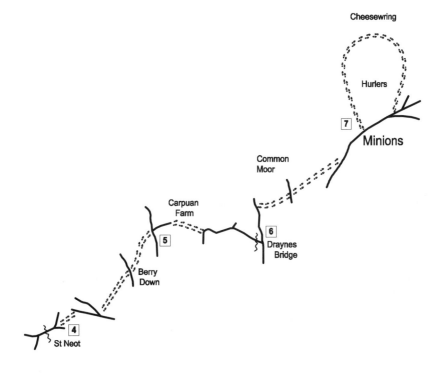

1: From the Old Schoolhouse in Cardinham village (SX 124 683) take the lane south briefly and as the lane bends right, leave it for a signed bridleway off left which passes through a garden and along a clear track. After crossing a stream, ascend on a grassy track which then becomes a farm track and keep straight, passing right of Castle Farm to reach a lane. Turn left and follow the lane to a cross road. Go left for just over a third of a mile then take a signed path off right (132 679). Follow a left hedge for two fields onto a lane. Turn left and ignoring turn-offs left and right along more minor lanes, reach a T-junction (144 681). Turn right, signed Mount, to shortly reach this small village (2.1m).

2: Continue eastwards through Mount and when the lane curves left, turn right along the access to South Bofindle farm (152 679). At the farm, follow the bridleway sign left to an enclosed farm track and at its end go through a gate on the left and follow the right boundary to a lane (156 677) (2.8m). The bridleway continues opposite on the access to Trengoffe Farm. At the farm go through a gate and turn right to find an enclosed track. Pass through stone posts then follow the left wall to a gate and descend on the enclosed track (sometimes with water running down it) to a bridge across a substantial stream. Cross and ascend to a gate onto a lane (159 672) (3.2m).

3: Turn right along the lane ascending steeply. Just after passing an isolated house ignore a turn off right and follow the lane as it curves left to Trenay at the bottom. Beyond, the lane ascends and just keep going until a building on the left is reached (169 670) (4.1m). Just after this, take the signed bridleway off left and almost immediately take a walkers' gate off right onto Goonzion Downs. Head east-of-North, close(ish) to the left boundary of the access land, to reach a bridleway waymark. Follow this directional sign and after a few yards, curve right to the next waymark. Beyond, go half-right to reach a walkers' gate onto a lane (174 676). Go left briefly and then turn off right at the bridleway sign. Go east, parallel to a road on the left and when the sign for a road junction is spotted, branch left to a bridleway gate. Beyond, immediately turn right on a delightful, signed footpath track which follows a right boundary to a gate and then a left boundary curving left to descend to a walkers' gate. Descend steps to a lane which is followed down to meet a road. Turn right through St Neot village following the major road as it curves left then right to cross the River Neot (185 679) (5.4m) with the London Inn and the church just beyond on the left.

4: Turn up left on the lane just before the London Inn and in a short distance turn off right on a signed ascending track. When this meets a lane, turn right to a lane junction (192 681) (6m). Here, enter the field opposite and go straight across it to a gate. In the next field, converge on the right boundary and follow it to a stile top right. Cross and follow the right boundary for a short distance to a stile on the right onto a lane. Turn left briefly then take a signed path off right into a field. Follow the left hedge to a stile in the corner and cross onto open access Berry Down. Go straight ahead on a path but then leave it to follow the right boundary. There's no path here other than the odd sheep track and the ground is uneven but this should not present a problem. Eventually when close to a road, some fencing is met. Follow the fencing left and exit Berry Down as best you can opposite a lane junction (202 689) (6.8m). (If you don't fancy the cross-country walk across the down, continue on the footpath across it which exits onto the lane (200 692), then turn right for 350 yds to the lane junction.)

5: Take the lane opposite to Carpuan farm. At the farm, continue beyond it on the track, following the permissive path signs, and shortly turn right as directed through a gate into open access land. Follow the path without losing height to find a mossy stone stile just left of the top left wall corner. Cross and go straight ahead south-of-East to a waymarked gate, continuing straight ahead to a stile. Beyond, go just right of straight ahead to a stile, then keep right of a mound to reach a stile. Finally, follow a left fence to a stile with steps onto a lane at Draynes (214 690) (7.6m). Turn left. The lane soon curves right to run eastwards. Ignore all turn offs to the left to maintain an eastwards direction. Eventually a cottage on the left called 'Riverwood' is passed. After another 200 yds, use a gap in the bank on the right to reach a ledge in the woodland and climb another short bank to a higher (better) ledge and path. Turn left along a path parallel to the road, rejoining the road when opposite a car park entrance. Turn right and in a few yards cross Draynes Bridge and reach a T-junction (8.7m).

6: Turn left for 320 yds to take the second footpath on the right into Bulland Downs (trying the first path right lands you in a terrible tangle of undergrowth). The path is waymarked and walked. It heads south-of East across the downs to an exit stile off right. Beyond, follow a stream, pass through a gate on the right then follow a left boundary to a kissing gate onto a track. Leave the track for a grassy track over the stream and then follow the right bank of the stream to a lane (236 694) (9.4m). Take the signed path opposite right, go through a gate labelled 'South Trekeive' and having passed the house, curve left to the stream which is then followed to a walkers' gate. Beyond, pass along a surfaced track at the back of the houses of Common Moor. A brief distance after the track becomes a lane, go left at a right of way sign and return to the stream. Turn right along the stream until a lane is met. Here turn left, cross the stream and pass through a farm gate onto a farm track (240 697). Follow the track until a footpath sign off half-right (near the stream) is spotted. Take this to the stream and then follow the stream to a footbridge crossing. After crossing a stile, go left of straight ahead past a post to a waymarked gate. Then go up a left fence, passing a house, through a gate and forward along an access drive to meet a surfaced white road. Go right to maintain an eastwards direction. When the track curves sharp right (247 700) (10.2m), carry straight on, cross a cattle grid into open access land and follow the main track as it curves right to a road (10.5m). Turn left and follow parallel to the road on the moorland verges for less than a mile into Minions (261 712) (11.4m).

7: To walk to the Hurlers and the Cheesewring, take the track signed 'Hurlers', passed as Minions is entered, branching off right after a short distance to inspect the stones. Then proceed to the left side of the hill ahead, aiming for the stones above the quarry and ascend to the top of Stowe Hill (258 725). After inspecting the Cheesewring perched on its top (awesome) and admiring the view (magnificent), return by the track visible from the top by the isolated tree. Having repeated the descent past the quarry, aim for the transmitter behind Minions to find the track and just follow this to return to the village.

Stage 7
Minions to (near) Lamerton

VIA: **Caradon Hill, Tamar Valley Discovery Trail and Horsebridge**
DISTANCE: **14.9m [103.3m]**
ASCENT: **1590ft**   **DESCENT:**   **2000ft**
EXPLORER: **109 (Bodmin Moor), 108 (Lower Tamar Valley)**
LANDRANGER: 201 (Plymouth)

After a week's walking there's a feeling that you will never get out of Cornwall! However, towards the end of this stage, the traverse of Cornwall is completed and it marks a significant landmark on the journey to John O'Groats. The fact that Cornwall is a very long county can be gauged from the fact that while 10% of the walk has been completed, the end-to-ender is still very much in south-west England. The River Tamar marks the end of Cornwall with the ancient bridge crossing at Horsebridge used to enter Devon. On our journey this stage was memorable for the swirling winds and driving heavy rain which was definitely 'in yer face'. Therefore the fire, soup and tea at the Royal Inn pub just inside Devon were more than welcome, and fortunately our B&B accommodation was less than four miles further on.

The paths in the area crossed are not exactly abundant so the route uses what's available, including a new path provided by the Duchy of Cornwall, which in the prevailing conditions, was ankle deep in mud. After leaving Bodmin Moor by crossing Caradon Hill, the route mainly passes through farmland of varying quality. The only place of any size passed through is the large village of Pensilva early in the day. After Pensilva, the route goes east-northeast through Golberdon to Old Mill. It then turns east to Luckett to pick up the Tamar Valley Discovery Trail which loosely follows the River Tamar northwards to Horsebridge. In Devon, the route leaves the Discovery Trail to reach Sydenham Damerel, but then follows it north to Youngcott before finally leaving it to turn east and finish the day about a mile west of Lamerton. The Blacksmiths Arms on the B-road at Lamerton serves meals.

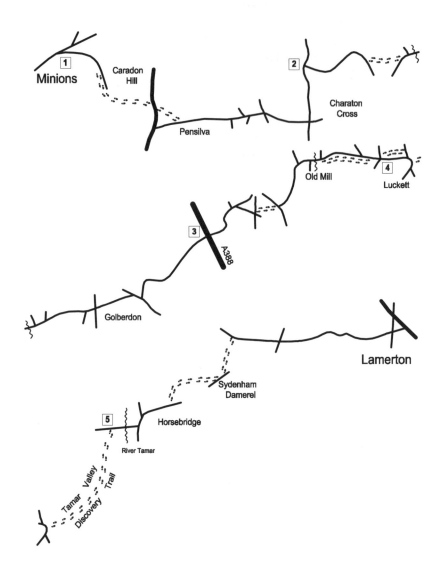

1: From Minions village (SX 261 712) turn right on the lane by the Minions Stores & Tearooms. The lane ascends towards the wireless mast. When the lane curves left, leave it by going half right to the wall on the right and follow the grassy easy-walking ground beside the wall south-eastwards. When an access drive is met turn right and very shortly, on joining another track, keep right to reach a B-road. Take a short grassy path opposite right to reach a minor road and turn left through the large village of Pensilva. Near the end of the village, at the Victoria Inn, follow the sign to Golberdon. After just less than 0.5 mile at the next cross-road, named Charaton Cross, turn left, signed Plushabridge (but carry straight on for a shortcut to Golberdon). After 700 yds, just after Penharget Cottage (300 705) (3.3m), turn right on a white road.

2: Follow the surfaced white road ignoring tracks off left. Eventually, the road curves significantly right passing Mill Lawn on the left. Just after this farm, turn left on a signed path (310 708) (4m). Pass through a gate into a field and cross it north-of-East to a stone stile. In the next field follow the right hedge to a farm gate onto a track. This very shortly leads through the yard of Scrawsden Farm and onto its access drive which is followed to a lane. Turn left descending to Kerney Bridge. Stay on the 'major' lane ascending to the small village of Golberdon. At the end of the village at a cross-road, keep on the 'major' lane by going straight on for about a mile to reach a T-junction (340 717) (6m). Go right here (signed Maders) and then shortly take the first left. Follow this very minor lane which soon bends right, north-eastwards, to the main A388 road (351 725) (7m).

3: Cross to the lane opposite. Ignore a turn off left and continue north-east to a lane off right which is taken (358 731). Ascend to a cross-road, turn left for 110 yds and then take a signed footpath off right into a field. Cross to the bottom right field corner. Go through the gap here and continue in the same direction to a gap out onto a lane junction. Take the descending lane opposite to Trehill and beyond continue to a T-junction (367 738) (8.5m). Turn right, ignore a turn-off right shortly afterwards and continue to Old Mill where its stream is crossed. Beyond, start to ascend a very steep hill. Immediately after a lane off left, go over steps on the right and take a permissive path (thoughtfully provided by the Duchy of Cornwall) which runs parallel to the ascending lane. Cross a parking area and continue on the Duchy path, rejoining the lane where there's wooden fencing on the left, just before the path curves right to diverge from the lane. Continue along the lane eastwards until a more major lane is met at a staggered cross-road (382 737) (9.5m).

4: Turn left here for 100 yds (away from Luckett) to take a signed path off right. Pass up a house drive to a two-stile arrangement into a field. Go straight ahead to a gate and in the next field follow the right boundary to a stile on the right onto a track. Turn left, pass through a gate ahead and follow the right hedge to a gap into the next field. Continue along the right edge to join a track and exit onto a lane via a gate. Turn right and descend through Luckett ignoring a turn off right. Just as the bridge is approached, turn left on a track (389 737) (10m) and join the Tamar Valley Discovery Trail, which uses an Apple for its signs. Enter a meadow and keep by the left hedge to a stile. Cross and follow the signed and well trodden path across rough ground into a field. Here follow the right boundary and exit to meet a track. Go straight on (i.e. right) and follow the track through a gate continuing on it all the way to meet a lane. Turn right and almost immediately cross the River Tamar into Devon (400 749) (11.2m).

5: Just over the bridge turn left. Pass the pub following signs to Sydenham Damerel, and ignoring a turn off left opposite the pub, keep ascending on the main lane for another 1/3 mile, turning off left onto a tarmac 'No Through Road' (406 753). Pass left of a farm entrance and then ignore a branch off right to another residence so as to continue descending, on the now rough and unsurfaced track, to meet a minor lane at the bottom. Turn right and follow the lane to meet a road in Sydenham Damerel. Turn left for a few yards and then turn off left down an 'Unsuitable For Motors' track, rejoining the Tamar Way Discovery Trail. Follow the clear (unsurfaced) track to and past Youngcott Cottage and out onto a lane (409 769) (13m). Turn right leaving the Discovery Trail for good. Follow the lane eastwards and go straight across at a cross-road. Ascend to the next cross-road and turn left to shortly reach B&B accommodation on the right, just before the B3362 road (436 774).

Stage 8
(near) Lamerton to Okehampton

VIA: Brent Tor, Lydford Gorge and West Devon Way
DISTANCE: 17.4m [120.7m]
ASCENT: 1840ft   DESCENT: 1870ft
EXPLORER: 108(Lower Tamar Valley)112 (Launceston)OL28 (Dartmoor)
LANDRANGER: 201 (Plymouth), 191 (Okehampton)

This stage can be described as the Dartmoor Day and has many outstanding highlights. From Lamerton, the route heads north-eastish to reach the western edge of the Dartmoor National Park and climbs Brent Tor to visit the isolated church on its top. At 1,100 ft, this tor with its church rises high above its surroundings and can thus be seen from a considerable distance away. The route continues northwards along the western fringes of the moor, picking up the West Devon Way (WDW) after passing through the village of North Brentor. When the Way reaches a lane there is a route choice of either taking the lane northwards to Lydford or reaching the village via Lydford Gorge; the distances are about the same. The gorge costs if you are not a National Trust member, but is highly recommended as the gorge walk is spectacular and exciting with its narrow path and tunnels perched over the steep drop to the rushing water below. We opted for the gorge and the NT café at its north end.

After leaving Lydford, the route again takes to the WDW which goes northwards but outside the national park. The WDW is temporarily left so as to re-enter Dartmoor south of Sourton village and ascend to just below Sourton Tors. Beyond, the WDW is re-joined but here we found it not well signed and it was necessary to pay close attention to the map. The route becomes navigationally easier as it drops towards the hamlet of Meldon. After crossing over the A30, the route runs through farmland before crossing a golf course where the walkers follow a path between two painted blue lines to keep them on the straight and narrow. The golf course entrance leads to a road on the southern edge of the pleasant, bustling, small, tourist town of Okehampton. We had thought we might stay at Okehampton's Youth Hostel, but investigation showed that a nearby B&B was cheaper and offered more luxurious facilities.

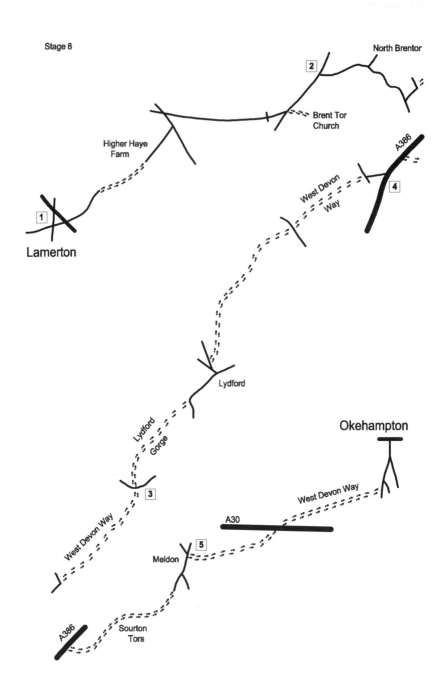

North Brentor

2

Brent Tor
Church

A386

4

Higher Haye
Farm

West Devon
Way

1

Lamerton

Lydford

Okehampton

Lydford
Gorge

West Devon Way

3

West Devon Way

A30

5

Meldon

A386   Sourton
Tors

1: Continue (SX 436 774) to the B-road and turn right for 200 yds to a cross-road. Turn left, signed 'No Through Road'. Follow the lane which is surfaced as far as Hurlditch Court and continues as an unsurfaced track beyond, mainly enclosed. After Higher Haye farm (444 786) the track becomes a lane which is followed in the same north-northeast direction to reach a T-junction (1.9m). Turn left for a 1/4 mile to a cross-road and turn right, east-northeast. After 1.2m go straight across at a cross-road and shortly reach a car park on the right. Cut through the small car park (toilets) and cross the lane to the gate opposite. Follow the well-trodden, easy path up Brent Tor to the church and then return the same way to the lane (4m). Turn right. Having passed the now closed Brentor Inn, take the next turn right (474 812) (signed Brentor and Mary Tavy).

2: Follow the main lane down to North Brentor's War Memorial and turn right, signed Mary Tavy. Fork right at the church, cross a cattle grid and turn left on a lane (487 811) (5.5m). Ignore a left fork to houses almost immediately and ascend gently on the lane. When the lane turns sharp left (493 816) (6m), continue straight on north-east on a good track across the moors following the WDW directional sign showing Brent Tor with its church. Follow the stony track, until diverted right to follow the left boundary of a residence, before returning to the track again. After the track crosses a small ford, it gradually comes closer to a left boundary. Look for a waymarked gate on the left and take this onto a track shortly leading to a lane (503 831) (7.1m). This is where there is the route choice. Turn left for Lydford Gorge (but turn right to miss the gorge and take the lane to Lydford village).

3: Assuming the gorge is chosen, its southern entrance is very shortly reached on the right (toilets/ café). After entering, take the first path left, pass under a railway bridge and continue on the main path until a right branch leads via steps to the White Lady Waterfall. Cross the river on a bridge and turn right towards the Devil's Cauldron passing the Tunnel Falls on the way. It's a one-way route – enjoy. Either reach the north exit (café/toilets) via the signed 'short way' or go via Devil's Cauldron (recommended). Exit through the car park to the lane through Lydford village. Turn left and ascend steeply past the church and castle, continuing on to the war memorial. Turn left here and shortly fork right at the derestricted sign, signed Watergate; there is also a WDW sign here (9m). Follow the lane for just over a 1/4 mile and immediately after a house on the right named 'Bolts House', take a signed byway off right (512 856). Follow this to a track T-junction. Turn right to a gate and then branch left as directed to a gate. Now go straight ahead on the byway now enclosed. Cross a lane to continue on the byway opposite and eventually reach a further lane (527 890). Here, turn left briefly and almost immediately right at a T-junction leaving the WDW. Follow the lane to shortly reach the busy A386 road (528 891) (11.7m).

4: Turn left along the A-road for 390 yds and immediately after the Country Hotel sign, turn right on an unsurfaced track, curving left to cross over a disused railway (traffic-free cycle route). Continue through a farm gate onto the open moorland. Here, turn left and loosely follow the left wall using the grassy paths on the ground. Keep the left wall in sight with Sourton Crags above on the right. Cross a 'gap' on the left where the WDW is again joined and keep on in the same direction in company with the left wall until a broken down wall at right angles is met. Turn right and follow this broken down wall south-of-East until it meets another wall. Turn left along this right wall over rough ground to a (WDW waymarked) farm gate. Beyond, enter an enclosed track. After another gate, follow the left boundary to a further gate and onto an enclosed track. After a farm entrance, the track becomes a lane (557 919) which leads straight down under the viaduct into Meldon (14.7m).

5: Just after Meldon's cottages, turn off right on a signed bridleway to Meldon Woods (560 924). Follow the track through a gate and look for a waymarked path off left. Pass through a gate and follow the path through the wood, initially high above the river, but then descending to cross the West Okement River by a footbridge. Beyond, turn left, following the river. On approaching the A30, the path curves right into a car park. Cross this onto its access lane and follow the lane left over the A30 (567 931) (15.6m). Immediately after crossing, turn right on a farm track. Follow it, diverting right around a farm as directed to reach its far side. The track continues along a left boundary reaching a gate onto a golf course. Follow the bridleway path across it; it's marked by blue lines on each side of the path. After passing left of the club house it meets the golf course's access track. Follow this left to meet Tors Road on the edge of Okehampton. Turn left and Tors Road runs into Station Road which has accommodation (588 949). Continuing down Station Road leads into the centre of Okehampton.

Stage 9
Okehampton to Clannaborough Barton

VIA: Tarka Trail, Bow and Two Moors Way
DISTANCE: 15.3m [136m]
ASCENT: 1380ft   **DESCENT:** 1560ft
EXPLORER: 113 (Okehampton)
LANDRANGER: 191 (Okehampton)

From Okehampton to South Tawton, parts of the Tarka Trail are used. Initially, the route continues eastwards through Dartmoor to the small village of Belstone and then follows the River Taw. It was wet from above and below and the rough riverside path was slippery and muddy making progress slow, so it was a relief to eventually reach the end of this section at Sticklepath village. For the remainder of the stage, the direction is predominantly north-east. After reaching South Tawton, the A30 is crossed by a path through a long dark tunnel beside a significant stream; gates are used to shut the tunnel if the water level gets too high and it was just below foot level on the day. Dartmoor is left at this point and it's lush Devonshire farmland that is now the feature of the landscape.

Quiet lanes, farm tracks and a Roman Road (also a farm track) are used to reach Bow; the Roman Road crosses the River Yeo and we were relieved to find a good footbridge as the map only shows a ford. From Bow, footpaths lead to the Two Moors Way which is followed to the main road at Clannaborough Barton. Crediton is the obvious place for a B&B but if you don't fancy organising a pick-up or taking the poor bus service, there is a B&B at Morchard Road, a further 2 miles along the route. We were fortunate to be able to stay with my relatives for the next couple of stages.

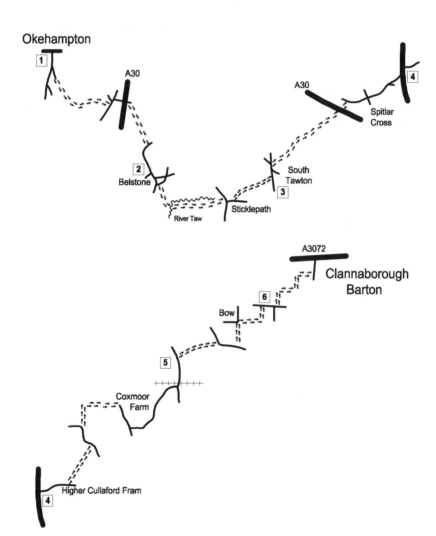

1: Proceed down Station Road (SX 588 949) and at the bottom turn right into Mill Road, signed 'College'. Immediately after passing to the left of the mill and its waterwheel, climb steps on the right and turn right on a lane. Keep right to pass between the side of Okehampton's college and the mill leat. On reaching a sign post, take the paved path indicated. On meeting a track, go straight across on the now unsurfaced path which eventually runs parallel to the East Okement River on the right. When the path meets a lane, turn left and shortly meet another lane. Turn right for a few yards and then go sharp right, signed Tordown. Immediately pass under a railway bridge and then under the A30 and 240 yds later take a walkers' gate off right (607 948) (1.5m). Cross a stream then follow the obvious path into a field and ascend by the right hedge for two fields. In the following field, follow the left fence and cross the next field to a farm gate leading out to a lane. Turn right following the lane to Belstone village (619 935) (2.6m).

2: In the village keep left until a telephone and post box on the left. Here turn right, keep left of The Tors pub and reach a small triangular piece of grassy moorland on the left very shortly afterwards. Cross this following the left wall, cross the road met into a small parking area and turn right to take the gently descending track leading down to a footbridge over the River Taw. Cross the footbridge, turn left and follow a track to the right of a wall, parallel to the river. Keep close to the river to eventually reach and cross a footbridge. The river is then followed for a short while on the north side before a footbridge resumes travel along the river on the south side. Eventually, a path T-junction is reached. Turn left here and follow the path to a lane in Sticklepath (644 940) (4.3m). Take the lane opposite right and soon go left on an unsurfaced track, signed 'Tarka Trail'. The track ascends to a lane in South Tawton village.

3: Turn left through the village and shortly after the derestriction sign, fork right on an unsurfaced track bearing an 'Unsuitable for Motor Vehicles' notice and also bearing a Quarry Cottage sign. Follow the track, turning left as directed. Pass the cottage and continue straight ahead to a footpath sign. Keep ahead following the sign into and through a long and dark underpass of the A30 on a path beside a stream. On emerging, follow the track parallel to the stream to reach a stile onto a lane (657 952) (5.5m) and turn right ascending for a long half mile to a cross-road at Spitlar Cross. Go straight on here and after a further long half mile at a lane fork, branch left for a half mile to meet the main A3124 road (676 967) (7.2m).

4: Go left briefly and then take a minor road off right. Follow this for 2/3mile to a turn off left at Higher Cullaford Farm (684 973) (7.9m) on a track signed 'Unmetalled Road'. The enclosed track, wet in places, emerges on a lane at Brandis Corner (693 987) (9m). Turn left following the lane until the lane turns sharp left to run westwards (694 994). Here, continue straight ahead, north, on a track for 300 yds then turn right through a farm gate onto a straight field track which is to the right of a ditch; this is the Roman Road. When a footbridge is reached use it to cross the River Yeo. Beyond, follow the now enclosed farm track to meet the end of a lane serving Coxmoor Farm (703 996) (10.1m). Turn right along the lane and at a T-junction (707 989) turn left (signed Bow). Follow signs to Bow at the next lane junction, curve left to pass under a railway line.

5: Follow the lane for a further quarter of a mile to a signed footpath off right (SS 717 005) (12m). Follow the track to a signed walkers' gate on the left leading into an irregularly shaped field. Follow the right hedge along four edges to a walkers' gate and in the next field, follow the right hedge to a walkers' gate onto a lane. Turn right briefly and then turn off left onto a signed path. Follow the right hedge to a footbridge and take the clear wide path continuation on the other side. When the path meets an access track at a corner, go straight ahead on the track and shortly reach a lane at a corner with a cross on the right (722 013) (12.8m). Turn right and when the lane swings sharp left almost immediately, carry straight on along a signed footpath. Follow the concrete track, going straight on through a scruffy yard and enter a field (waymarked). The path now followed is both waymarked and trodden. Follow the right hedge, north-of-East, for two fields, then pass through a waymarked farm gate. Gently diverge from the right boundary to a stile on the opposite side of the field. Follow the trodden path across the next field to a stile, then follow the left hedge until turning left at a directional waymark to a walkers' gate. Beyond, follow a right boundary which curves right to a walkers' gate. The path now passes between a left boundary and a house onto an access drive which is followed to a lane (13.5m).

6: Turn right and follow the lane east for nearly 2/3 mile to a signed footpath off left (740 017) immediately before a couple of houses. Follow the ascending track which curves right to Sweetfield. Follow the track as it curves left past Sweetfield and look for a walkers's gate on the left into a field. Turn right along the hedge briefly, then left at a waymark where the Two Moors Way is joined. Cross the field as indicated, passing a waymarked telegraph pole. Go through a hedge gap into the next field and follow the right hedge. Follow the track down and right, as directed on the Moors Way sign, out onto a lane with Clannaborough Barton's church opposite. Turn left and shortly reach the main A3072 road (746 028).

Stage 10
Clannaborough Barton to Bickleigh

VIA: Two Moors Way, Kennerleigh and Cadeleigh Court
DISTANCE: 16.3m [152.3m]
ASCENT: 1600ft   **DESCENT:**   1930ft
EXPLORER: 113 (Okehampton), 114 (Exeter & Exe Valley)
LANDRANGER: 191 (Okehampton), 192 (Exeter)

This stage continues the march across mid-Devon and again the landscape is pastoral. The route follows the   Two Moors Way to near Morchard Road before leaving it for a mixture of quiet lanes, farm tracks and footpaths on a predominantly eastwards route which connects the small hamlets and villages of Oldborough, Kennerleigh, Poughill, Upham and Cadeleigh Court, before dropping to cross the River Dart and very shortly afterwards the Exe by Bickleigh Bridge. This is not a highly populated area so we were surprised to find a shop in Kennerleigh. Other than that, there are no facilities until the stage end at Bickleigh Mill where you can get an excellent pot of tea and cakes. It is not a particularly well-walked area but like other parts of Devon we walked in, we found the paths were all there and well signed. Finally, we were blessed with a decent day of weather with some sun which was most welcome.

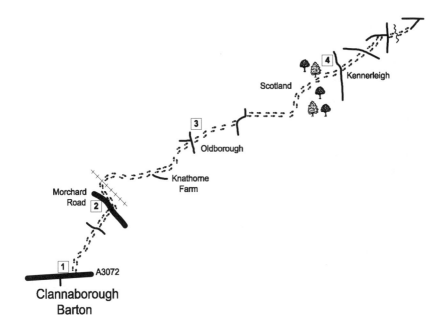

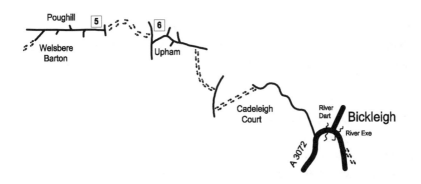

1: From the main A3072 road at Clannaborough Barton (SS 746 028) turn right towards Copplestone and after 160 yds turn left on a 'No Through Road' to a T-junction. Here turn right for 280 yds on a farm track and left into a field at a Two Moors Way sign to follow the farm track along the left hedge. At the bottom-most point of the field turn right and then left as directed through a walkers' gate for a path through woodland. Beyond, enter a field and follow the right hedge to a gate into a wood. Follow the path to a footbridge, go across a field just east-of-North to a gate in the corner. Then follow the right hedge to a lane (751 041). Turn right for 250 yds, then turn left at a footpath sign. Cross the field half-right to reach and follow the right hedge to a stile onto the main A377 road (1.4m).

2: Turn left along the verge for a short distance, then turn right at a path sign and follow the path parallel to the main road which soon runs beside the railway line. The village of Morchard Road is just ahead, but turn right as directed, over the railway bridge and follow the farm access towards Shobrooke Farm until a signed footpath off left is reached. Follow the field left boundary round two sides to a ladder stile. Cross and follow the left hedge to a wood and turn right along the wood edge. Leave the Two Moors Way (which turns left) by carrying straight on over a stile signed to Knathorne. Follow the left hedge to a stile. Turn left to a double stile, then follow the left hedge down a long field. Go through the left of two farm gates into a field and half-right to shortly reach a farm track which is followed right to and through a farmyard. Beyond, keep straight on along an enclosed unsurfaced farm track, signed as a bridleway, which is followed to a lane. Turn right for a few yards to meet a lane in the hamlet of Oldborough (773 063) (3.9m).

3: Turn left briefly and then go right through a farm gate. Follow the directional sign to cross the field to a waymarked farm gate. Go just left of straight ahead in the field entered to a stile, then go straight up the field to find and follow the left hedge to farm buildings. There's now a leftwards circle to reach its access drive, so turn left through a gate, then half-right as directed and along a left fence to a farm track, whereupon turn right into the farmyard. Turn left through the yard onto the farm's access drive which is taken to a lane (783 065) (4.6m). Turn left for 140 yds and then turn off right on a signed restricted byway which is followed eastwards to a gate through Moor Farm. The track twists right and left through the farmyard (signed) to pass through a gate on its far side. Continue to a byway T-junction (806 069) (6.2m) and turn left for 230 yds to a waymarked path off right, immediately after passing the building named Scotland (807 070). The path goes eastwards making for and following the tree boundary on the left to a waymark into the woods. Follow the well waymarked path to a footbridge over a stream and then follow waymarks ascending steeply through woodland into a field. Turn left and follow the left boundary for two fields to meet a track. Turn right and follow the track which becomes a lane to a lane T-junction in the small village of Kennerleigh (820 074) (7.3m); the village store is on the left at this junction.

4: Turn left for 70 yds and then turn right at a footpath sign. In the field entered, turn right to pass the buildings and continue along the field just north-of-East to a waymarked gate. Follow the left hedge down one field and also partway down the next to a gate on the left where the hedge side is swapped. Thereafter the right hedge is followed to a lane (827 077). Turn right briefly then left on a path along the left field boundary and out onto a lane. Turn right steeply downhill for 120 yds, turning right onto a lane and almost immediately left on a signed bridleway track, which soon turns left through a gate waymarked 'County Road'. When the two paths part, follow the bridleway sign to a stream ford (no bridge). Across, follow the County Road sign up the right hedge to a gate onto a (muddy) track. Follow the track eastwards passing Welsbere Barton farm where the track becomes a public road. This is followed to a T-junction (847 084) (9.3m). Turn right and follow the lane eastwards through Poughill village. At the end of the village, go straight on, eastwards on a lane signed to Upton Barton. This descends and at the bottom gets to a T-junction (865 085) (10.4m).

5: Take the track opposite climbing steeply. Branch left on a track at the first buildings and left again at a footpath waymark. On shortly approaching a farm gate, turn right to a gate leading back onto the track around the buildings perimeter. Turn left on this track and look for a gap on the left in the hedge. Leave the track to climb over a lowered electric fence and head half-right across a field to a gate in the far corner to rejoin the track; it's not a right of way but it's far easier to keep on the track to a barn where the track turns left to reach the same point. Turn left (or keep on) along the track and enter a field. Follow the left field edge eastwards for three fields. The path follows the left hedge in the fourth field, but comes to a difficult overgrown stile onto a track so you may feel justified in using the adjacent track from the end of the third field. The track leads down to the lane at Upham but is not a right of way. From the 'difficult' stile, the right of way crosses the track and continues opposite. It crosses two small fields northwards and then turns right along a left fence down to a lane (881 084) (11.6m).

6: Turn right and shortly reach the hamlet of Upham. Here take the first lane off left (signed Cadeleigh) and proceed generally eastwards, ignoring turn-offs, to a T-junction (898 081) (12.8m). Turn right (signed for Cadeleigh and Bickleigh) and continue eastwards for nearly 3/4 mile. Shortly after a lane comes in on the left (and before Cadeleigh village), turn right at a signed public footpath which initially is a surfaced lane (909 080). When the lane bends right, go straight on along an enclosed path called Back Lane which descends to a lane (911 075) (14m). Turn right on the lane for 410 yds and then turn left at a public footpath sign along a concrete farm track. When the Manor House at Cadeleigh Court is reached, follow the waymarks to a track round the back of it and into a field. Go half-right across the field to a gate onto an enclosed grassy track which eventually meets a track. Turn left on this improving track which becomes surfaced and leads up to a lane (931 078) (15.6m). Turn right and on meeting a main road after over 1/3 mile, turn left over the River Dart and shortly reach the Exeter to Tiverton main road. Turn right crossing the River Exe by lovely Bickleigh Bridge. Across, immediately branch left off the main road onto a surfaced lane signed to Bickleigh Mill. This leads through a parking area to the mill (938 075).

Stage 11
Bickleigh to Hagley Bridge

VIA: Exe Valley Way, Knightshayes Court and Bampton Down
DISTANCE: 16.1m [168.4m]
ASCENT: 1950ft   DESCENT: 1700ft
EXPLORER: 114 (Exeter & Exe Valley), 128 (Taunton)
LANDRANGER: 192 (Exeter), 181 (Minehead)

This stage promises an enticing day's walking starting with a walk northwards following the River Exe on the Exe Valley Way as far as Tiverton. The route continues north to join a Sustrans cycle route to, through and beyond the grounds of the National Trust's Knightshayes Court and onto a bridle track across the ridge of Bampton Down. Beyond, Dark Lane is followed eastwards over an unmarked entry into Somerset where the West Deane Way is joined. This Way is followed northwards by the River Tone to a B&B at Hagley Bridge. On the day we undertook this, it was such a miserable day with wall to wall heavy rain that only one of our hosts walked with us to Tiverton, the other opted for the breakfast washing up! Refreshments can be had at both Tiverton and Knightshayes Court. We opted for very welcome tea and soup at the latter, and it has to be said that being inside in the dry for a short period, was the highlight of the day as there weren't many distant views in the prevailing conditions.

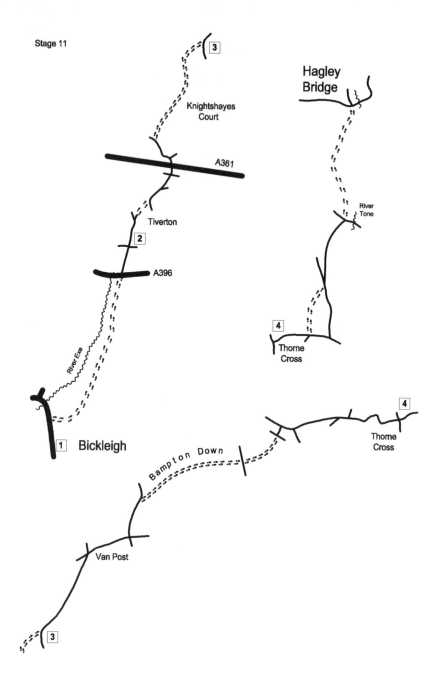

Hagley
Bridge

Knightshayes
Court

A361

River
Tone

Tiverton

2

A396

4

Thorne
Cross

River Exe

1 Bickleigh

Bampton Down

4

Thorne
Cross

Van Post

3

1: Continue on the lane to just past Bickleigh Mill (SS 938 075) and take the signed path off left on the Exe Valley Way. The low level, well-marked path generally keeps close to the River Exe. The only uncertainty in the path comes just after passing through a walkers' gate where the way goes left briefly towards the Exe before turning right. Eventually the path passes to the right of a sewage plant. Beyond, follow the concrete farm track which eventually becomes a lane. After the River Exe splits on the southern edge of Tiverton, follow the Exe Valley Way sign left over the 'side' stream and follow the street up to a footbridge over the A396. Beyond, continue following St Andrew Street to Tiverton's main shopping street (3.7m).

2: Go left for a few yards then leave the Exe Valley Way by turning right into St Peter Street (do not cross the Exe!). On reaching a road junction, turn left so as to keep to the right of the parish church's grounds. Shortly after passing a sign to the Castle, branch right on an ascending surfaced lane named Park Hill which leads into a park. Follow the path through Peoples Park and out onto Park Road. Turn left and ignoring turn-offs, particularly a turn-off right down Carew Road, reach a T-junction. Turn right for a few yards, then left on a road to Chettiscombe. Follow the lane over the A361 (960 142) and immediately beyond ignore a turn-off right by going straight on towards Knightshayes Court (5m). After 1/4 mile turn off right along Knightshayes drive following Sustrans Cycle Route 3. This passes left of the Court buildings and continues towards The Stables where there is a café and toilets. Follow the cycle route signs which turn left just before the café. Continue to follow the cycle signs keeping straight ahead, northwards, on the track which becomes unsurfaced. The track ascends gently to a track T-junction. Go right as directed to shortly meet a lane (963 169) (6.9m).

3: Turn left for 1.5 miles to the Van Post Hill cross-road (974 190) (8.4m). Turn right for just over 1/3 mile to the next cross-road. Turn left and after 700 yds when the lane bends left, go straight on along a good unsigned, unsurfaced track. Follow this east-of-North and north-of-East along Bampton Down, ignoring a track turn-off left. Cross a lane and continue to a lane junction (ST 006 214) (11.3m). Take the lane opposite (signed Clayhanger) and follow it as it swings right after 270 yds (signed Clayhanger). After a further 350 yds, turn off left along an unpromising lane called Dark Lane which is more like a farm track than a minor road. The surface improves after the entrance to Hearne

Farm. Keep heading eastwards on the lane. When the main lane swings left to Clayhanger (018 217), keep straight on signed to Thorne Cross. On reaching the cross-road at Thorne Cross, go straight across leaving Devon for Somerset (032 214) (13.2m).

4: Continue eastwards on the lane for a further 2/3 mile to where there's a lane off right (042 213) and here turn off left on a signed track which is the continuation of Dark Lane. Follow this to meet a lane junction. Go straight across for a few yards to meet a further lane and turn left joining the West Deane Way. The lane descends to the River Tone (15.1m). Don't cross the river bridge, but instead turn left briefly on the lane to Clayhanger and then take a signed restricted byway off it right. Follow this parallel to the river using a footbridge to cross a side stream and reach a track junction. Take the bridleway track opposite, signed West Deane Way, and ascend a short distance to a directional sign off right leading via a gate into a field. The right of way follows the right boundary and becomes a cattle track along this boundary leading to a gate. However, if it's ankle deep in mud, as it was on the day, you can reach the gate by following the hedge to the left of the track on the field side. Having passed through the gate into the next field, follow the right boundary to a waymark onto a track along a left boundary. This is followed by a short stretch by the River Tone to the lane at Hagley Bridge (056 238). The route continues by turning right, but Hagley Bridge's B&B is a very short distance to the left and an evening meal can be had at Waterrow a mile away.

Stage 12
Hagley Bridge to Waterpits

VIA: Wiveliscombe, Ash Priors Common and Cothelstone Hill
DISTANCE: 15m [183.4m]
ASCENT: 2240ft   DESCENT: 1980ft
EXPLORER: 128 (Taunton), 140 (Quantocks & Bridgwater)
LANDRANGER: 181 (Minehead), 182 (Weston-super-Mare)

Having entered the third county, there's a definite feeling of progress. Today's stage heads generally east-north-eastwards across rural Somerset. It soon leaves the West Deane Way for a more direct route to Wiveliscombe which lies just south of the eastern end of the Exmoor National Park. From here the route heads north-of-East through the tiny village of Fitzhead. We had hoped to stop at the pub in Fitzhead shown on the map, but a local lady told us it had been knocked down some years ago! She then very kindly offered us a brew and remained cheerful, despite us emptying her plate of chocolate biscuits. We sat in her wonderful, large, peaceful garden which seemed the perfect example of an English Country Garden. Such kindness and visions remain long in the memory.

After Fitzhead, Ash Prior Common is the next destination and on to the small town of Bishops Lydeard at the foot of the Quantock Hills. From here, the only serious climb of the stage commences up through the hamlet of Cothelstone and on to the summit of Cothelstone Hill on the eastern side of the Quantock Hills. There's a fine panoramic view from the top enhanced by the nearby grazing Exmoor ponies. The stage finishes in the hills at Waterpits and there's a pub a short distance away serving food in the evenings.

The weather on this day was a pleasant contrast to the less than lovely conditions of the previous day and this was a great relief.

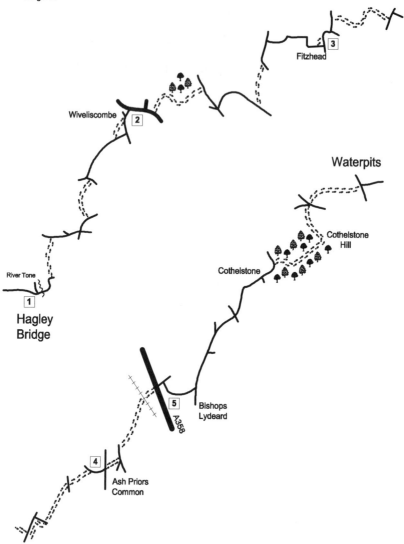

Fitzhead

3

Waterpits

Wiveliscombe

2

Cothelstone
Hill

Cothelstone

River Tone

1

Hagley
Bridge

5

Bishops
Lydeard

A358

4

Ash Priors
Common

1: From Hagley Bridge (ST 056 238) turn right to cross the River Tone and follow the lane for a short distance to a bend right and here take a signed path off left. On very shortly reaching a building, turn right up steps as directed onto a path which enters a field. Follow the left boundary along two sides to a stile in the field corner into a wood. Follow the clear path through the wood above the River Tone, cross a stile and go left as directed to reach a standing stone. Here, go left to pass by the base of viaduct buttresses for a disused railway line. Pass close to the river and turn left onto a brief track which meets a lane (055 248) (0.7m). Leave the West Deane Way here by turning right, north-of-East, to a cross-road at Hellings Cross. Turn left, signed Wiveliscombe. After nearly quarter of a mile, turn left immediately after a barn on the left onto a signed restricted byway which goes generally north to meet a lane (064 259) (1.8m). Turn left and ignore a turn-off left in a very short distance. Follow the lane for over a mile to the second footpath off left through a gate on the left of two; the path is signed. Follow the right hedge for a few yards to a gate in the hedge. Cross, then go a quarter-left aiming just to the right of Wiveliscombe's church to reach a stile. This leads to a further stile onto a lane. Turn right briefly to meet a road on the town's outskirts. Turn left. Wiveliscombe's centre is ahead (with a café and Co-op shop), but is missed by the e2e route which branches off right into Russell's. This continues into Rotton Row, passing left of the church and meets a B-road (083 277) (3.7m).

2: Turn right. Ignore the B-road left to Watchet and just before the roundabout, turn left before the substation onto a signed gravel path which continues across an estate road to meet a path. Turn right and soon go through a gate into a field. Follow the well-walked ascending path half-left and then contour close to the left hedge. The path curves left to cross the hedge and the path then splits. Turn right to follow the right boundary and descend to cross a lane onto a track. Follow the track as it curves round the edge of woodland and continues along a field edge to a lane. Turn right to a cross-road of lanes (by old sandstone buttresses for a dismantled railway) and turn left. A descent to cross a stream is followed by a long ascent. Near the top of the rise, go half-left on a signed, unsurfaced restricted byway, having a steep ascent before a gentler descent, to a lane at Cat's Ash (114 282) (6.2m). Turn left to Fitzhead and take the first right at Knights Farm. Then turn off right by a letterbox to pass to the right of the church. Just after the entry to the last house on the left and before reaching a T-junction, look for and take a short, well-hidden quarter-left path which short cuts across the T-junction corner to a lane; if you miss this path go on to the T-junction.

3: Turn left and at the far end of the village, take the first lane off left (124 285). Tyler's Lane runs north but is left after 140 yds for a signed path off right. Follow the track and continue straight ahead along a right boundary. The path then enters a large field where the right boundary is followed east-southeast. At its end, keep left of a pond and don't pass through a hedge gap. Instead turn left to follow the right hedge to a stile in the hedge. Beyond, take the right path of two and proceed just left of straight ahead in a north-of-East direction to a stile in the diagonal opposite field corner (this is not as on the map). A right hedge is then followed east-southeast for two fields to a lane (135 285) (8m). Cross to the path opposite, but turn left along the crop edge and at a signpost turn right along the crop edge, again parallel to the road. Leave the path for the lane via a gate and turn right briefly before turning left through a gate onto a signed track. The track continues in the next field and having crossed a stream reaches a signed path fork. Go half-right along the track to a gate gap and follow the waymark to another field gap. From here, go half-left up a bank on a distinct crop gap to a barn. Keeping to the right of the barn, turn right on a short track to gates onto a rough lane (145 290) (9m). Turn left and after a short distance turn right on a signed path. Follow the trodden path to a walkers' gate. In the field entered, go briefly left by the hedge then cross the field north-of-East to a walkers' gate (to the left of the field gate) onto a lane. Turn right and shortly reach a small triangular junction. Keep right and on meeting a lane, take the track opposite left onto lovely Ash Priors Common (149 291).

4: Keep right of the cottages and follow the trodden path parallel to the left boundary of this open access area. On meeting a lane turn left to very shortly meet a T-junction. Turn left and after a short distance turn right onto a track signed as a path. Follow the track into a yard and turn right to a walkers' gate where the path splits. Take the left of the two signed paths and follow the left boundary to a walkers' gate. Beyond, follow the left hedge and then continue in the same direction, between the house on the left and a lone tree, onto the house's access drive which is followed. The waymarked unsurfaced track meets and crosses a surfaced track and continues into a field where it follows the left hedge with an army of solar panels to the right; Bishops Lydeard's church can be viewed incongruously poking out beyond the panels. The track leads to a walkers' gate over the West Somerset Railway line. Beyond, turn left on a good path along a left boundary to the main A358 road (163 301) (10.5m).

5: Cross with care to the road opposite. It almost immediately curves right. When it gets to a T-junction, turn left along Bishop Lydeard's High Street. At the end of the town, branch right at a fork (signed Bridgwater). At a cross-roads go straight on, signed Cothelstone and Bridgwater, ascending towards the Quantock Hills. Keep to the major road, pass the place sign for Cothelstone and continue through this hamlet to where the road bends sharp left (184 319) (12.6m) and here take a signed bridleway off right. Follow the main track up through the wood and turn sharp right (with a track ascending straight ahead). The track ascends, turns left and then seems to reach many forks. Keep left here and the excellent track running north-east soon becomes clear again. Keep straight on across two forest tracks and then join a forest track briefly and continue north-east beyond. On reaching a marker post near the top of the wood, turn right and shortly afterwards go through a walkers' gate on the left (193 324) (13.4m). Take the wide grassy track left across open ground, which diverges gently away from the fence on the left and eventually reaches a mound with a few stones on top, marking the position of Cothelstone Folly on the top of Cothelstone Hill (190 327). Go straight on, left of the mound, to a gap in a small bank to pick up the start of a trodden path which goes steeply down north-northwest to a stile. The path continues ahead, crosses a bridleway and continues to exit onto the road immediately to the right of a minor road junction. Take the unsurfaced track opposite right (189 331) (14m) and follow it to meet a track. Turn left and continue to a multi-track junction. The required track is straight on, quickly descending to the edge of the wood, which it then follows. Beyond, the track continues to a lane junction. Take the lane opposite and Manor Farm is at the bottom on the left (207 333), with the Travellers Rest pub beyond at the top of a steep ascent.

Stage 13
Waterpits to Cossington

VIA: Broomfield, The Meads and paths through Bridgwater
DISTANCE: 14.6m [198m]
ASCENT: 670ft   DESCENT: 1210ft
EXPLORER: 140 (Quantocks & Bridgwater)
LANDRANGER: 182 (Weston-super-Mare)

This is another day in Somerset but is a stage of contrasts. It starts in the Quantock Hills and after the lovely village of Broomfield there's a good section of hill paths to Goathurst village. Thereafter the route follows Cobb's Cross Stream over flat farmland. The land directly to the south-west of Bridgwater is called The Meads. The River Parrett is crossed in Bridgwater, this being the first crossing point from the coast. Bridgwater, in my opinion is unattractive, so the stage takes a walkers' route through Bridgwater which entirely misses its centre. Sticking to the route, the only place passed for stocking-up is a very large Morrisons complete with a café. After Bridgwater, the landscape changes as the crossing of the Somerset Levels is commenced. This low-lying wetland region is dominated by the man-made channels provided to drain the area. These, as well as hedges and fences, are used as land boundaries. Some of the drains, such as the King's Sedgemoor Drain which is crossed on this stage, are substantial being many yards wide and their size is indicative of the amount of water siphoned off the ground. After reaching the small village of Bawdrip, the route leaves the levels for the larger village of Cossington on the low ridge named the Polden Hills.

On the day we walked this, we started in rain but by the time we reached Goathurst the weather had temporarily improved. We were doing really well until we came to a plank footbridge over Cobb's Cross Stream that was completely submerged under water. The water came way over the top of our boots so we swapped them for our sandals and went across gingerly, carefully feeling with our sandals for the position of the plank completely hidden under water. Once across, there were water meadows to cross with the emphasis on the water, so we kept our sandals on until we arrived at Mr Morrisons. We hastened into the Ladies in order to get ourselves cleaned up before we sat down to eat and dry out. Whilst in the toilets, numerous women whizzed in and out. What amused us was that nobody batted an eyelid, as if seeing two middle-aged women each with a wet, muddy foot in a washbasin, was a perfectly everyday occurrence! This was not the only time on our journey that we were grateful for the shelter, café and facilities of Mr Morrisons, so it's definitely a case of three cheers for this particular supermarket.

Waterpits

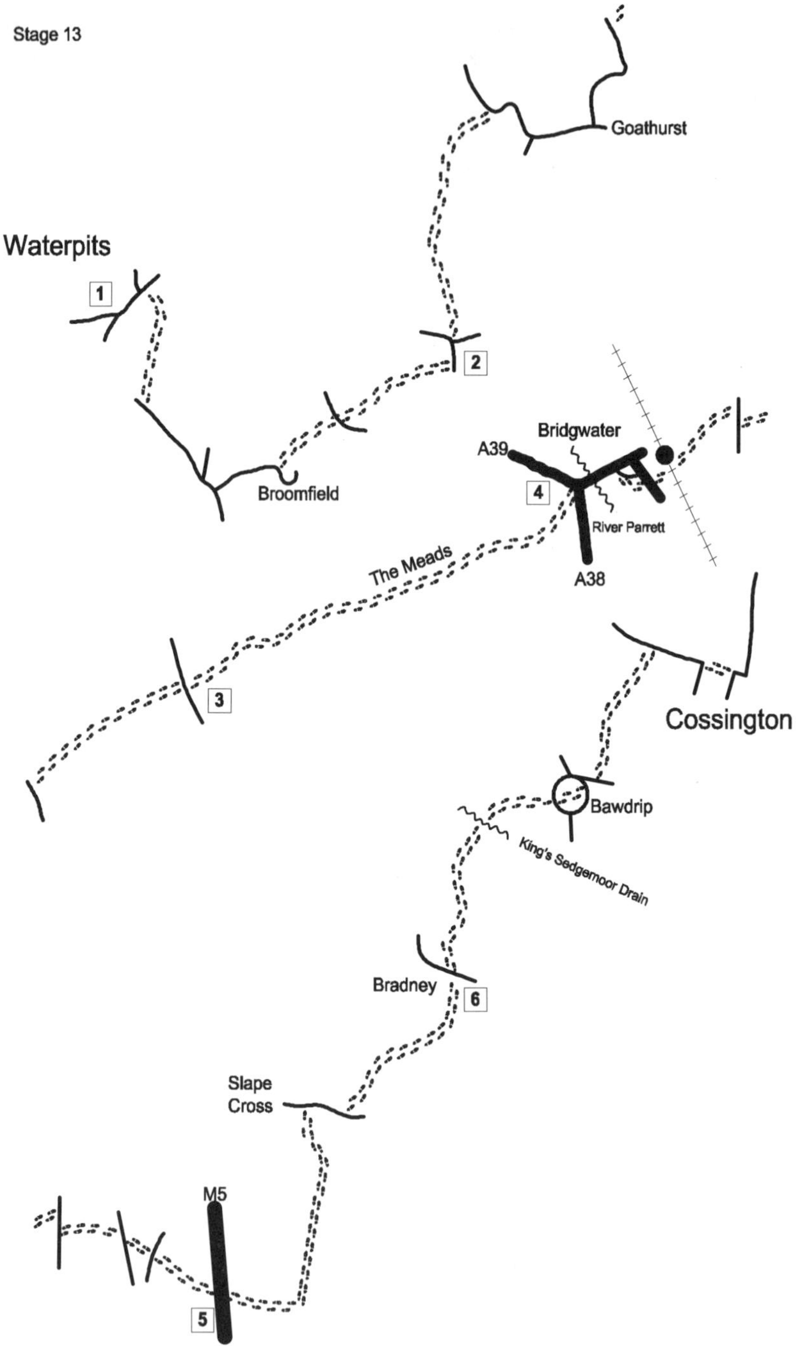

Goathurst

1

Broomfield

2

Bridgwater

A39

4

River Parrett

The Meads

A38

3

Cossington

Bawdrip

King's Sedgemoor Drain

Bradney

6

Slape
Cross

M5

5

1: From Manor Farm (ST 207 333) continue east steeply up the lane for 300 yds to a T-junction. Turn left, pass the Travellers Rest, pass a lane off left and immediately after this turn right at a path sign on to the National Trust's Broomfield Hill. Ascend on a clear path close to the Trust's left boundary, pass through a walkers' gate and beyond continue ascending by the left boundary. After the path's highest point, the path descends, again close to the left boundary. When a walkers' gate is reached, with a lot of paths, continue in the same direction passing a very large old tree and shortly afterwards meet a lane (211 326). Turn left to a lane junction and turn left here signed Fyne Court. Immediately before Broomfield Church, turn left along a very short track along its right railing and turn right through a walkers' gate into a National Trust field marked Fyne Court. Turn left and follow the left wall to a walkers' gate and take the descending track beyond to a walkers' gate. Through, the track descends very gently across grassland towards a stream on the left and keeps to the right of the stream to reach a lane (228 323) (2.2m). Cross to the ascending path opposite through a wood, which initially is to the left of a track, before the path crosses it opposite left and then continues to an unsigned path T-junction with the track just to the left. Turn <u>right</u> here and eventually reach a waymark; follow this passing to the left of netting and exit the wood into a field. Follow the waymark along the left boundary, cross a stile to follow a right field boundary and then proceed ahead as signed to a lane. Turn left briefly to a T-junction (239 327) (3m).

2: Go left for a few yards and then turn off right on a waymarked bridleway track. Pass through two gates then follow the track along a right hedge. Pass through a waymarked gate and descend gently along a left boundary with a Christmas tree plantation beyond. The clear track becomes enclosed and is followed down to a car park. Here, take a walkers' gate just to the right and follow the enclosed path to a farm track. Turn right to shortly meet a lane (246 345) (4.4m). Turn right to a T-junction and turn left to Goathurst (signed Bridgwater). In Goathurst village (256 343), turn left (signed Bridgwater) to pass its church. Continue beyond the village on the lane and take a signed path on the right just before a wood on the right. In the field entered follow the left hedge down a long field. At the field end, cross a stile on the left over a stream named Cobb's Cross Stream. Now follow the right boundary of a long field until the stream curves right, at which point carry straight on to exit onto a lane via a field gate (271 350) (6.4m).

3: Turn right briefly and then go left at a footpath sign. Go half-right to a footbridge over the stream in the field corner, then turn left along the left boundary to a plank bridge over the stream. Over, turn right; the houses on the edge of Bridgwater can be viewed on the left. After a short distance go a quarter-left to a waymarked post guarding a plank bridge over the stream. Cross and pass through the wooden walkers' gate on the right. Follow the left hedge to a stile, cross and then cross the next field, heading towards the visible tower block, to reach walkers' gates guarding a footbridge. In the next field cross to the diagonal opposite corner to find a farm gate incorporating a metal walkers' gate (just to the left of a large tree). Cross to the next field and follow the left hedge to a footbridge and a metal walkers' gate. Beyond, go half-right to an embankment. Follow the embankment beside a drain, ignoring a metal walkers' gate at the corner of allotments. If the fields are not saturated, veer half right from the embankment to a hedge turn and follow the left edge over a farm crossing of a drain (which can be horrendously muddy); continue parallel to the left field edge to a footbridge, then cross a stile (which is opposite a prominent red building) onto the canal towpath and turn right. If the farm crossing of the drain is too dreadful, continue on the embankment to its end and turn left over a footbridge onto a lane. Proceed up the lane briefly, take the first right into Albert Street and immediately before the canal bridge turn right to descend onto the canal towpath which is followed to the right. Whichever way is used to join the Bridgwater & Taunton canal, leave the canal shortly, just after Bridge 5 (299 365) (8.5m), returning on an ascending path to cross this bridge and continue straight on along a wide urban path beside a brick wall on the right and Morrisons on the left; the path passes a pedestrian entrance on the left into the supermarket. The passageway comes out where the main A38 and A39 roads fork.

4: Turn right, cross the A38 (Taunton Road) on a pelican crossing, then take the A38 (signed Bristol) over the River Parrett and immediately turn right down Cranleigh Gardens (passing to the left of the Lime Kiln Inn). Turn half-right just after the Medical Centre into Eastover Park, cutting across it on a path just north-of-East to a park exit into Liberty Place. Follow Liberty Place to meet St John's Street (which is the main A372 road) (306 370). Turn right and cross the road at a pelican crossing to take the road left towards Bridgwater Railway Station. However, before reaching the station, take the footbridge over the railway into Redgate Street. Follow Redgate Street straight ahead and just before it turns right to rejoin St John's Street, turn left on a tarmac walkers' and cyclists' path. The path crosses over an estate road and reaches some garages. Twist left and then right through the garages to emerge on Longstone Avenue. Turn left down Longstone Avenue, and then right along Fairfax Road to meet a dual carriageway named Parkway. Go right to use a zebra crossing and enter a children's play area and recreation ground opposite. Take the tarmac path along its left side and at the end continue straight ahead on a cycle and walkers' path which crosses an estate road and continues to eventually emerge into Avebury Drive. Go down this but turn right into Duncombe Close and take the passageway at the end which curves left to busy Eastern Avenue. Cross to the passageway opposite, which passes between houses, to emerge on Bower Lane with a field opposite and the M5 motorway beyond. Cross to the signed footpath opposite and take the clear path down the left side of the field to a stile. Cross and then cross a stile leading on to the curved motorway footbridge (323 370) (10.5m).

5: Over the motorway bridge, cross a stile then follow the right field boundary for two sides to a footbridge over a drain. Cross through a left gap and then follow a right boundary, passing left of the pylon. At the field end, turn left for a short distance along the right boundary but then cross the drain on the right by a plank bridge. Now, briefly turn right then left along the right field edge to a footbridge onto a track. Turn left and follow the track which eventually twists left and right to get to the lane at Slape Cross (329 380) (11.5m). Turn right, pass Nelson Lodge and look for a waymarked stile left which leads to a waymarked walkers' gate. Beyond, go just right of straight ahead to a stile and plank bridge in the field corner. Then it's left of straight ahead to a waymarked gate. Don't go through but turn right along the left hedge to a gate in the left hedge. Pass through and go just right of straight ahead to a gate. Cross and take the track across the field and then by the right hedge to a metal gate. Through, follow the left boundary which curves left and continues to a gate onto Bradney Lane (336 388).

6: Turn left for a few yards, then opposite Chapel Cottage turn right on a track and after a short distance turn right on a signed path. Go just left of straight ahead to a marker then straight ahead, as directed, to a stile and plank bridge in the field corner. Cross and turn left along the left boundary to a stile with a footbridge. Follow the path beyond to a track. Go left through a metal gate and then right over a bridge crossing King's Sedgemoor Drain (338 394) (12.7m). Go half-right on a trodden path to a 'Heath Robinson' stile cum planking arrangement, and then follow the trodden path to two more 'Heath Robinson' efforts in quick succession which lead into a between fences path onto a lane. Turn right and on meeting a lane, go opposite left along Church Path. Pass to the left of Bawdrip's church and on meeting a lane (Church Road) turn left. When the road curves left, turn off right on a lane having a Cycle Route 3 sign. After 320 yds, turn off left at a cycle route sign and follow the surfaced track, along a disused railway line, to its end and onto a lane on the edge of Cossington (14m). Turn right and just after Station Road comes in on the left, take a signed path off left. Descend and ascend to a lane. Turn left and Brookhayes Farm is soon seen on the right (360 408).

Stage 14
Cossington to Cheddar

VIA:	**Somerset Levels, Blackford and Brinscombe Hill**
DISTANCE:	**14m [212m]**
ASCENT:	**420ft** **DESCENT:** **460ft**
EXPLORER:	**140 (Quantocks & Bridgwater), 141 (Cheddar Gorge)**
LANDRANGER:	**182 (Weston-super-Mare)**

The Somerset Levels is an area barely above sea level. The area is characterised by its flatness and its network of drains which enables the land to be farmed. There are few paths so it is necessary, in places, to take to quiet lanes. The drains tend to be constructed in straight lines and this tends to be reflected in the path and road layout! From Cossington, the stage crosses the levels making for the small village of Blackford, the only village passed through on the day. The route continues northwards with no hills to negotiate until the ridge along Brinscombe Hill at around 160 ft, which overlooks Axbridge and Cheddar to the north. Even so, the hill is somewhat of a disappointment as the view is obstructed by a hedge for a good distance until the boundary side is swapped. After the hill, the River Axe is crossed and a track then leads to a path round Cheddar Reservoir and on into Cheddar village. Cheddar's famous gorge ensures that this is a place which caters well for tourists and it has a good range of accommodation and facilities for travellers.

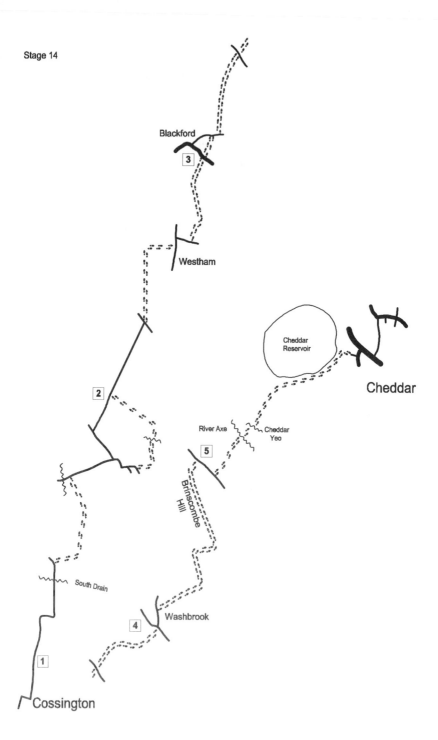

Stage 14

Blackford

3

Westham

Cheddar
Reservoir

2

River Axe
Cheddar
Yeo

5

Brinscombe
Hill

South Drain

4
Washbrook

1

Cossington

Cheddar

1: From Bell Lane in Cossington (ST 360 408) continue north on the lane. After 0.8 mile the lane swings sharp right to run east for 0.3 mile before turning left to run north and cross the enormously wide South Drain. Continue for a further 120 yds to a house on the right and immediately after turn right on a signed bridleway (367 432) (1.8m). Follow the stony track over a drain named Shaking Drove Sluice and after a further 270 yds follow the stony track as it swings left. The track runs to the right of a drain, becomes grassier and eventually reaches a gate. Pass through and continue ahead on the grass track to shortly reach a waymarked walkers' gate where the track ends. Go half-left to an embankment overlooking the Cripps River drain and follow this to the right, emerging on a lane at the embankment gate (369 444) (3m). Turn right along the road for 0.8 mile to meet River Road at a T-junction. Turn right, ignore a turn-off right and continue for a short distance to a sharp bend right (387 445) (4m). Turn left through a gate signed River House Farm (although the public footpath is unsigned). Turn right to follow the gravel farm access track. After crossing the River Brue, continue on the track along one-and-a-half sides of the house and then turn left on an enclosed trodden path where you may have to negotiate fallen trees. The path becomes a farm track and emerges on a lane (388 455) (5m).

2: Turn right to a T-junction. Here, take the footpath opposite through the waymarked farm gate. Go straight on past the barn to a farm gate, then follow the waymarked path along the left edge of two fields. Exit the second field via a waymarked gate on the left, followed by a waymarked gate on the right to reach a house drive. Turn right on this very briefly, then turn left up the left side of the house and through a waymarked walkers' gate (don't cross the drain). Go three-quarters left across the field (just north-of-East) to a drain crossing point marked by two stout wooden posts. Cross and follow the right field edge to another drain crossing point on the right, just before the large trees. Cross here into the adjoining field and follow the left hedge to a farm gate onto a lane (401 466). Turn left and shortly take a lane off right into the hamlet of Westham (6.3m). After 250 yds, turn left just after the postbox into Elm Tree Farm on a signed path. Pass straight through the farmyard and out onto a track which curves right along the back of the farm to enter a field. Go through the gap on the left into the adjacent field. The right of way goes half-right across the field, keeping to the right of a pond, to reach the field corner, but this can be very muddy and most people appear to follow the right hedge round two sides to reach the field corner. From here follow the right hedge in the next field to cross a footbridge. Now go just left of straight ahead across a field to a 'stile' by a gate. Go just left of straight ahead in the next field to a waymarked stile, straight across the following field to a stile by a gate, and then half-left along a long field to find and follow the left fence to a stile by a gate onto the B-road through Blackford (410 476) (7.2 m).

3: Turn right for a few yards and then turn left onto a signed path. Follow the left hedge to a stile. Cross and take the farm gate immediately right and follow the track to meet a road. Go right for a few yards, then left on a short, between-houses lane and through a double gate arrangement onto a signed restricted byway going northwards. Follow the right hedge into an enclosed track, which in turn leads into a field. Here the left hedge is followed across two fields into an enclosed track. The enclosed byway crosses a lane and the second footpath off left is taken, which is immediately before the start of wooden fencing of the grounds of a house. In the field entered, diverge gently from the right boundary to take a farm crossing over the stream at the bottom of the field and then turn left along the left edge to a walkers' gate. Go through and cross the footbridge into a field. Turn right along its right boundary out onto a lane junction at Washbrook (421 501) (9.2m).

4: Take Quab Lane opposite for 160 yds to a signed path off right. Cross the field strip and pass through a gap into the next field. Cross the next long field just north-of-East to pass through a wide field gap then go three-quarters left to a stile. In the following field turn right along the right hedge to a gate with a well hidden waymark. Cross and follow the left hedge until it turns, continuing straight ahead to a gate. Pass through and turn right along the right hedge in this and the next field to arrive at a waymarked gate marking a cross-path (428 504). Do not pass through but turn one-and-a-half left in the same field to a gap in the opposite diagonal field corner; you may by now have spotted the shortcut to the field gap by following the left boundary on entering the second field. The gap leads into a very short track to a gate. Pass through and go half-left to find and follow a right boundary to a gate. Pass through and contour the field to reach a stile in the top left corner. In the following field, go parallel to the right hedge to find its gate. Cross and immediately turn right to a gate which leads onto a private track. Don't take this but cross the track to take an enclosed waymarked descending track on the right, just after the private track. Just before a gate across the track, turn left into a field and ascend close to the right edge; this is Brinscombe Hill but there's no view because of the trees. Ignore a stile off right to continue to a metal gate where the boundary side is swapped so a view is obtained. The path descends gently along the left boundary to a stile. Then go half right to a gate and thence out onto a lane (420 523) (11.2m).

5: Turn right for 120 yds and then turn left on a signed track at Moor View Farm. Go through the gate ahead and follow the enclosed farm track to and over the pumping station bridge over the River Axe (423 526). Beyond, go straight on along a good enclosed track to a gate. Pass through and keeping parallel to the right drain, cross the field to the gate straight ahead. Cross the bank bridge over the Cheddar Yeo onto a drove track. When this unsurfaced track turns right, leave it for a stile on the left. Ascend the bank to a track around Cheddar Reservoir (12.6m) and follow the track to the right. Just before the tower, pass through a walkers' gate and descend right through a car park. Take its access drive and go straight ahead when it exits onto a lane. On reaching a T-junction, turn left for a few yards to meet the main A371 road. Turn right briefly then left up Barrows Road and at the T-junction at the top, turn right then shortly turn left up Upper North Street (457 539) (14m).

Stage 15
Cheddar to Long Ashton

VIA: **Mendips, Blagdon Lake and Monarch's Way**
DISTANCE: **15.2m [227.2m]**
ASCENT: **1960ft**   **DESCENT:**   **1960ft**
EXPLORER: **141 (Cheddar Gorge), 154 (Bristol West)**
LANDRANGER: **82 (Weston-super-Mare), 172 (Bristol & Bath)**

This stage is the final day in Somerset and offers a fine day's walking. It starts by a steep climb out of Cheddar, ascending the Mendip Hills to reach its highest point of 1066 ft at Beacon Batch. From there, the route drops to Blagdon village where there's a place for coffee and a general stores. After peaceful Blagdon Lake, a succession of paths, tracks and quiet roads lead past the Bungalow Inn (serving food) and on across Felton Common. Beyond, the route threads its way cross country to join the Monarch's Way at Barrow Gurney Reservoir. The Monarch's Way is left after crossing under the main A370 road, to make its way by path and cycle tracks to the stage finish at Long Ashton, just outside Bristol's boundary. The local pub provides accommodation and food. On the day the weather held until we left the Bungalow Inn when the heavens opened in spectacular fashion. Although this had stopped within an hour, field paths thereafter were wet and on the final approach to Long Ashton were so muddy as to be the wrong side of dreadful. This stage also marked the first use of the GPS to identify our exact location as we went slightly off-course in approaching Castle Farm late in the day.

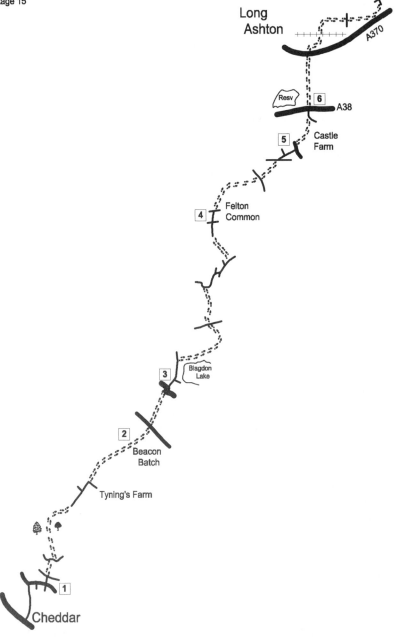

Long
Ashton

A370

Resv **6** A38

5 Castle
Farm

4 Felton
Common

3 Blagdon
Lake

2

Beacon
Batch

Tyning's Farm

1

Cheddar

1: Continue north along Upper North Street (ST 457 539) to a T-junction. Turn left briefly and then take a tarmac passageway off right, just to the left of the Kings Head pub. It passes between stone walls leading north to Warrens Hill lane. Turn right for 60 yds and just beyond the last bungalow on the left, turn left on an unsurfaced restricted byway (458 542). Follow this to reach a walkers' gate. Pass through to take a good ascending path through the wood. This rejoins the bridleway again which becomes surfaced after a quarry entrance. The bridleway is followed past Ashbridge Farm to a lane corner at Tyning's Gate (469 563) (2m). Go straight on (to the right) along the lane to a sharp bend right at Tyning's Farm. Go straight on here, ascending along a well-trodden restricted byway. At the top, go through a gate and take the broad green bridleway track to the right going east-northeast which gently diverges from the right boundary. Cross a signed bridleway track and at the next crossing point turn right along a sandy track to the trig point at Beacon Batch, the highest point on the Mendips (485 573) (3.2m).

2: Take the second track off clockwise from the approach track to re-meet the grassy bridleway and turn right on this to descend gently east-northeast, with lovely views towards Blagdon Lake. When a multi-bridleway junction is reached (491 577), turn left to a walkers' gate, then follow a wide track to a B-road (490 580). Go right for a short distance and then take Ellick Farm's access drive on the left (4m). Just before the farm, take a stile on the right and follow the left field boundary to pass into the next field. Here go diagonally right to a stile in the hedge (beyond the first telegraph pole). Cross the next field diagonally right to a stile (to the left of a lone large tree) and maintain the same direction in the next short field. In the next field follow the trodden path through the middle of the field, keeping to the left of the College. In the following field, descend to pass a right hedge corner and continue in this field curving slightly right to a stile. In the next field, again follow the trodden path, which keeps close to the right boundary before curving left on a trodden path to a gate at the bottom. Cross the adjacent stile and follow the left boundary to a kissing gate onto unsurfaced Post Office Lane. Turn right down this to the main road (500 592) in Blagdon village.

3: The main road is busy and there's no pavement, so unless you want its shop (which is to the right and just past the corner), cross to the Village Club opposite and use the path to the right, round this building, into the village's car park and out onto a lane (5m). Turn left, descend to Blagdon Lake and continue straight on north beside the lake. At the end of the dam, immediately go through a walkers' gate on the right to take an excellent path along the shoreline. Cross a side stream on a footbridge and continue on the shoreline path to the second footbridge. Don't cross but turn left to a walkers' gate into a field. Go up the field to a gate in the top right corner and in the next field go parallel to the left boundary to a stile by the gate onto a lane (508 611) (6.6m). Take the byway opposite with an 'Unsuitable for Motors' sign which soon becomes unsurfaced and has a steep rise initially. When this meets a lane (512 622) turn right and take the first right to a T-junction (515 625). Turn left and after 220 yds take the right fork. Proceed for another 180 yds and immediately after Cherry Tree Cottage on the left, follow a signed path off left (8m) to meet a lane. Turn right, follow the lane northwards going straight across at a cross-roads (signed Bristol) and on to a T-junction (512 640) (8.7m).

4: Go straight across onto an unsurfaced track (but turn right briefly if you want the Bungalow Inn). Follow the track to a track T-junction. Turn left for a few yards then right at the sign for Felton Common. There are a lot of paths but take the rightmost path and follow close to the common's right boundary. When a track T-junction is reached, follow the track left briefly and then curve right to remain close to the right boundary. Keep right at any branches and eventually get to a (padlocked) gate. Here take the track left briefly to a sign for the common (hopefully different to the one met at the entrance onto the common) and exit the common (524 650) onto an eastwards track which is followed for a quarter of a mile to a lane (528 650) (10m). Go right for a few yards then turn left onto a surfaced byway. When this shortly swings right, carry straight on along an unsurfaced path which meets a road (530 654). Go straight across to Raglan Lane which soon curves right. The route from here to the B-road is also used by Cycle Route 334 and is signed. The lane enters a village and reaches its village green. The exit road is far right of the green and is followed to meet a B-road (539 659) (11m).

5: Turn left briefly as far as Hanging Grove Farm on the left and take a footpath on the right. Go three-quarters left aiming to the right of a barn. Go through the gate and turn right, just north-of-East, to a waymarked gate into the next field. Follow the left hedge to a stile, cross and go half-right (north-east) to pass through a large field gap and maintain this direction to a waymarked gap near the topmost right corner of the field. Then go half-left as directed to take the right of two farm gates. Go through and follow the left hedge northwards until it turns left, at which point continue northwards across this and the next field to a gate onto the access lane to Castle Farm (548 668) (12m). Cross the access lane and into the farmyard opposite, dinking right to pass a barn. Don't go through the restricted byway gate ahead but pass through a walkers' gate just left of it. Go half-left onto a farm track and turn right to follow it into a field. Here follow the contouring track to a gate gap. Through, go half-left descending steeply to a stile to the left of a house. Beyond, follow the right hedge to a stile by a gate and exit onto Dundry Lane. Turn left to the A38 main road (547 680) (12.7m).

6: Turn right for a few yards and then turn left on a signed passageway joining the Monarch's Way. The passageway leads to a track round Barrow Gurney Reservoir, then through an area of woodland and into a field. Go a quarter-left to a walkers' gate in the left boundary, then half-right to a walkers' gate into another area of woodland. Beyond, follow a right field boundary to a walkers' gate into more woodland. In the field that follows, walk along the left hedge to a walkers' gate. Cross a stream and on through scrubland, veering right to an underpass of the A370 which is taken (544 694) (13.7m). Beyond leave the Monarch's Way (which goes left) and turn right crossing the stream and take the track (not the lower path). The track runs close and parallel to the A370. Ignore another crossing under the A370 and shortly afterwards, turn left as directed, up the left boundary of a field and over the railway line (546 700). Beyond, take the well-trodden path across the field to meet a tarmac track on the edge of Long Ashton. Turn right on Cycle Route 33. When the route is signed onto the road, keep beside the stream and rejoin the surfaced route which is followed to a lane (550 704) (14.7m). Go right to cross the stream and then immediately take the signed path off left. Follow the stream, cross it and continue to a walkers' gate. In the next field follow the line of the house backs and then head towards the church to find a walkers' gate. Beyond, follow a left boundary to a walkers' gate onto a track. The path continues opposite through a walkers' gate and again follow the left boundary to a walkers' gate into the church grounds. Turn left to take the tarmac path up the side of the church and exit out onto a lane. Proceed up the lane to a busy minor road and the Angel Inn is on the corner (552 710) (15.2m).

Stage 16
Long Ashton to Northwick

VIA: Clifton Suspension Bridge, Downs and Blaise Estate
DISTANCE: 13.9m [241.1m]
ASCENT: 930ft   DESCENT: 1010ft
EXPLORER: 154 (Bristol West)
LANDRANGER: 172 (Bristol & Bath)

This is a surprisingly good day's walking, using a largely green route to the west of the city of Bristol, to reach its north-west outskirts and continue to the hamlet of Northwick close to the River Severn. From Long Ashton, the route passes through the nearby delightful and large Ashton Court Estate, owned by the City of Bristol. This leads to Brunel's magnificent Clifton Suspension Bridge over the River Avon. Just after the bridge, the route crosses the fort area to the left and the Avon Gorge is best appreciated from here. An ex-colleague joined us at this point for three days. An enquiry as to what to bring resulted in the suggestions of good waterproofs and a sense of humour!

The city has a large area of Downs around Clifton and these are taken north-westwards to reach a bridleway lane which is followed to the suburb of Stoke Bishop. Pleasant urban paths then lead into the large Blaise Castle Estate; this parkland is also owned by the City of Bristol. Routes for recreational use tend to be signed as a Community Forest Path and from Bristol's suburb of Henbury, at the north end of the Blaise Castle Estate, one is taken northwards over the M5 motorway and Spaniorum Hill to reach the village of Easter Compton in Gloucestershire; this has a pub which we made for lunch. The route then leaves the Forest Path to thread its way along paths towards Pilning Railway Station before veering away to cross the M4 motorway and reach the hamlet of Northwick. Northwick has an imposing church tower, this being the only remains of its church. Our excellent B&B lay a short distance to the north.

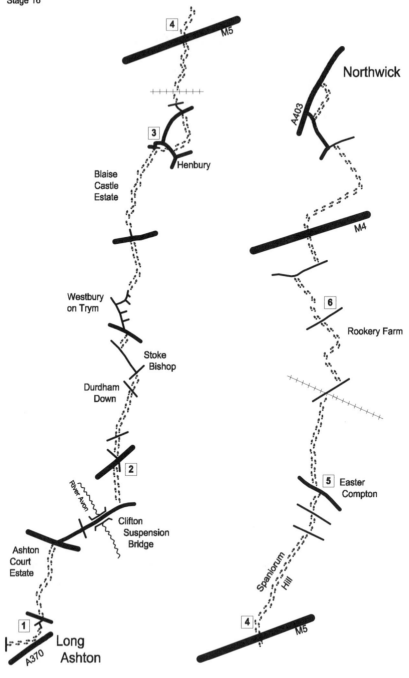

1: From the road junction at the Angel Inn in Long Ashton (ST 552 710), turn right to the B-road and cross over to the South Lodge entry into the Ashton Court Estate. Walk up the drive and after it turns left, turn right on an unsurfaced track which leads to the House garden. Pass through this and up an avenue to the House. At the far end of the House, turn left up the side of the car park and continue north to the base of a tree mound ahead. Circle the base anti-clockwise until reaching a gravel path with an iron gate on the left into the Red Deer Park. Through, follow the gravel path for a short distance looking for a white marker post off right. Follow the posts across a grassy path taking left branches at forks. This brings you to an exit of the Deer Park. Beyond, continue forward to shortly meet an access drive with North Lodge just to the right (558 727) (1.3m). From this park exit, cross the main road to take the road opposite, following it to and across the Clifton Suspension Bridge over the River Avon; there's a toll for motorists but it's free for pedestrians. Having crossed the bridge, immediately turn left on a surfaced path to the Observatory. Follow this left, parallel to the Avon, for a good viewpoint. Continue, curving right to pass to the left of an ancient fort, fork left at the far end of the fort to reach a surfaced walkers'/cycling track named 'The Promenade' and turn left. The Promenade runs close to a road on its right and emerges at a staggered cross-roads (566 739) (2.5m).

2: A good footpath onto Durdham Down leaves at this junction; it leaves from the right of the road opposite right (across the main road). Follow the path through bushes onto the open down then head east-of-North across the down (easy walking but no path). Cross Ladies Mile (road), where the railway tunnels beneath the road (566 745), and maintain this direction to cross Stoke Road and very shortly afterwards reach Saville Road (568 754) (3.4m) with the entry to Hollybush Lane opposite. Take Hollybush Lane which quickly becomes countrified and traffic-free. After nearly two thirds of a mile, two footpaths go off right. Take the second of these, just before the lane bends left. Follow this enclosed path to a road junction (563 764). Go left briefly on the B-road and then fork right onto Coombe Lane. After 310 yds, take the third street off right and follow Red House Lane, which turns sharp left, to its end. Take the track continuation to a cross-track (565 771). Turn left and follow the track initially along the edge of a cemetery and keep on in this direction, crossing a residential street (Sandyleaze), to then pass between houses and garages to reach the main A4162 road (561 775) (5m). Turn left briefly, take the next right into Canford Lane and take a footpath off left, just before a block of flats, signed Blaise Estate. Descend and turn right to a footbridge over a side stream. Cross, turn left along the side stream to cross a footbridge over the main stream, Hazel Brook. Ascend half-right up stone steps to a surfaced valley path. Turn right on this path which follows parallel to the brook passing through The Gorge as well as past a lily pond and later Tarn Lake. When the path reaches the Old Mill, cross Hazel Brook and continue on the surfaced path to Blaise Museum; toilets and a café are left of the museum towards the car park. Pass to the left of the museum and exit onto a road junction (562 788) (6.2m).

3: Take Church Lane immediately to the right and when it turns left, turn right up the cobbled access into Henbury Church grounds and take the path left. Take the first exit left and descend steps into Rectory Gardens Road which is followed. Near its end, fork left to meet the B-road and cross Henbury Road (565 789) to the access entrance opposite into scrubland. Take a path half-right to reach a tarmac track. Go right on this, very shortly cross a stream and then turn left alongside the stream, initially on a tarmac track but then on a good path. On reaching a footbridge, cross the stream and shortly after go right at a path fork to enter Lowlis Close. At its end, go briefly right then left (Community Path sign) up a passageway and continue in the same direction along Langfield Close to very shortly reach a B-road (565 794). Turn right briefly then left (Community Path sign) into Greenlands Way following it as it curves left. At the top of this road, cross Meadowland Road to a footpath track opposite. This almost immediately crosses the railway line (563 797) (7m), and then turns right along a right hedge to a walkers' gate. Beyond, follow a right wooden fence to a gate and then go just right of straight ahead to a waymarked gate. The right boundary is followed over the next two fields to reach a surfaced lane. Turn left and follow the track over the M5 motorway to a cross-track.

4: Turn right and then pass through a kissing gate left into a field. Follow the left hedge for two fields into a wooded area. Branch left at a fork in the wood to a waymarked kissing gate. In the field entered, follow the path to a waymarked field gate where the path forks (564 815). Take the right of the two paths, cross a track to a walkers' gate opposite. Go just left of straight ahead to a walkers' gate (with a view of the 'new' Severn Bridge) and then proceed half-right on a gently descending path to a gate in the bottom right diagonal corner. In the succeeding two fields follow the right boundary into an enclosed path to a lane (568 819). Turn right briefly then take a track left over a footbridge with a postbox on its far side! Continue onwards on an enclosed path to a kissing gate and then go half-right on a trodden path to a kissing gate. In the following field follow a right boundary, with Easter Compton's church ahead, to a walkers' gate onto a lane. Take the path opposite, into and through the church gounds passing to the right of the church and out on a tarmac path to the B-road in the village (572 824) (9.3m). The end-to-end route leaves the Community Forest Path here.

5: Turn left for 180 yds, passing the Fox Inn, then turn right along a tarmac track with a gate bearing the name 'Collinwood'. Cross a stile, then go half-left along a well-mown path to a stile. In the next field, go half-right across rough ground to a waymarked gate. Through, go straight ahead a few yards to another gate (not signed). Pass through, proceed half-right to the diagonal opposite far corner and in the following field follow the left hedge to a stile with a footbridge. Now go three-quarters left, crossing a farm access track, to reach a stile with a footbridge. Cross and go one-quarter right towards a farm to reach a stile. Cross and go just right of straight ahead to a stile with footbridge, then turn three-quarters right to pass to the right of Brynleaze Farm. Just to the right of the farm go through the first gate on the right then turn left along the left hedge to a stile with footbridge. Continue to follow the left hedge until it turns left, at which point go over the padlocked gate straight ahead (to the right of a brick barn) to reach a bridleway lane (574 840) (10.3m). Turn left briefly and then go right to pass under the railway line. Beyond, continue for another 100 yds and then turn left on an enclosed signed bridleway track. After 400 yds the track turns right to shortly reach Rookery Farm (575 846). Here the track turns left, becomes surfaced and is followed to a minor road (570 850) (11.2m).

6: Continue on the enclosed surfaced track opposite. At a farm gate to Gumhurn Farm, turn right as directed, and follow the now unsurfaced but enclosed track in a generally west-northwest direction, to emerge on a lane at a bend. Turn right for 160 yds and then turn off left opposite a farm (12m) on a stony bridleway track which soon crosses the M4 motorway (564 860). Beyond, follow the track to the right. The track is generally north-eastish but does turn right briefly along a wood edge. Just over a quarter of a mile after the M4 crossing, turn left off the track through a metal walkers' gate. Go a quarter-left to a metal walkers' gate in the diagonally opposite field corner. From there, go half-right (aiming to the right of a distant barn) to a walkers' gate by the field gate to emerge on a lane (563 865). Turn left to a B-road, passing Manor Farm on the right. Turn right into the hamlet of Northwick. On reaching its church on the right (559 867) (13m), take a signed path off right along the left hedge of the graveyard. Enter a field and follow the right hedge down a long field. Cross a stile onto a rough between-hedges grassy lane. Turn left here and keep going across stiles and through gaps to reach the main A403 road (558 872). Turn right along the cycle path to the right of the main road and the Northwick Pig Farm B&B is on the right after 360 yds (560 875).

Stage 17
Northwick to St Briavels

VIA: Severn Road Bridge, Gloucestershire Way and Miss Graces Lane
DISTANCE: 15.5m [256.6m]
ASCENT: 2270ft   **DESCENT:**   1610ft
EXPLORER: 154 (Bristol West), OL14 (Wye Valley)
LANDRANGER: 172 (Bristol & Bath), 162 (Gloucester & Forest of Dean)

This was by far the worst day of weather on the whole journey. The official forecasts for that day describe it as 'a day of very strong gusts of wind from the north-east with accompanying persistent rain'. I was very worried that the Severn Bridge would be closed due to the conditions. This would have seriously disrupted the walk's itinerary, as the next crossing point of the River Severn is at Gloucester many miles to the north. As it was, having taken the Severn Way along the river to the bridge, we found that the bridge was open to cars but not lorries; even so, there were speed and lane restrictions. The pedestrian and cycle lane was open as we went across and we were literally blown sideways by the gusts, so we were grateful to have substantial side barriers on each side; views were fairly non-existent due to the large curtain of rain falling from the skies. So what should have been a highlight, marking the completion of the south-western part of the journey with magnificent views up the Bristol Channel as the River Severn and Wye are crossed, turned out to be a frightening experience and it was a relief to reach the other side. The bridge was completely closed shortly after we crossed.

Monmouthshire lies on the far side of the bridge and it's a couple of miles by a well-trodden route, now part of the Wales Coast Path, into Chepstow, where we patronised a local coffee shop and attempted to get slightly drier. Beyond, the River Wye is crossed almost immediately and Gloucestershire is entered. Having done the Offa's Dyke Path twice, the Gloucestershire Way seemed an obvious route choice this time. It was here that we met up for the rest of the stage with two more wet walking companions, determined to join in the fun of getting even wetter. In my view the route chosen for the Gloucestershire Way is not particularly inspiring and features a lot of woodland. Thus it is only loosely followed to woodland called the Parson's Allotment before it is left for a far more open landscape. The end-to-end route takes to the wonderfully named Miss Graces Lane which is an excellent track northwards. The Offa's Dyke Path is briefly joined on Madgett Hill, but left for a succession of brilliant ascending paths and tracks northwards which cross Hewelsfield Common to reach the hamlet of Coldharbour, just south of the stage's finish. At St Briavels, one quarter of the overall distance has been completed – progress indeed! We arrived in St Briavels wet to the core, and had booked into its Youth Hostel as staying in a Norman Castle is a unique experience. Since the hostel had no properly functioning drying room, it's not an experience that any of us will be repeating.

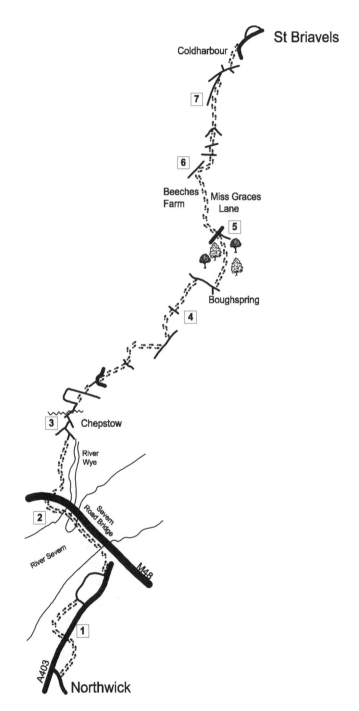

St Briavels

Coldharbour

7

6

Beeches
Farm

Miss Graces
Lane

5

Boughspring

4

3 Chepstow

River
Wye

Severn
Road
Bridge

2

River Severn

M48

1

A403

Northwick

1: From Northwick Pig Farm (ST 560 875) turn left and go south on the cycle path beside the A403 main road for a third of a mile to a signed bridleway track off right (557 870). After 320 yds this meets an embankment overlooking the River Severn. Turn right along the embankment joining the Severn Way. The embankment is followed to a quiet minor road. Here, follow the Severn Way and Cycle Route 4 left along the road for a mile then turn left on a track named Bridge Access Road (570 891) (2.3m). Follow the directional signs for Cycle Route 4 to the cycle lane on the left of the M48 motorway. This is the cycle lane that is usually open. However, if the lane on the left side is signed as closed, cross the motorway on the provided bridge and use the lane on the other side. The track to the left side turns left parallel to the M48 and on to the cycle and walkers' lane of the Severn Road Bridge. Normally the views are very enjoyable with the Bristol Channel to the left and Wales straight ahead. After crossing over the River Severn, the first land the bridge passes over is an outpost of Gloucestershire. This is followed by the River Wye and finally the bridge crosses into Monmouthshire in Wales.

2: From the bridge, descend on the cycle path to meet a lane. Turn right and pass under the motorway (538 915). Carry straight on, ignoring the first turn-off right, and curve right with the (urban) road along Caerwent Lane (5m). From the end of this street, the route into Chepstow is well waymarked by Wales Coast Path signs. At the end of Caerwent Lane turn right and then right into Tenby Lane. Turn left up the left side of a playing field and continue along a good track through woodland, to the right of housing. Keep going on the main track, parallel to the River Wye, following the yellow waymark signs and getting occasional views to the right of the river. Eventually the track descends close to the railway line on the right. Continue straight ahead through bollards, go straight across a lane coming down from the left and pick up a steep tarmac path ahead which ascends to Raglan Way. Turn right and at the T-junction at the top turn left for a short distance, then turn right on a good track to the right of Little Gables. This soon becomes surfaced and just keep going straight ahead, sometimes near housing, sometimes near factories but the way to go is always clear. The path goes to the left of a quarry where awesome cliffs to the right can be seen. Just after the quarry, curve left onto a wide tarred cycle path as indicated. The cycle path is followed into Wye Crescent. At the end, turn left into Hardwick Avenue. When the Wales Coast Path is signed right, go straight ahead, still on Hardwick Avenue, to an underpass for the A48 (532 936) (6.7m). Beyond, climb up steps to Hardwick Terrace. This very shortly meets a street. Turn right here, pass through a medieval town gate and continue through the pedestrian area forming the centre of Chepstow.

3: Descend to the bottom of Chepstow's main shopping centre (St Mary Street). Turn left into Upper Church Street to a T-junction and turn right into Bridge Street. Follow Bridge Street, ignoring turn offs to the right, to the bridge over the River Wye. Cross the river into Gloucestershire and immediately take an ascending, wide surfaced passageway off right. Ignore a passageway off right to reach a fast road at the top and cross to take the surfaced path opposite. This quickly joins a lane which is followed to a B-road. Go left here for 200 yds then turn right into Elm Road (540 950) (7.8m). After a few yards, follow the Gloucester Way (GW) cathedral sign left for a between-houses path to a stile. In the field entered, follow the right fence until it turns, then go straight ahead to cross a grass track and come alongside a right field boundary which is followed to a metal kissing gate. Now take the trodden path across a crop field to reach its farm gate onto a lane. Go straight across through the gate opposite and leave the GW temporarily, by going straight across the field, aiming for the visible stile on the far side (to the right of a white house). Cross and go straight on ascending alongside a left fence to a kissing gate onto a woodland track. Turn left here, ascending to a double gate. Pass through to a track and turn left to a metal gate onto a lane (544 957). Turn right following the lane to its end. Here, go through a metal walkers' gate (just to the right of a children's play area), go half-left to meet and then follow the left hedge down to a stile. Cross, go slightly left of straight ahead across the field on a trodden path. Exit the field at a farm gate and go forward a few yards to meet a lane where the GW is rejoined. Turn left for 280 yds then go left through a metal walkers' gate into a field on a signed path. Turn right to follow the right edge for a short distance until the trodden path veers right through the hedge to follow the right fence through a narrow belt of woodland; the track of a disused railway lies in the dip beyond the right fencing. Pass through a metal walkers' gate and follow the right hedge to a metal walkers' gate onto a lane (551 963) (9.1m).

4: Go left briefly and then right at the GW sign onto an ascending grassy track to reach a stile. Cross into a field and turn right along the trodden path for a short distance to a metal walkers' gate into the next field, where the left edge is followed to a metal walkers' gate. In the next field, again follow the left hedge and cross a farm track at its end to reach a metal walkers' gate. Pass through and again take to the left boundary to find a metal walkers' gate. Beyond, follow the left edge until veering left at a waymark post to a left wall, which is followed to a stile onto an access drive. Turn right and follow the drive to meet a lane (554 973). Turn right as directed. Ignore a lane turn off right and just after this turn off left on a GW signed grassy path beside a left hedge. Cross a stile and follow the left edge to a stile. Cross and go straight on along a right boundary. When the hedge ends, continue in the same direction to a metal walkers' gate beside a farm gate. In the next field follow the left hedge for a few yards, then go just left of straight ahead on a trodden path just west-of-North (which passes to the right of a small group of trees) to reach a track leading half-left into a plantation. Take this track which follows a left fence to a stile into the wonderfully named Parson's Allotment. After a few yards, there's a track fork (557 980) (10.5m). Take the left branch and leave the GW for good. Keep to the main, very good track, ignoring turn-offs until a track fork is reached (557 984). Branch right here on the lesser track (the left fork leads north-west to a B-road). Follow the path until close to the road when a left fork is taken to very shortly exit the wood onto the B-road, opposite a church graveyard (556 988) (11m); the exit point is close to the plantation's north-west corner.

5: Turn right briefly and take the signed footpath off left opposite Rosemary Lane. Go forward on the enclosed path to a stile into a field, then go straight ahead along the right boundary to a waymark. Cross the right boundary as directed and turn left on an enclosed gravel path to emerge on Miss Graces Lane. Turn right on the lane which almost immediately becomes unsurfaced. Follow the lane, with its excellent easy walking and good views, to Beeches Farm, ignoring turns offs. At the farm keep straight on along the track to a waymarked walkers' gate. Walk past the campsite toilets in the direction of the waymark and then follow the left field edge to a cross-path. Go straight on here through a metal walkers' gate and follow the left hedge down to a stile onto the Offa's Dyke National Trail. Turn right. After a short distance, the path descends half-left to exit woodland and then continues the half-left descent of Madgett Hill. At the bottom, go over a stile then follow the left hedge into an enclosed track to reach a fingerpost. Turn right here, as directed, to find a wide gap in bracken which descends to a metal walkers' gate guarding a footbridge. Cross and follow the Offa's Dyke acorn waymark to ascend half-left, turning right at the top to follow the waymark onto a lane (SO 545 015) (13m).

6: Turn right for 10 yds then turn right on a signed restricted byway, leaving the Offa's Dyke path. Proceed along the unsurfaced access track and eventually reach a house with an access drive coming in from the left. Go straight on, pass a sign saying 'To Spring Vale Only' and 50 yds beyond this go left on an unsigned trodden enclosed path which ascends to a gravel access drive. Turn left here and ascend to a lane (549 020). Turn right for 200 yds then turn left on a signed path. Follow the enclosed path to a stile and then follow a right wall up two fields to a 'stile' out onto a lane. Turn right and almost immediately left on a lovely enclosed (unsigned) bridleway. Ascend to a top lane. Turn right and at the end of the wall on the left, turn left on an unsigned enclosed path which ascends to meet an access track. Turn left for about 10 yds and then turn right on the path continuation which is signed as a restricted byway. Ascend on this enclosed track and at the top of the climb meet a path. Turn right and then immediately left. Shortly afterwards the main track curves right, but go straight on here along a path towards a visible white house; the path is not as well-walked as the others and so may be a bit overgrown. The path becomes a grassy track which passes to the left of the house and meets its access track. Turn left here onto Sandy Lane (552 031) (14.4m).

7: Almost immediately take a signed path right into a field. Turn left and follow the left hedge which runs along the lane for two fields. Then cross a stile to re-meet Sandy Lane. Turn right and on meeting a lane turn right. Ignore a lane off left to follow the sign to St Briavels. Later, ignore a turn off right signed to Chepstow. Just beyond this, take a signed footpath off half-left (not the byway) (556 039) (15m). Cross the stile into a field following the right hedge initially. When the hedge curves right, continue straight ahead to a stile, aiming for the school's small green steeple. Beyond the stile go straight ahead on a farm track which curves right to stiles onto a B-road at the start of St Briavels village. Turn left and follow the pavement then lane past the school entrance. Keep left down High Street and ignoring a lane off left after the bus shelter, curve right and shortly take an enclosed green track off left immediately before the village's inn (The George); the castle which is a Youth Hostel can be viewed on the left. On meeting a lane (559 046) (15.5m), the Youth Hostel entrance is on the left and the B&B is to the right.

Stage 18
St Briavels to Ross-on-Wye

VIA: Symonds Yat, Kerne Bridge and Wye Valley Walk
DISTANCE: 16.4m [273m]
ASCENT: 2780ft DESCENT: 3280ft
EXPLORER: OL14 (Wye Valley)
LANDRANGER: 162 (Gloucester & Forest of Dean)

This stage, which is predominantly northwards, combined the largest amount of ascent of all the stages with a relatively high mileage and turned out to be our longest day. It was a relief to have a decent day after the gales and torrential rain of the preceding day. However conditions underfoot were mucky and wet, particularly to and along an overflowing River Wye. This is an area of short sharp ascents and descents. Since St Briavels is at the top of a hill, the day begins with a sharp descent to Mork to be immediately followed by a sharp rise. The route heads generally north on paths to the village of Whitecliff, then skirts to the west of Coleford to enter Ellis Reddings Wood in the Forest of Dean. A long, beautiful traverse on a well-waymarked path along the forest edge now follows culminating in the arrival at Symonds Yat. Without doubt, the highlight of the day is the stunning high viewpoint from Symonds Yat over the Wye Valley, and this point is just over the halfway point of the stage. As well as the views and nice surroundings, the site boasts a refreshment cabin and nearby toilets.

From the Yat, the route descends steeply to the River Wye, crossing out of Gloucestershire into Herefordshire. The Wye is then followed to Huntsham Bridge. After crossing the Wye, Kerne Bridge which also spans the Wye, is the next objective and because the direct route is along a busy and fast B-road used by heavy traffic, paths are taken to minimise the time that needs to be spent on the section of this road that is without a pavement. From Kerne Bridge, the Wye Valley Way (WVW) is loosely followed to Ross-on-Wye. Surprisingly, given its name, this part of the WVW keeps well above the river so requiring a climb up from Kerne Bridge. It is a delightful trail, very well-signed and hence easy to follow. The approach to Ross involves a stiff, rough climb up through the wood of Chase Hill. The top of the hill was the site of an iron age fort thought to be occupied around the fourth century BC. However the right of way skirts round the fort perimeter and stays below the summit. The route continues into Merrivale Wood, where the WVW is left for a shorter and more interesting route into the picturesque market town of Ross-on-Wye. When close to the town centre, the route passes the end of the wonderfully named 'Old Maids Walk' but no zimmer frames were spotted.

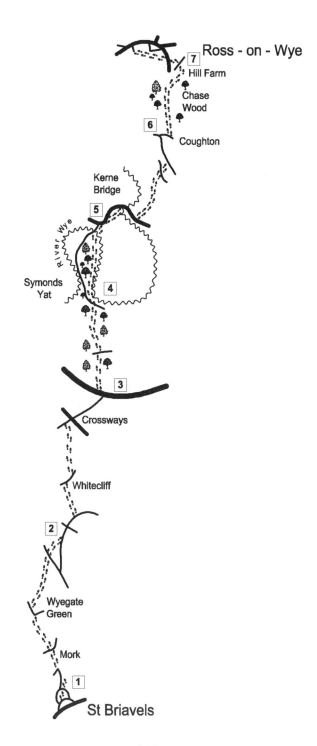

Ross - on - Wye

7 Hill Farm

Chase Wood

6

Coughton

Kerne Bridge

5

River Wye

Symonds Yat

4

3

Crossways

Whitecliff

2

Wyegate Green

Mork

1

St Briavels

1: From where the green track meets the lane (SO 559 046) in St Briavels, take the signed path opposite left into the church grounds. Follow the surfaced path, which curves left passing to the right of the church, and continuing past a seat to a gate exit onto Mork Road. Turn right. After a quarter of a mile, just before a sharp left bend, turn right on Mork Lane signed as 'Unsuitable for Motor Vehicles'. The lane soon becomes unsurfaced and descends steeply to a footbridge just before meeting the lane at Mork (555 056). Turn left briefly, turning right at a restricted byway sign to join a steep ascending surfaced lane which becomes unsurfaced. This emerges onto a lane corner at Wyegate Green. Continue straight on (left) for 240 yds to an east-northeast footpath signed off right (552 067) (1.5m). Follow the right fence in the first field. The path continues opposite left in the next field, following to the left of rough, slightly raised ground indicating the old position of a hedge; the stile is just to the left of a line of trees. Now follow the clearly trodden path to a field gap and continue along a grass strip. Maintain the same direction in the next field to reach a stile out onto a lane in the field corner (561 076). Turn left on the lane for 270 yds and at a left bend, turn right on a signed path. Follow the trodden path across the field to a gate gap in the far left corner, then go half-right on a trodden path to a gate onto a lane (566 081). Turn left down a hill and go straight across onto Pingry Lane at a cross-road (3m).

2: Beyond, continue for just over a third of a mile, ignoring a 'No Through Road' off left just after the residence of Dunfightin, to reach a signed footpath off left (569 089). The footpath is tricky to follow, but keep to the left side of the pond and ascend the short bank to pass through the line of trees at its top. Turn right along the tree line briefly and having passed through a hedge, turn half-left uphill across a field to a field turn (which is just to the right of a lone tree in the field). Turn right along a right fence to a field gate. Pass through and then follow the left boundary round two sides to take the field gate in the corner. Now contour briefly anticlockwise to the right, then continue straight ahead along a cattle trod to slowly converge on a wood edge on the right and find a stile. Cross to take a lovely path along the wood edge to a stile. Beyond take the trodden, gently descending path to a stile and out onto a lane (566 099). Turn right for 500 yds. Pass through the small village of Whitecliff and shortly after passing Whitecliff Furnace, turn off left at the footpath sign (569 102) (4.5m). Pass through the gate and ascend on a path to a ledge. Follow the trodden path left, passing kilns, and then turn right as directed to meet an old railway track. Turn right along the line but almost immediately leave it by branching left as signed. Ascend into a field and find a stile in the top left corner. Go across the next field to a stile (aiming for the left of a house) and reach a track. Turn right on this enclosed track which becomes a lane. At the end of a recreation field turn left and follow its right hedge (with a cemetery the other side of the hedge). Cross a stile in the corner and cross a field on a wide path to Owen Farm. Cross the farm drive into a field and follow its left boundary to a stile by a gate out onto a lane (567 113) (5.3m). Turn right and on shortly reaching a cross-road, go straight across the B-road. Continue to shortly reach a main road and take the footpath opposite right.

3: Follow the left fence to a stile into the forest ahead. Take the middle path to a wide forest track which has a stone base (569 120). There's now an excellent footpath with occasional waymarks all the way to Symonds Yat. Turn right and follow the track to a wide forest road. Turn left, pass through a barrier and go left, as signed, to meet a track. Turn left (with a caravan park to the right) and pass through a gate. Shortly after this the track branches. Fork right as directed and reach a lane (568 130) (6.6m). The right of way continues opposite right and branch right almost immediately (signed). The path here is a lovely, contouring track through beautiful mixed-deciduous woodland. At a track junction, go straight across as directed by the waymark and go straight on at the next cross-track. The track passes to the right of a house (Mailscot Lodge) and on meeting a track here, turn left as indicated. Eventually, a lane is met and the path continues opposite. Follow this, passing just to the left of a farm, into and through the Symonds Yat car park to a signpost. Here go right for the 'historic view' and the refreshment cabin (it's left for the toilets). From the cabin take the footbridge on the right and then turn left for the classic view from the Yat (565 160) (8.8m).

4: Return to the log cabin and follow the directional sign to the River Wye. Descend on steps to a track. The steps continue downwards opposite left to reach a track T-junction. Follow the sign to Ross by turning right here and shortly reach a lane. Continue on the path opposite which curves right. Follow it to the right of a cottage and through woods, branching left at a sign to Ross and carrying on down steep steps to a track. The path continues opposite left, descending through woods and out into the open by the River Wye. Join the WVW for a short time by turning left along a grassy track by the river. Follow the path past a cottage and shortly after at a path branch, leave the WVW (which forks left here), by branching right towards the Wye. Enter a grassy meadow from the wood and follow the bank of the Wye. Eventually when a hedge is reached, follow the left hedge to a lone tree then veer a quarter-right to a stile by the river. Cross and follow the trodden path close to the Wye through a makeshift gate and on to a plank bridge with steps up to a lane by Huntsham Bridge. If the Wye is flooded, you may need to follow the right boundary of the hedge and in the succeeding fields follow their right edge to reach the plank bridge. Turn right crossing the Wye on Huntsham Bridge (568 182) (10.3m). Ignore the footpath sign off right immediately over the bridge, carry on for another 40 yds and turn right over a stile onto an enclosed, unsigned permissive path which leads into a field. Here, turn left up the field by the left fence to a walkers' gate. Go straight on as directed onto an access track, veering slightly left before the entrance to a waymarked gate. Go straight on to another waymarked gate and foward to an access track which is followed to a stile onto a busy, fast B-road; the B-road is narrow, has no pavement here and is a route for HGVs, so take particular care.

5: Turn right for an unpleasant 220 yds escaping down a track off right (573 186), opposite where a footpath goes off left. When the track bends left, carry straight on along a signed enclosed path which ascends. At a fork, branch left as directed and soon after this, the path continues as an access track, still ascending. On meeting a lane, turn left. Fork left at a branch and keep left again, on very shortly meeting a lane, to continue descending towards Goodrich village. Turn right to follow the pedestrian sign to Kerne Bridge, descend to the pavement on the B-road and follow the pavement to and across Kerne Bridge (581 192) (11.7m). Having crossed, immediately take the gravel footpath off right running parallel to the busy B-road. Follow this enclosed path to emerge in the Bishopswood Village Hall car park. Exit through its gate and immediately turn left up the side of an ordinary car park to exit left at the top onto a short path leading to the B-road. Take the lane opposite left. After a few yards go left on an ascending track to a house and then turn right up steps to an access drive. Follow this right to a junction of access drives. Take the path opposite and after a few yards turn left (temporarily leaving the WVW). Follow the path to a drive and turn right. Follow the track to meet an access drive (where the WVW is rejoined). Turn left downhill and when nearly at the B-road, turn right on a concrete access track, continuing straight on when it turns right. The path goes through woodland and crosses a drive to continue opposite. Eventually the path reaches a lane (596 205) (13.3m). The path continues opposite left, up the access drive of Linden Lea house. Just before the house, turn left to pass up its side. Now proceed steeply on steps down its left hedge, cross a stile and go through a short patch of woodland to a stile. Descend the field to a stile bottom left, then go steeply up by the left hedge to a stile onto an enclosed track on the left. This is followed to a lane (599 206). Leave the WVW here by turning left and descending to a T-junction. Turn right, signed Pontshill, into the hamlet of Coughton (14m).

6: After 210 yds take a signed path off left, rejoining the WVW (600 212). Go up the permissive farm track and through walkers' gates into a field. Follow the trodden path along the left boundary to a walkers' gate and continue into the right leg of Chase Wood. At the top of the leg, curve briefly left and then turn right up a steeply ascending path and keep going, bearing right at a waymark. The path levels off and meets a track junction. Here, go straight ahead on the WVW which passes to the right of the summit and starts to slowly descend, curving gently left. Continue to pass a barrier and very shortly reach a track junction with Hill Farm on the right (604 229) (15.1m). Go straight ahead on the WVW. Pass through a walkers' gate. Shortly after, ignore the WVW marker right by turning left on a good path which descends down steeply through Merrivale Wood to a fork. Here branch right down steps to reach a track at the slope bottom. Turn right briefly and take a kissing gate into a field on the left. Follow the right hedge to a disused railway line at the end of the field. Cross the line into Lakeside Drive which is followed to meet Merrivale Lane.

7: Go right here for a few yards and then turn left (to the right of two garages) on an urban path which emerges on Eastfield Road. Turn right on Eastfield Road. After passing The Avenue (a road) and Galen House on the left, curve left on a short, surfaced track which emerges on a street. An urban path continues across the road emerging on Kent Avenue. Continue forward a short distance to meet a B-road. Cross and take the signed pedestrian path going half-right to The Prospect (and many other places). When this reaches a lane, turn right and on very shortly reaching a lane off right called Old Maids Walk, take the surfaced path half-left through church grounds. Pass left round two sides of Ross's church and then escape left down steps into St Mary's Street. Turn right briefly to meet Ross-on-Wye's High Street with its Market Place to the right. However, the e2e continues by turning left to shortly reach a T-junction. Here, turn left and almost immediately right into Wye Street (597 242) (16.4m).

Stage 19

Ross-on-Wye to Hereford Railway Station

VIA: Sellack, Little Dewchurch and Dinedor Camp
DISTANCE: 16m [289m]
ASCENT: 1490ft   DESCENT: 1470ft
EXPLORER: 189 (Hereford & Ross-on-Wye)
LANDRANGER: 162 (Gloucester), 149 (Hereford & Leominster)

Today's stage takes in rural Herefordshire as it moves to Hereford. The route commences along the River Wye, passing an elegant modern metal sculpture of three mallard ducks, and crosses Ross's bridge over the Wye. The route then goes north-west to cut across a large loop of the Wye and crosses the river again at Sellack Bridge. After King's Caple village, the Wye is again crossed at Hoarwithy. It was again raining heavily and we sheltered in the cloister of its church. We were surprised to see a group of people approaching, but learnt that they had arrived for a tour of and lecture on the church's unique Italianate architecture. We were invited to join in, but on learning that there wouldn't be coffee and biscuits, we declined!

The Herefordshire Trail, which was joined just before Hoarwithy village, is now followed to Little Dewchurch. This posed some unforeseen problems as a bridleway we followed emerged on a lane awash with water; I was looking round for the bridge across the 'stream' still thinking we were on part of the bridleway! Further on, along a right of way through a crop field, my companion's feet and legs sank into the morass and got boots full of grit and mud for her trouble. Roads and paths beyond Little Dewchurch lead to the ascent of Dinedor Hill, which has an ancient hill fort on its summit, although difficult to discern. The northern side of the hill overlooks Hereford and paths lead down to its suburb of Lower Bullingham. A path from here is shown along the river but it does not exist. Instead it is necessary to take back streets to Putson, where the river path can be taken through Bishop's Meadow to the distinctive Victoria footbridge, built to celebrate Queen Victoria's diamond jubilee in 1898. A short walk through the streets leads to (a Morrisons and) the railway station. From here we chose to take the train home and have a rest day. Hereford has plenty of B&B's and there is one on the route, (about) half a mile into stage 20.

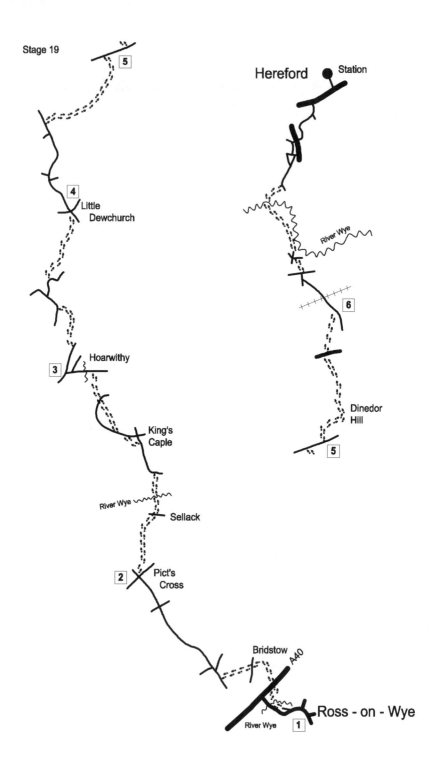

Stage 19

Hereford ● Station

5

4 Little
Dewchurch

6

Hoarwithy
3

King's
Caple

Dinedor
Hill

River Wye

5

River Wye

Sellack

2 Pict's
Cross

Bridstow A40

Ross - on - Wye

River Wye 1

1: Proceed down Wye Street (SO 597 242) turning off right as soon as possible to a footpath along the river. Follow the path to the left ascending steps to meet a B-road just before Wilton Bridge. Cross the river on the bridge and then immediately take the footpath on the right, following the well-marked Herefordshire Trail (HT) apple signs; Wilton Castle is visible on the left. After the path crosses the stream twice, follow to the left of the stream on a permissive path which passes under the A40. Then turn left, parallel to the A40, to meet the right of way. (If the underpass is flooded, as it was for us, reach this point by passing up the field to a stile and cross the A40 with care to the path opposite). Turn right (or go straight on) on the field path going north along the back-of-the houses to a gate. Pass and follow the left boundary until houses on the left, at which point curve left to a farm drive. Cross to take the concrete access drive and soon a walkers' gate left. Go round the bottom of a mound, then aim for Bridstow's church. Pass through a walkers' gate and take the trodden field path to the left of the church to reach a lane (585 248). Take the footpath opposite and follow right edges to a minor road (580 247) (1.7m). Turn right and follow the 'major' road (leaving the HT) to Pict's Cross (561 267) (3.5m) marked by its war memorial. Go straight across here for 100 yds and then take the next footpath off right, rejoining the HT.

2: Go across the field just east-of-North to a field turn, then follow the right hedge. When it turns, go straight ahead on a trodden field path to a wood. Take the track through the wood to a walkers' gate, then the path along the stream to the lane at Sellack (566 276). Turn left past its church and immediately after turn right on a trodden path through fields. Cross a footbridge, proceed forward to cross the River Wye by elegant Sellack Bridge and follow the path beyond to a lane. Leave the HT by turning left along the lane for nearly half a mile to a footpath off left, just before the first house on the right (562 288) (5m). Follow the trodden path in the field westwards to a drive. Cross the drive to a stile opposite and follow the path, branching left to a lane with King's Caple church (559 288) opposite. Turn left, keep right at a branch and turn off right onto a path (553 289). Follow the trodden path across a field into the next field where the path is along the left fence, then curve left onto a track and thence out to a lane at Ruxton. Turn left for a short distance and then turn off right along a right fence. In the next field go three-quarters left to meet a track and rejoin the HT. Turn right to a lane (550 295). Turn left and almost immediately cross the Wye by Hoarwithy Bridge. Ignore a lane off right and continue to meet a road in the village (6.5m).

3: Turn right uphill passing Hoarwithy's church, pass the derestriction sign and turn left on a path (546 297). Follow right boundaries to a building. Keep left round its boundary and then continue along the right edge to a stile. Cross and follow the right boundary along the top of a drop to the left. On reaching a track turn left and descend to shortly meet a lane (540 300). Turn right and take the first lane right just after Prothither Farm. After 120 yds, when the lane bends sharp right, turn left at a sign into a field. Follow the left edge in this and in the next field until the boundary side followed is swapped to the right. In the next long field, keep with the right hedge to a stile. Beyond, follow the left edge to a field turn and then go straight ahead to a stile. Then follow the left edge for one and a bit fields to a stile. Cross, go a quarter-left to a marker post and turn right along the left field edge, accompanying a stream. On reaching a farm track, cross to the path opposite then go a quarter-left across a field to exit at a road junction (534 318) (8.5m) in Little Dewchurch village. The Herefordshire Trail is left for good here.

4: Take the second road on the left, signed for Hereford and this 'major' road north-west is followed for nearly 2m to a signed path off right (519 341) (10.4m); the path is a quarter of a mile after passing the lane off left to Aconbury Court and its church. In the field entered, go half-left to a lone tree then descend half-right to a wood and follow the right edge of the wood. When the wood edge turns right, go straight ahead to a stile and continue straight ahead keeping to the left of the stream. In the next field, keep to the base of a mound on which there are pylons, gradually curving left (away from the stream) to a stile. In the next field go straight on, aiming for the far left corner of the field where the access drive of Tar's Mill Farm can be joined. Turn right on this, following it to a lane (525 358). Turn right on the lane for 280 yds (12m) and then take the signed footpath off left (just before a line of trees on the right) onto Dinedor Hill.

5: Follow the right hedge line up the hill to a stile. Over, turn right along the right hedge to a stile. Don't cross but turn left along the right hedge ascending to a gate near the top corner of the field. Cross a stile here and go straight up briefly, through house grounds, to a stile on the right into a field. Follow the left hedge, and ignore a path off left, to continue by the hedge to the next stile. Across, follow the left hedge to a stile into a wood and descend through the wood to a track. The path continues opposite. Twist left as directed and then turn right down a left field edge to a walkers' gate into an orchard where the left hedge is followed. At the bottom, turn left to a walkers' gate and follow the path on a circuitous route to the underpass of a new road. Beyond, go through a walkers' gate left then one right and follow the right field edge until directed right into an adjacent field. Here, go beside the left edge to a gravel path to the right of a stream and thence out onto Watery Lane (523 378) (13.7m) on the south-eastern fringe of Hereford.

6: Turn left, pass under a railway line and continue to a T-junction. Turn right and shortly meet a busier road. Turn left and immediately after the Wye Inn (on the right), turn half-right down a passageway into River View Road. Turn left along River View and take the first road left to very shortly meet Putson Avenue. Turn right to meet Hinton Road and turn right to shortly reach a fork at a mini roundabout. Fork right, signed 'Hinton Road leading to Peregrine Close/Acacia Close'. At the end, when the road turns right into Acacia Close, carry straight on along a tarmac path which soon turns left along the river and out into parkland. Continue to elegant Victoria Bridge (513 394) (15m), the first bridge met over the River Wye. Cross this footbridge and go ahead to a junction of Mill Street left and Nelson Street right. Follow the line of Mill Street which curves left into Cantaloupe Street and continues to meet St Owen's Street. Go opposite right into (unnamed) narrow Gaol Street and follow it as it curves left, until it's possible to turn briefly right at the end of a car park, to meet a main road named Bath Street. Go opposite left into Symonds Street, take the first left into Vaughan Street to a T-junction and turn right into Kyrle Street. Kyrle Street curves left (by the hospital) into Union Street which is followed to shortly meet a busy main road named Commercial Road. Cross and turn right. For the railway station (515 406), turn left into Station Approach and then right as directed, while the end-to-end route of the next stage continues down Commercial Road.

Stage 20
Hereford Railway Station to Leominster YHA

VIA: Sutton St Nicholas, Bodenham and Stoke Prior
DISTANCE: 16.3m [305.3m]
ASCENT: 900ft   DESCENT: 860ft
EXPLORER: 202 (Leominster)
LANDRANGER: 149 (Hereford & Leominster)

We returned to Hereford by train and knew, as we surveyed the area between Leominster and Hereford from the train, that there was extensive flooding. It was another day of wall to wall heavy rain. The amount of flooding was borne home on attempting to leave Hereford, as the field the path passed through was awash with water, with ducks swimming past waving. After going round this section by road, we picked up the planned route again and whilst the paths and roads were under water, sometimes over boot level, we got as far as the path down into Bodenham. The fields here were just completely covered with water; you would have needed a boat or a swimming costume to get across. So having already done quite a bit of extra mileage from detouring round the water, and with the necessity of now doing more, we abandoned the planned route and took to the lanes to get to Leominster. It was the only stage where we were forced to abandon the planned route. Although we experienced rain further on, there was nothing to match the downpours we experienced up to this point, and as we moved further north, the underfoot conditions gradually improved indicating that less rain had fallen here. So in many ways, we regarded this day as a watershed!

Subsequently, we went to do the entire stage of the planned route later in the year and it is this that is described here. It is not dramatic but nevertheless a very satisfying day's walking. Hereford is left via Aylestone Hill Park and then the route takes a footpath to the River Lugg. After crossing the Lugg, a drove track northwards to Sutton St Nicholas is followed. From there, the route passes the old fort at Sutton Walls and the orchards typical of the area, to the lane junction at Hawkersland Cross. Beyond, the route heads north on paths and bridleways to reach the large village of Bodenham with a subsequent path parallel to the Lugg. The hamlet of Bowley Town is the next objective and then it's a lane walk northwards to Risbury Bridge, with paths from there past ancient Risbury fort to Stoke Prior village. The pub at Stoke Prior is unlikely to be open so it's onwards mainly by path to a riverside path beside the River Lugg which leads to Leominster's railway station. The town is some distance to the west, but we continued northwards to the self-catering Youth Hostel close to Leominster's priory church. This Is a relatively new hostel and had good facilities with a decent drying room.

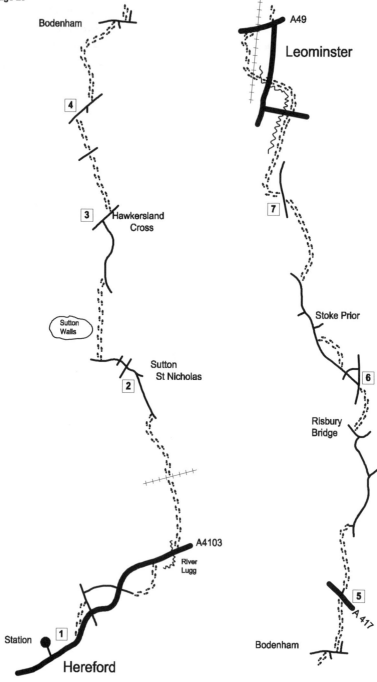

Stage 20

Bodenham

4

3 Hawkersland
Cross

Sutton
Walls

Sutton
St Nicholas

2

A4103

River
Lugg

Station 1

Hereford

A49

Leominster

7

Stoke Prior

6

Risbury
Bridge

5

A 417

Bodenham

1: From the railway station (SO 515 406), return to the junction with Commercial Road and turn left to continue up Commercial Road, crossing the railway line. Commercial Road becomes Aylestone Hill and immediately after crossing Moreland Avenue on the left, turn left into Aylestone Park. Follow the surfaced path through the park and pass out onto a road through the car park entrance/exit. Turn left and take the first road right which is Overbury Road. At its end meet a road and continue opposite on Walney Lane, a 'No Through Road'. At the lane end, go through two stone pillars onto an unsigned path which very shortly reaches a kissing gate. Descend ahead on a well-trodden path to cross a footbridge into a field. Here take the trodden path a quarter-left to reach the River Lugg and then turn left to a farm gate onto a main road (to the right of a telegraph pole). Turn right on a narrow pavement along the main road. Immediately after the River Lugg is crossed, take a signed bridleway track off left (532 418) (1.9m). Follow the track to a gate and pass through to two gates. Take the right gate signed 'Drovers Way, Public Bridle Path'. Follow the enclosed path to a gate. Beyond, follow the grassy track, enclosed by a drain on either side, to a railway crossing. The enclosed track continues straight ahead across the line. Ignore two turn offs right to eventually meet a good track (536 446). Turn left here and the track quickly becomes a rough lane which is followed into Sutton St Nicholas village where it curves right to reach a T-junction by the church (534 454) (4.2m).

2: Turn left to a cross-road. Go straight across and after another third of a mile take a signed bridleway off right also signed 'To Ordis Court' (528 458); the bridleway is opposite a signed path off left. When the access track soon curves right to the court, carry straight on along a gently ascending track. At a fingerpost, leave the bridleway which curves right for the signed footpath straight on. Enter a field and ascend along the left hedge; at the top, the ancient settlement of Sutton Walls Fort is to the left. Descend along the left hedge to a field turn and go straight ahead through the gap here into an orchard. The path continues to the left of the grassy strip straight ahead, along a row of trees to the right, and joins a gravel access track. Continue straight ahead on this and when the access track curves right, follow it as directed by the waymark. Pass a barn, then a couple of houses and exit via a stile onto a lane. Turn left and follow the lane to a T-junction at Hawkersland Cross (532 480) (6.2m).

3: Turn right briefly then left on a signed bridleway track. Pass a scout hut and when the track curves, go straight on along an enclosed grassy track between hedges to the right of a farm track. Follow this without interruption as it descends and then ascends to meet a bridleway path (530 489). Turn left for 110 yds and just after a paddock in the field on the right, turn right over a stile onto a field path. Go parallel to the right hedge to a kissing gate, then across the next field parallel to the right hedge to a stile. Now go straight on descending to a stile at the bottom right corner onto a rough lane. Turn right briefly to a gate off left with a hidden footpath sign. Go a quarter-left to shortly reach a farm crossing over a small stream. Then go three-quarters right, passing well to the right of a lone tree in the middle of the field, and pick up a trodden path leading to a stile. Cross and follow the right hedge to a stile. Cross and diverge gently from the left hedge to a stile by a gate. Cross and go a quarter-left to a stile into a cottage garden, with a sign saying 'Trespassers Welcome, Garden Open'! Go straight ahead onto the paved garden path which passes to the right of the house and curves right to meet its access track. Turn left to a stile by a gate and follow the grass track beyond for a short distance to a footbridge on the right. Cross and go straight on along the left hedge of two fields. Then go a quarter-left in the next field to a stile in the top left corner. In the subsequent field follow the left hedge to a kissing gate onto a lane (525 499) (7.6m).

4: Turn right for a quarter of a mile to just after a turn off right signed to Litmarsh and turn left on a track signed to Berrington Spring Water. Follow the track as it curves right and a few yards further on, turn off left over a stile on a signed path. Follow the left fencing to a garden seat, then immediately turn right to ascend along a right hedge to a signed entry point into woodland. Follow the good, well-trodden path through the woodland. It descends steeply on steps to walkers' gates guarding a footbridge. Cross to exit the woodland into a field. Take the trodden path slightly right of straight ahead, aiming to the right of the church, to reach a footbridge over the River Lugg. Cross and follow the path ahead through a gate into the grounds of Bodenham's church. Follow the left edge of the grounds around two sides passing its lych gate and exit via a gate into a field. Follow the left edge of the long field until the fencing turns left. At this point go straight ahead to a hedge gap and continue in the same direction to meet a hedge at a kissing gate. Beyond, follow the path now enclosed and waymarked to another kissing gate. Then follow the right edge to a kissing gate out onto the road through Bodenham (534 512). Turn right, cross the River Lugg, ignore a lane turn off right and 110 yds after this, turn left on a signed path (9m). Cross a footbridge and follow the provided wide path through a crop field to a waymarked stile; initially the path is close to the river but then diverges from it. Cross the next field a quarter-right to a footbridge and beyond go straight on towards a sign on the main road; the stile onto the road is in a field corner just to the right of the sign (538 520) (9.6m).

5: Turn right briefly on the busy, fast main road and then turn left on a 'No Through Road'. Go straight ahead ascending up the lane which ends shortly and continues as a path to shortly reach a waymarked stile into a field. Here, go half-right to a walkers' gate near the top right corner of the field. Then follow the right edge across two fields to reach and cross a farm track to the farm gate opposite. Again go up the right edge which has a small field turn to reach a stile and then follow the right hedge to a farm gate. Curve left onto an access track running along a left hedge and when this shortly meets a lane at the hamlet of Bowley Town, turn right to shortly reach a road (540 532) (10.6m). Turn left and follow the road for one and a third miles, ignoring two turn offs signed for Risbury. After the second turn off the road descends to Risbury Bridge over the Humber Brook. Immediately before the bridge, turn right over a stile onto a signed path (540 550) (11.9m). The path follows to the right of the brook, but then veers half-right passing a waymark on the tree in the garden to reach a farm gate. Through, go parallel to the stream, ignoring a footbridge off left. The path enters a meadow where it leaves the brook to go straight across on a trodden path to a waymarked stile; Risbury Fort is on the hill to the right. Beyond the stile, cross a small patch of woodland to a footbridge with a waymarked walkers' gate and then follow the left field edge; the building ahead in the field is called Gob's Castle (539 556)! Shortly after passing this building, turn left through a farm gate and go half-right towards the right end of the woodland ahead to reach a waymarked stile (visible from the field's brow). Cross and turn left (as directed) down the left edge to a farm gate on the right. Pass through and follow the trodden path through a thin strip of woodland to a walkers' gate with a footbridge over a stream. Beyond, turn right on a trodden path which ascends to meet a field hedge. Here, turn to follow the right edge until a waymarked stile on the right. Cross, turn left and follow the left hedge round two sides to a stile on the left onto a road junction (532 560) (12.8m).

6: Cross to take the more minor lane opposite and go straight across at a cross-road. Continue on the lane towards Stoke Prior village for another 250 yds and then turn right over a stile on a signed path. Follow the left hedge which soon turns left. Descend to a stile and enter an orchard. Go straight ahead, following the left edge of the orchard beside a left ditch, until the ditch can be crossed by a farm crossing. Officially the right of way goes half-right from here to a stile out onto a lane. However, if the side ditch is too wet and deep to cross, continue along the side ditch (towards the cottage) to a crossing point and then on to the stile. Turn right on the lane and ignoring a turn off right, descend to the road junction in Stoke Prior. Here turn right, signed Leominster. Follow the lane past the village pub, The Lamb, which is unlikely to be open and continue for another third of a mile. Go past a farm drive on the right and take the next farm gate right onto a signed track (518 571) (14m). At the next farm gate, cross a stile and continue along the track running down the left edge of an orchard to a stile. In the next field follow its left edge curving left onto an ascending track into a narrow belt of woodland. On leaving the woodland, continue straight ahead on a rough grass track along a left boundary to reach a waymarked farm gate. Through, go a quarter-right to pass through a hedge gap and then follow a trodden path to a farm gate with a waymarked stile; the large town visible is Leominster. From the stile continue ahead, descending on a grassy track parallel to the left edge and then drop down into a small gully. Turn left to a stile and over, follow the gully path which passes left of Eaton House and out onto the road (511 579).

7: Turn right for 210 yds and take Eaton Hall's access drive off left (unsigned). At a fork branch right and immediately right over a stile into a field. Head across the field in a curving left arc to a stile in the corner by the River Lugg. Cross and follow the rough path by the river to a stile. Over, go half-right to a signed difficult stile (or follow the river curve) and then follow the river passing over a stile and through a makeshift gate to reach a stile onto the main A44 road (15.3m). Cross to the better river path opposite, keeping left at any forks in order to stay near the river; the noise you can hear is from the A49 trunk road. Eventually the path branches left to go under the A49. Beyond, stay with the river for a short distance before ascending steps to a footbridge crossing the river (503 589). Over, turn right at a path T-junction to a footbridge over the railway line, close to Leominster's station and reach a road corner by the White Lion Inn. For accommodation in the town, carry straight on westwards up Etnam Street to the town centre. For the YHA and the route continuation, follow the path sign to the right, passing up the left side of the inn, and continue by the side of the railway line on a grotty path. This soon improves as it enters parkland and the major path is followed, curving left to pass along the back of The Old Priory. Just past here, exit the park through an access gate on the left and go forward to meet a lane named 'The Priory' with Leominster's Parish Church opposite (498 593). The route continues right but for the YHA turn left a short distance (499 593) (16.3m).

Stage 21

Leominster YHA to Onibury

VIA: Orleton, Mortimer Forest and Bromfield
DISTANCE: 18m [323.3m]
ASCENT: 1550ft   **DESCENT:**   1450ft
EXPLORER: 202 (Leominster), 203 (Ludlow)
LANDRANGER: 149 (Hereford), 137 (Church Stretton & Ludlow)

Although the distance for this stage seems relatively large, we found it an 'easy' 18 miles, both underfoot and navigationally. We therefore made good time and completed it in under eight hours. The stage finishes at Onibury and so avoids Ludlow. This is deliberate. Ludlow is a delightful town but the routes to and from it are not in my view attractive or interesting. From Leominster, the route makes its way northwards using paths and tracks to the attractive village of Orleton. Unfortunately, it appears to have no facilities at the time you are likely to pass. From Orleton the route ascends gently to join the Mortimer Trail and this is followed up to and across elevated Hanway Common. Very shortly after entering the Mortimer Forest, the Trail is left for forest tracks leading to High Vinnalls car park. The stage now makes its way to the entry into Shropshire, this being marked by a sign. From here the route descends to join a delightful walk through estate parkland which crosses the River Teme near Bromfield. Field paths are then taken to the hamlet of Wootton and on to the end of the stage at the village of Onibury. There is no accommodation at Onibury, but there is a regular bus service between Shrewsbury and Ludlow, with Ludlow being the obvious place to stay and stock up. The bus stop at Onibury is well equipped having seats and a good shelter.

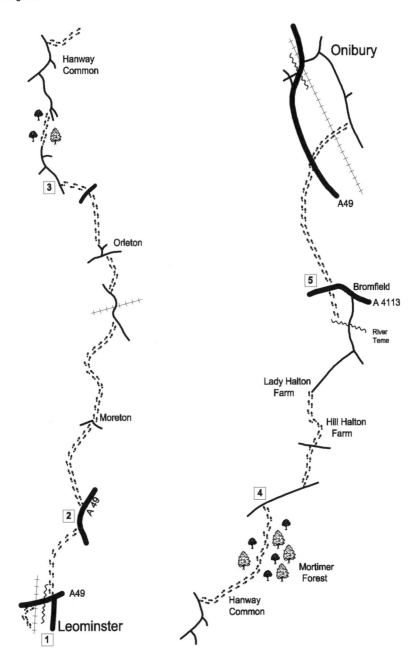

Hanway Common

3

Orleton

Moreton

2 A49

A49

Leominster

1

Onibury

A49

5 Bromfield
A 4113

River Teme

Lady Halton Farm

Hill Halton Farm

4

Mortimer Forest

Hanway Common

1: From the YHA (SO 499 593), walk back to the park exit on The Priory (lane). Continue for a few more yards and then turn right down a 'No Through Road' also called The Priory. Shortly reach and cross an iron bridge over Kenwater, then turn right along this stream to emerge on the main A44 road (500 595). Turn right, cross the railway on a level crossing and then the River Lugg. Immediately after crossing the Lugg, turn left on a footpath (502 596), which starts as a track to a bridge over Ridgemoor Brook, and then turns right along a right field hedge with the brook beyond. Continue by the right boundary in the next field and in the succeeding field until a footbridge right crossing the brook. From the bridge go half-left to cross another footbridge and then half-right aiming for a barn (506 608). Here turn left, north, along a left boundary. In the next field curve right to an embankment which is then followed in this and the next field, dropping left at the end into a sunken track which has a stile left onto an enclosed track. This is followed to the right to the busy and fast main A49 road (511 615) (1.8m). Turn left along the main road for a half mile. Pass a footpath off left to Park Farm and 90 yds beyond take a bridleway off left (511 621) into a field.

2: Go half-right, passing a lone tree, to reach a waymarked gate. Continue in the same direction in the next field to meet the right boundary at a field turn and the right boundary is then followed. Keep with right boundaries north-northwest as the bridleway passes Keepers Cottage, goes through a small patch of woodland then follows a wood edge and continues north to meet a lane at the hamlet of Moreton (503 641) (3.7m). Go straight across on the bridleway continuation and pick up a path beside right railings which leads to a bridleway gate. The route of the bridleway track is clear from here. Keep straight on to a T-junction and take the signed bridleway track opposite. Later, ignore a branch track left into woodland. A little later, turn left as signed, for the bridleway (504 648). Beyond, follow the right field edge when the track is not enclosed to emerge on Tunnel Lane (503 659) (5m). Go left along the lane, cross over the railway line, continue for another 390 yds (ignoring a path off right) and then take an enclosed, unsigned bridleway path off right (498 666). The path leads through a gate and left onto a farm access drive which is followed to the road beside Orleton's church (495 672) (6m). Turn left through the village and opposite a telephone box, turn right up Mortimer Close. When it shortly forks, turn left into Mortimer Drive. At its end, turn left into Millbrook Close and almost immediately turn right on a path between wide-apart hedges. After the path crosses a stream, go opposite left on a path into woodland and maintain this north-west direction into a recreation field. Follow the right hedge briefly to a plank bridge off right (before the sports pavilion) and in the large field entered, follow the visible path north-northwest to a B-road (489 676). Take the path opposite and follow the left hedge to a walkers' gate. The path turns westwards here, but continues to follow the left hedge for three fields to a stile onto a farm track which leads to Green Lane (479 678) (7m).

3: Turn right and in a short distance right again at a fork. When the Mortimer Trail joins the lane from the left, continue on the lane for another 80 yds to a T-junction (475 682). Go left here (the Trail goes right) and follow the rough lane, signed 'Waterloo', north to a notice saying 'Private Road'. Here take the rightmost of three possible openings, which is a bridleway. Descend on the access drive to April's House passing it on the left. Continue beyond through a gate to a good, ascending woodland track on the right side of a valley. This meets a lane and rejoins the Mortimer Trail (473 691) (8.1m). Turn left and follow the lane to a T-junction. Turn right for 380 yds and join a lane (472 699) but after 180 yds, at Fircroft, take an enclosed bridleway off right and follow this into and along a narrow strip of land keeping to its left side. When the field opens out, go half-left to cut off the field corner and reach the left boundary which is followed to the right; the open land being crossed is Hanway Common. Cross a farm access drive (476 708) (9.6m) and continue along the left boundary to a gate into Mortimer Forest. Beyond, follow a good track with forest only on the right. When the forest appears on both sides of the track, continue forward on the track following Mortimer Way signs, to shortly reach a gravel forest road. Turn left, and ignore the Mortimer Way turn-off right after a few yards, so as to continue on the forest road as it contours the west side of Vinnalls hill west-of-North. After just over two-thirds of a mile, a severe left bend is reached. Here, take a grassy track on the right which reaches a forest road. Go straight across to very shortly meet a forest road and turn right, following signs to the car park, to emerge on a busy minor road by Vinnalls Car Park (474 732) (11.2m).

4: Turn right along the road for just under two thirds of a mile then turn off left (482 738) where Shropshire is entered. Descend north on a good bridleway through a now felled area of woodland. Cross two forestry tracks and finally descend through a dip in a field turning half-left near the bottom to exit onto a lane (482 743). Turn right for 90 yds, then turn off left on a just west-of-North bridleway. Go straight on at a bridleway/path fork and then turn left just before the buildings of Hill Halton farm. Descend to cross a stream and beyond, ascend to Lady Halton farm. Take a gate on the right immediately before the buildings and keep just to the right of the buildings. Turn left immediately after the house to meet a lane (13m). Turn right for three-quarters of a mile to a T-junction (487 760). Here, turn left (signed 'Bromfield') along a delightful estate road through parkland for over half a mile and cross the River Teme (481 767). Immediately after, turn off left on a footpath signed 'Shropshire Way to Craven Arms'. Follow the trodden path along the river and pass into a field. Follow the path along the left field edge to meet a track and turn right on the track to reach the main A4113 road (473 769) (15m).

5: Go opposite left into a very long field and follow the right boundary around two sides. Just before a wood is reached at the end of the second side, look for a (well-disguised) stile in the hedge to the right. Cross and follow the left field boundary to a concrete farm track. Turn right here (16m), follow the track for 90 yds and then turn left on a concrete track (461 775) which is the access to Cookeridge farm. Just as Cookeridge's gate is reached, go slightly right of straight ahead to follow the left field hedge. On shortly reaching the end of the field, turn right and follow the field edge for 220 yds, to where the field starts to curve right, and look for a well-disguised footbridge over the stream on the left. Cross and turn half-left along the left field boundary. On reaching the end of the field, turn right and follow the left hedge boundary north-east down two fields. At the bottom of the second field, turn left and follow the right hedge boundary for one field with the A49 trunk road on the other side of the hedge. Exit the field by its gate onto the main road (458 783) (17m). Cross with care to take the footpath opposite left. Go through the walkers' gate and proceed straight ahead down a slight slope to a walkers' gate which leads onto a track. Go left on this very briefly before branching off right to a sturdy footbridge over the River Onny. Turn right for a few yards along the river, then branch off left to pass under the railway line and continue straight across the field to a walkers gate onto Back Lane (461 785). Turn left and ignoring a lane turn-off right, follow the lane into Onibury village. Ignore another turn off right to shortly reach the main A49 road at Onibury (454 791) (18m).

Stage 22
Onibury to Bridges YHA

VIA: **Stokesay Castle, Long Mynd and Adstone Hill**
DISTANCE: **16.4m [339.7m]**
ASCENT: **2610ft** DESCENT: **2100ft**
EXPLORER: **203 (Ludlow), 217 (Long Mynd)**
LANDRANGER: **137 (Church Stretton & Ludlow)**

This is a really good day's walking with the ascent of and walk along the Long Mynd ridge being the highlight, although the ridge walk over Adstone Hill later on is also very fine. The route picks up the Shropshire Way. This is a trail which seems to be in a constant state of flux, and everyone I've met who's done it, has done a slightly different route. Therefore, the route picks up and follows what I think is the current route from Onibury to above Craven Arms passing Stokesay Castle and then takes to the original route to Bridges; understandably, the former is better signed than the latter. I really like the original route signs of a white buzzard on a black background, with the buzzard pointing in the direction you need to take. The new signs have an indeterminate looking bird within a footpath or bridleway directional marker and to my eyes are not nearly as distinctive or classy.

Stokesay Castle is a fortified 13th century manor house and is worth a visit if you have the time. Beyond the castle, the route passes half a mile from the small, unappealing town of Craven Arms which has few facilities, so is best missed unless you need its railway station. Near Craven Arms we were delighted to meet up with close members of my family and members of our walking group, for the walk to Bridges through land designated as being an area of outstanding natural beauty. It was a fine but a blisteringly cold day, particularly on the Long Mynd ridge, which rises to nearly 1700 ft. Bridges is tiny but beautifully situated and does have a pub. The only accommodation is the independently run Youth Hostel which provides meals.

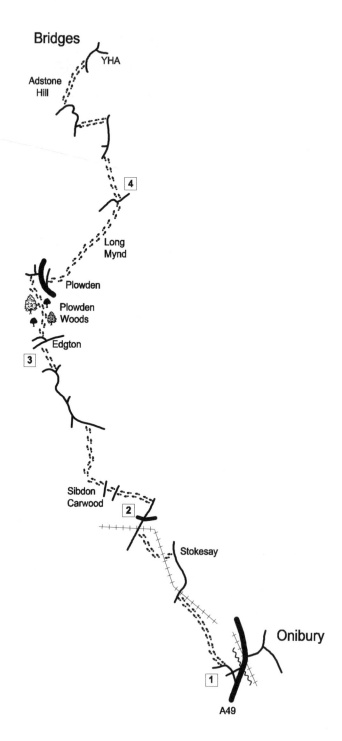

Bridges

YHA

Adstone
Hill

4

Long
Mynd

Plowden

Plowden
Woods

Edgton

3

Sibdon
Carwood

2

Stokesay

Onibury

1

A49

1: From the A49 at Onibury (SO 454 791), turn left over the level crossing at Onibury, then cross the River Onny and 90 yds beyond, turn right on a minor road. After 110 yds turn right on a lane signed 'Aldon'. Shortly, just after the lane bends left, take a signed path off right. Go through the farmyard of Stepaside to a walkers' gate. Follow the footpath sign to get to an enclosed path leading into a field. Here go to the bottom right corner, near the railway line. Beyond, follow the right field edge across two fields and then it's half-left to follow the right edge of a wood. Continue to follow round the edge of the wood until a stile on the right, into the wood, where the Shropshire Way is joined. Cross and descend half-right on a track through the wood, branching right to an exit stile into a field. Go three-quarters left across the field on a trodden path to a stile, and cross the next field on the trodden path. In the succeeding field go slightly right of straight ahead to a track which passes lime kilns and then descends to the railway line. Continue by the line to a line crossing, then turn left on a lane. Opposite Stokesay Castle (435 817) (2.4m), turn left on a track which passes to the right of a pond and under the railway. Beyond, follow right boundaries, as signed, into a wood where the right edge is followed to a signed stile off right into a field. Follow the right hedge to the railway line and turn left along it to a minor road (423 825) which is the old Roman Road of Watling Street. Turn right under the railway line and very shortly meet a B-road (3.5m).

2: Craven Arms is half a mile to the right but the route continues on the lane opposite right. This shortly joins a road and after 160 yds turn left on a signed path. Follow left boundaries until a pass through to the opposite side is indicated. Beyond, head just left of straight ahead to a stile onto a lane (415 830) (4.2m). The path continues opposite going half-left to a gate onto a lane (412 830); the buildings of Sibdon Carwood are just to the right. The path continues opposite going just right of straight ahead to a stile with a footbridge. Beyond, follow the telegraph lines west-northwest then follow the left hedge to a gate into a field (not as on the map). Cross the field to the left of a tree line with a ditch and when the tree line ends, continue straight ahead, just north-of-West, to a gate. Through, turn left along the left boundary, which passes through Oldfield Wood, into a field and then follows the wood edge. At the end of the field when the field boundary turns right (403 835), go straight on to the left of a ruined red brick building to a gate (5m). Through, turn right by the right hedge and when it turns right, go straight ahead to pick up and follow the right edge again. The boundary passes to the left of Sibdon Wood and after accompanying the wood edge on the right for 100 yds (403 840), turn half-left across the field to a stile (402 842). Cross and turn right along the right fence to a gate onto a track which descends to a lane (402 846) (5.7m). Turn left. Ignore a lane coming in from the left and one off right to reach a T-junction (393 854). Take the stile opposite and follow the left hedge to a gate. Through, ascend by the left hedge to a stile, and then follow the left edge with a steep descent via steps to a track. Go left until near a farm, when turn right as directed, through a gate and up a track to a lane at Edgton (389 859) (7m).

3: Take the lane opposite but very soon after it curves left, take a signed path off right (388 860) into a field. Follow right field edges to a stile into Plowden Woods. Follow a short path through the wood onto a forest track and turn left following the main track. This joins a forest road which is followed to a lane. Turn right (381 871) (8m) to meet a minor road and turn right over the River Onny to shortly reach the main A489 road (8.5m). Turn right down the main road for 400 yds and then turn onto a lane coming in from the left (383 875). Soon the lane bends sharp right and immediately after a cattle grid, turn right on a bridleway signed 'Long Mynd'. Follow the track to a gate and through, ascend to the next gate on the track. Go slightly left of straight ahead to meet and follow the left fence to a gate on the left. Beyond, take the ascending track to a gate. Pass through and continue on the good track with a wood to the right; there's quite a steep gradient to the left. The ridge route is historic and is reckoned to have been in use by traders for 5,000 years avoiding the soggy valleys, hence its Port Way name on maps. Continue on the track and eventually reaching a track junction with a gliding club ahead. Turn left, signed 'Starboard Way', to avoid walking on the gliding club access road. Follow the grassy track which soon turns right. Follow the northwards track as it passes behind the caravan park attached to the gliding club, and continue beyond curving gently right to meet the gliding club's access road. Turn left for a few yards to the public road (405 919) (12.2m).

4: Go right briefly then turn off half-left on a signed bridleway. Follow the good path diagonally downhill to a lane at the bottom of the Long Mynd (403 929). Turn right and on shortly meeting a lane (13m), go straight on for 750 yds and then turn off left on a path opposite Stanbatch Cottage (402 937).

Follow the right boundary along three fields joining an access track in the third out onto a lane. Turn right and follow the lane as it turns sharp left, and then sharp right to reach Adstone farm. Immediately past the farm, follow the lane as it turns left. After ascending for 310 yds pass through a signed gate on the right (389 941) (14.7m) which gives access to a good grassy track up Adstone Hill, initially alongside a distinctive row of trees on the left; there are good views back to the Long Mynd. The ridge track north along the top of Adstone Hill is now followed until it veers right descending. At this point, continue straight ahead so as to keep with the top of the ridge. Eventually the ridge descends down alongside a right hedge to a short track out onto a lane (391 961). The lane is followed to the left to shortly arrive in Bridges. Turn right at the lane junction to reach the YHA on the right (395 964) (16.4m).

Stage 23
Bridges YHA to Shrewsbury (Coton Hill)

VIA: Golden Valley, Lyth Hill and River Severn
DISTANCE: 16.1m [355.8m]
ASCENT: 1000ft   DESCENT: 1670ft
EXPLORER: 217 (Long Mynd), 241 (Shrewsbury)
LANDRANGER: 137 (Church Stretton & Ludlow), 126 (Shrewsbury)

This is another high quality walk. It follows the well-signed Shropshire Way up lovely Golden Valley to the ridge on Betchcott Hills, and then gradually descends to the Shropshire Plain, passing out of the Shropshire Hills area of outstanding natural beauty. After reaching Lyth Hill, the Marches Way (alas no longer shown on the latest maps) is picked up and followed through the village of Hook-a-Gate to the outskirts of Shrewsbury. This is a nicer route than flogging through Bayston Hill on the Shropshire Way. From the outskirts, surprisingly nice urban paths are used to reach the River Severn, which is followed through Shrewsbury to its centre. It is then a short walk to its suburb of Coton Hill on the edge of countryside. There's a hotel at Coton Hill and we walked into the centre for a meal in the evening.

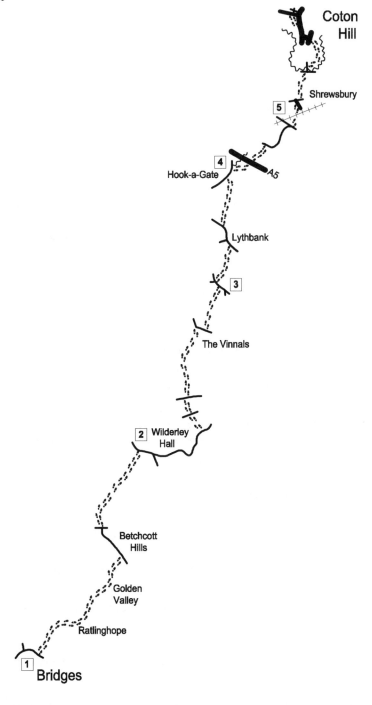

Coton Hill

Shrewsbury

5

4

A5

Hook-a-Gate

Lythbank

3

The Vinnals

2 Wilderley Hall

Betchcott Hills

Golden Valley

Ratlinghope

1 Bridges

1: From the YHA (SO 395 964) turn right along the lane for 260 yds and then take a footpath off left (397 964) just before the lane crosses a brook. Follow the path parallel to and to the left of Darnford Brook. Cross a track to Ratlinghope and continue opposite. Further on, when a footbridge over the stream is reached, turn left as directed, away from the stream, ascending gently on a grassy track by a right fence. The path continues contouring round the hill following the line of the brook below on the right. Turn off left as directed on a path which gently ascends and meet a farm track near Lower Darnford farm (416 978) (1.7m). Turn left on the track as signed, pass through two gates and go half-right passing to the right of an old hedge line. Cross a plank bridge, then turn left as indicated, on a grassy path up the hill. At a path fork, take the lower path to contour to a waymarked stile and follow the trodden path which ascends up Golden Valley to a lane running along the Betchcott Hills ridge (420 985) (2.3m); the lane is another ancient Port Way route. Turn left for three-quarters of a mile to a T-junction and take the signed path opposite. Go half-right to a walkers' gate with a footbridge in the right hedge. Through, go half-left to the left side of the trees and pass down the left side of the trees to a gate. Beyond, follow the left hedge line through a walkers' gate and continue by this boundary until an indistinct waymark indicates a half-right turn towards the farm. Pass through a walkers' gate, cross a farm track to the path opposite, and follow a right hedge to a gate onto a track which is followed to a lane at Wilderley Hall (SJ 434 017) (5.1m).

2: Turn right. Shortly reach a lane branch and fork left, signed 'Stapleton'. After a further 1.2 miles, pass Keepers Cottage on the right and then look for and take a walkers' gate off left (451 026) (6.5m) (before the farm). Follow the right edge to a walkers' gate with a footbridge. Over, go half-right to and along a right hedge to a walkers' gate with a footbridge (left of the corner). Then follow a right edge out onto a lane. The path continues in the field opposite where left boundaries are followed to cross another lane (449 035) (7m). Continue opposite, following the trodden path which starts along a left edge but carries straight on when the edge turns left. When the path meets a track, cross onto the enclosed bridleway opposite which becomes a farm track to The Vinnals. At The Vinnals, turn left to pass by the left side of the house onto its access drive, which is followed to meet a lane in the hamlet of Lower Common (454 054) (8.4m). Turn right for 170 yds to just after the last house on the left and take a field path off left. Follow the left edge before swapping boundary sides for the right. Follow the grassy track initially along the right boundary before it diverges to a walkers' gate onto an enclosed path to an access drive. Turn left for a few yards to meet a track and turn left, north-northeast, to a minor road (460 062) (9m) in the hamlet of Exfords Green.

3: Turn left here for 70 yds and then turn off right onto a rough lane. Follow the track as it swings right and reaches a waymarked bridleway fork (462 065). The Shropshire Way is exited here by taking the left bridleway. Follow the enclosed bridleway which becomes an access track past houses to meet a lane in the hamlet of Lythbank. Turn left down the lane and after 170 yds keep right at a fork and join the Marches Way. After a further third of a mile, turn off right (459 076) on an unsigned track, opposite a lone house on the left. The access track is signed to 'Lower Lythwood Hall'. On reaching its entrance, the track turns half-left to the left of the entrance and runs north-northwest to a stile into a field (10.5m). Follow the trodden path east-of-North to three trees and from there continue in the same direction past a lone tree to a now visible stile. In the next field follow the right hedge, then join a track briefly before turning right through a walkers' gate and following the right hedge round two sides of the field. In the next field go a quarter-right to continue in the same north-northeast direction across the middle of a field on a well-trodden path to reach a waymark on the opposite field boundary. Turn left here along the right fence to a stile. From here descend to a gate on a well-trodden path with a small stream to the right. Then go straight ahead on a track, pass through another gate and descend to a road at Hook-a-Gate (464 090) (11.4m).

4: Turn right for nearly half a mile; the stream crossed is the Rea Brook. At a layby on the right take a signed footpath off right (468 096), cross the Rea Brook and after another 200 yds, turn off left on an unsigned trodden path (12m). Cross rough ground to a visible stile near the brook and enter a field. Follow the left boundary on a good track parallel to the brook (ignore a signed path left closer to the brook which is quite badly eroded). Follow the track under the Shrewsbury bypass and beyond, continue to follow a good path along the left boundary, which keeps with the brook. At a path fork (476 098), take the left fork to a footbridge over Rea Brook and follow the path beyond to a minor road on the outskirts of Shrewsbury (478 100) (12.6m). Turn right and follow the road as it turns left. Follow Washford Road all the way down to where it turns half-right to become Alexandra Avenue. Here, carry straight on along a much narrower Washford Road and follow it right to meet Station Road. Cross to the Recreation Ground opposite and follow it along its right side, turning right at the end onto an urban footpath. On reaching a street, take the continuation footpath opposite. This reaches a crossing point of the single track Welshpool to Shrewsbury railway line. Cross, using the provided swing gates, and enter a playing field. Turn right and follow the edge of the field to half way along the next side where there is an exit point on the right onto a busy B-road (486 111) (13.6m) with a roundabout off to the left.

5: Cross the road when convenient and walk towards the roundabout but before reaching it, take a footpath passage off right, just after the cemetery, and emerge on the minor road from the roundabout. Turn right briefly, then cross to a cyclists' dismount sign and take a delightful surfaced urban footpath which descends to Rad Brook and then ascends to a path fork. Here go right to emerge at a road junction. Go straight across onto the private road leading to Kingsland Bridge over the River Severn (488 121). There's a charge for motorists but it is now free for pedestrians; formerly the toll for crossing the bridge on foot was 1p earning it the nickname of Penny Bridge. From the bridge, continue to the road junction at the top, noting the stone wall on the right while ascending. Do a U-turn and take the tarmac passageway on the other side of the stone wall viewed, following it down to the River Severn (489 121) (14.6m). Turn left on the wide track along the river. Pass under a footbridge (Greyfriars Bridge), then under English Bridge, and continue until a foot/cycle access point off left onto a steeply ascending lane. Ascend St Mary's Water Lane and turn right into Windsor Place to meet Shrewsbury's Castle Street. Turn right past the Castle entrance and continue to a major road junction (494 129) (15.6m), with the railway station on the right. Go left for a few yards then turn right onto the A528 signed for Ellesmere. The main road goes beside the Severn for some of the time (so it could be worse). Opposite the Bird-in-Hand pub, take an urban path off left called the Pig Trough(!) and turn right off this to reach a B-road. Go straight across onto Corporation Lane. This shortly meets Coton Crescent. The route continues straight across on Corporation Lane, but the Sydney House Hotel (491 135) (16.1m) is a short distance to the right along Coton Crescent.

Stage 24
Shrewsbury (Coton Hill) to Wem

VIA: **Marches Way and Shropshire Way**
DISTANCE: **12.8m [368.6m]**
ASCENT: **690ft**   **DESCENT:**   **620ft**
EXPLORER: **241 (Shrewsbury)**
LANDRANGER:**126 (Shrewsbury)**

This is a day of crossing the Shropshire Plain with the only rise of any note at lovely Grinshill late in the stage. I never find the Shropshire Way exit from Shrewsbury very interesting so the end-to-end route takes to The Marches Way, which leaves Shrewsbury at Coton Hill, and is followed northwards through farmland to near Bomere Heath. More farmland paths, north-east through Preston Gubbals, then provide a link onto the Shropshire Way, which passes north through attractively situated Grinshill and on to the small, quiet market town of Wem. Beyond Grinshill, I was surprised at the state of the paths on this section of the Shropshire Way indicating it is not well-walked thereabouts. This is not difficult walking and is a relaxing day after three fairly long and more strenuous days. As you would expect, Wem has both accommodation and eating places.

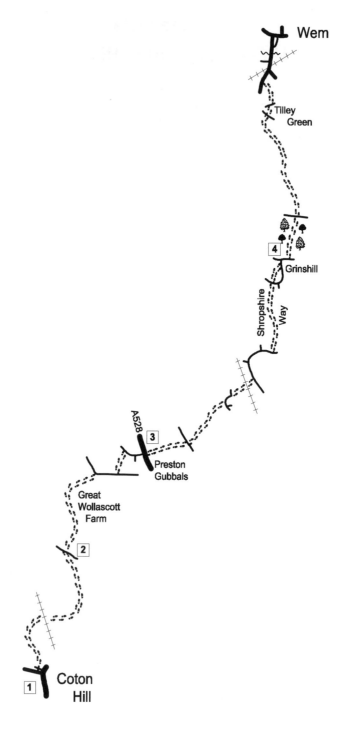

Wem

Tilley
Green

4 Grinshill

Shropshire Way

A528

3

Preston
Gubbals

Great
Wollascott
Farm

2

1 Coton
Hill

1: From (SJ 491 135), return to where Coton Crescent meets Corporation Lane and turn right to following the continuation of Corporation Lane, which soon becomes unsurfaced and quickly reaches the countryside north of Shrewsbury. Follow the lane to where it forks, take the path waymark right and shortly enter a field. Follow the path signs to pass right of Coton Grange and on beside the railway line. After a further two fields and a patch of scrubland close to the railway line, enter a field. Go left of straight ahead to a lone tree and continue in the same direction to a stile. In the next field, curve right on a track to a walkers' gate by the railway and continue on the track, turning right on a bridge over the railway (486 152) (1.2m). Beyond, continue on the track which becomes surfaced. When the track swings right, just before Crosshill farm, turn off left on a signed field path (494 153). Go parallel to the left hedge to a stile (passing left of trees around a pond) and maintain this northwards direction in the next field to a field gap. In the succeeding field, go left along the left edge (with Hencott Wood beyond). A gap leads into the next field where a trodden path, west-of-North, leads to the top left field corner. Pass into the next field and curve right into a field with a waymark. Here follow the right hand edge looking for an exit gap on the right onto a road (489 169) (2.7m).

2: The path continues opposite. Go half-left on a trodden field path. Continue northwards by going just right of straight ahead in the next field. In the following field, go just left of straight ahead to meet a fence and turn left by the fence to a stile. Cross, turn half-right, north-west, to a stile in the far right field corner. Cross, follow the left edge until it turns left, and continue straight on. In the next field, head north-west past the lone tree and continue in this direction to find a stile. Then go just left of straight ahead towards the barns of Great Wollascott Farm to reach and cross a stile. Go just right of straight ahead in the same north-west direction to a stile and beyond, follow the left fence. Take the right gate of two (waymarked), cross a concrete yard and continue straight ahead on a concrete track, following it when it turns right (481 186) (4m) to a gate into a field. Through, go straight across, north-east, to take the gate opposite, then in the following field go just left of straight ahead to a gate onto a lane (486 190). Turn right along Broomhall Lane for a quarter of a mile then turn off left through a waymarked gate. Go half-right to a stile on a trodden path. Beyond, go half-left to a gate and beyond, cross the field entered, aiming to the left of a barn and following the right hedge around it, to a stile onto a lane (490 196). Turn right through Preston Gubbals curving left to the main A528 road (5m).

3: Turn right briefly to a waymarked stile off left into a field, but if this is obstructed on the field side, enter via its gate. Aim north-of-East, to the right of the little copse and to the left of a marshy pond to get to the edge of woodland. Follow the wood edge to the right to reach a gap into the next field. Here, pick up and follow a good track which is followed all the way to a lane (504 201). Turn right for 120 yds and immediately after the last house on the left turn off left onto a signed path (6m). Follow the left hedge briefly and then cross a (difficult) stile or gate on the left. Turn right to follow the edge round to the first gate on the right (waymarked). Cross and head half-left, north-northeast, towards trees to reach a stile. Cross, head north-northeast, keeping right of the trees, to reach and cross a stile. Now maintain the same direction by going half-right across the field towards a lone house and cross a stile out onto Haston Road (509 206). Turn left here and follow the lane for 380 yds to a signed path off right. Follow the left boundary down the field to a second ditch crossing point on the left. Cross and go half-right (keeping left of a pond area) to a stile onto a railway line. Cross the line with care and in the field entered, follow the left edge to a stile onto a lane (7m). Turn left, ignore two lane turn-offs left and 320 yds after the second turn-off, turn left on a good signed farm track along a right hedge, joining the Shropshire Way (519 217). The field track continues in the next field, but now follows the left edge to pass through a walkers' gate; the wooded hill ahead is Grinshill Hill. Turn right along the right hedge for two sides and follow the track by the right hedge in the next field to a lane (519 229) (8.5m). Take the path opposite right. Go a quarter-right to a stile. Cross and pass up the left hedge to another stile which leads onto a (grim) enclosed path which is followed to a lane (521 231). Turn left and follow the lane to a T-junction in Grinshill.

4: Turn right briefly then left on a track passing to the right of Grinshill Church. Continue along the track to a seat around a tree, turn right above the tree and curve left to meet and follow a track (with a stone wall to its right). Ascend gently on the track to a Shropshire Way sign pointing half-left. Here, leave the track for the signed path which ascends above the track. Watch carefully for Shropshire Way left and right directional signs in the wood as you ascend steeply to a track. The path continues opposite left. Follow the right boundaries until the boundary side swaps to the left and this is followed to a minor road (522 244) (9.5m). The footpath continues opposite right. Follow the right boundary along two fields and then follow a mown path north-northwest across a field which passes left of a pond and exits onto a track. The path continues opposite along left hedges to reach a grass track (519 253). The sign says straight on, but go right for a short distance on the track, then turn off left at a walkers' gate. Follow left boundaries and then a right boundary for one field in a west-of-North direction. In the following field, go west-northwest on a between-crops path and in the succeeding field go three-quarters right, northwards, on an easy to follow path to a walkers' gate, left of the field corner. Continue northwards across a small field and turn half-right, eastwards, across another small field to emerge on a lane opposite a red brick house (512 272) (11.4m). Take the grass track opposite which leads into a field. Go past a telegraph pole, then aim for the right of the house ahead and pass up its left hedge, to a stile in the corner onto a lane (513 274). The path continues opposite going north-northwest across a large field on a cut path to a walkers' gate just left of white Pankeymoor Cottage. Turn left down the cottage's access drive to a B-road (510 279) (12m). Turn right down the B-road. Turn left under the railway bridge and continue to cross the River Roden followed by its side stream. Just after this, turn right into Drawwell Lane and then second left into Leek Street, following this to meet High Street. Turn right briefly to where a passageway turns up left (before the B-road turns left to Whitchurch); the next stage continues on the Shropshire Way along this passageway (514 290).

Stage 25
Wem to Bell o' th' Hill

VIA: Shropshire Way, Canal and Wolvesacre Hall
DISTANCE: 12.8m [381.4m]
ASCENT: 460ft   **DESCENT:** 390ft
EXPLORER: 241 (Shrewsbury), 257 (Crewe & Nantwich)
LANDRANGER: 126 (Shrewsbury), 117 (Chester & Wrexham)

Shropshire is left in this stage and Cheshire is entered after a very brief excursion into Flintshire. This is very much lush farmland territory. From Wem, the Shropshire Way is followed northwards to just north of Whixall. From here footpaths lead to the Shropshire Union Canal and this is where we parted with two friends who had joined us. Relaxed and easy walking along the canal towards Whitchurch was enhanced by it being a lovely sunny day. The route keeps to the west of Whitchurch and leaves the canal for paths to Wolvesacre Hall and then paths north to join the Bishop Bennet Way. The Bishop Bennet Way was set up for horse riders, but can also be used by cyclists and walkers. Thus one would expect bridleway tracks and so it was a surprise that the section taken into Bell o' th' Hill mainly comprised field paths. From Bell o' th' Hill to Bolton (on Eden) in Cumbria, we were more than fortunate to be near enough to home, relatives or friends to be able to have accommodation with pick-ups and drop-offs . However, the route was planned so that as far as possible, accommodation would be accessible from a stage end. Thus the Sandstone Trail accommodation list (dated 2010) has a B&B address in tiny Bell o' th' Hill www.sandstonetrail.com/sandstone-trail-accommodation/. The village also has a pub (closed on Mondays) which serves food.

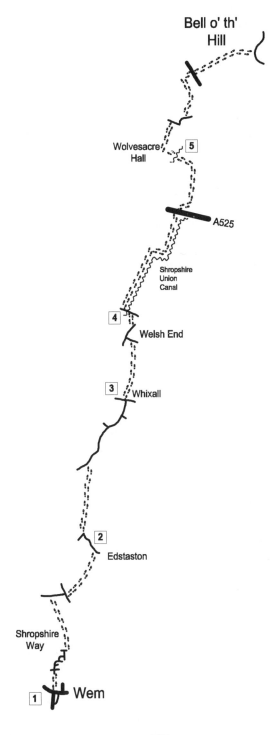

Bell o' th'
Hill

5

Wolvesacre
Hall

A525

Shropshire
Union
Canal

4

Welsh End

3 Whixall

2

Edstaston

Shropshire
Way

1 Wem

1: From Wem's High Street take the passageway between Castle Inn and the Opticians (SJ 514 290). Follow this northwards and eventually it meets a road. Go straight across onto Wemsbrook Road, a 'No Through Road', and take the second right into Marlcroft. Take the first left off Marlcroft and follow the road round to a T-junction. Turn left for a passageway marked 'The Shropshire Way' and at its end meet a road. Turn right into another passageway which becomes a well-walked buzzard-signed field path. After one and a half fields, the path crosses the right hedge boundary and turns left along the hedge boundary to a stile. Thereafter, cross fields west-of-North on the trodden path, finally keeping left of a house to reach a lane (510 308). From now on, the paths are not well-walked but the Shropshire Way is signed. Turn right to a T-junction, go left briefly and then turn off right onto a path which follows the left hedge boundary. Go half-left in the next field following a trodden cow-path. In the next field go three-quarters left to cut off the field corner, cross to the next field and follow the right boundary to a crossing in the field corner. The path now turns north, going half-left on a cut crop path, to a stile by a gate half-way along the field edge. Cross, go right of straight ahead (aiming just to the left of the white house visible ahead) and along a right fence to a stile, leading via a short track, to a lane opposite the church at Edstaston (518 320) (2.3m).

2: Turn left and follow the lane until a hairpin bend left (515 324). Here, go right on a track (the signpost on the right is hidden by the hedge) and almost immediately reach a track fork leading to properties. Go left, signed 'The Park'. The access to The Park soon goes off right but go through the gate half-right. Go half-right across the small field to a stile to the left of the corner. Cross the drive and continue for a few yards in the same half-right direction to a stile. Cross and continue straight ahead, ignoring any left forks, to pass down a long avenue of trees to a waymark. Carry straight on as indicated along an enclosed path at the back of a large chicken farm. Ignore the first turn-off right to continue to a stile at the end of the enclosed path. Cross into a field and go half-left to the top left field corner. Cross to the next field and follow the left edge to a gate which leads via a brief track to a lane (511 335) (3.5m). Turn right, ignore a lane off left and shortly after passing a pond on the right, ignore Gilbert Lane off on the right so as to reach a T-junction in Whixall (515 344) (4.1m).

3: Go opposite left onto a signed, overgrown, enclosed track and after 110 yds emerge at the end of a lane. Go straight across to a gate and take the signed path half-left, which keeps left of a barn at Church Farm, to reach a concrete farm track. The right of way crosses the track and continues north to pass to the right of a pond surrounded by trees and so reach a stile by the gate. In the next field go straight across, parallel to the farm track, to the next stile. In the following field, go half-left to a stile to the right of the gate. Cross and leave the Shropshire Way by going a quarter-right, west-of-North, to gently converge on the left boundary at the top of the field (by a pole) and escape over a stile in a hedge gap. Go north to an oak tree and continue to a plank bridge and stile in the hedge (to the left of the corner). Go a quarter-right to the next stile and then follow a trodden path through scrubland onto a lane in the hamlet of Welsh End (513 359) (5m). Turn left for a short distance to a T-junction. Turn right for 350 yds and just after the signed path off right, take a signed path off left, just after Pheasant Farm on the left. Go half-right to stiles just to the right of a pond. Cross and go half-right to a stile, a few yards to the right of a large tree. Cross and go straight ahead to a minor road (512 365). Turn left and very shortly cross the Shropshire Union Canal. Having crossed, immediately turn right, descend to the towpath (5.5m) and follow it northwards to the left.

4: After three miles of unaccustomed easy walking on the towpath, leave the canal by a stile off left as bridge 35 is approached (518 407) (8.5m) and rejoin the Shropshire Way. Go half-right to a gate and pass through to reach Blackhoe Cottages and then follow its access track, passing the Alfresco Kitchen Café, and continuing to the busy and fast A525 road (518 412). Cross this busy road, go left briefly and then take a signed path off right. This turns right to pass round the left side of a pond and reach a metal walkers' gate. Go slightly left of straight ahead to the next metal gate and out onto the drive of Hadley Farm. Turn left passing up the left side of the farmhouse. Go through the gate ahead and continue past the farm buildings. Towards the end of the last barn, keep left to a walkers' gate. Pass down a field close to the right fence to a walkers' gate at the bottom. Follow the right fence briefly, then go left over Red Brook on a footbridge and continue slightly right of straight on following the bridleway sign. Go over a stile (or through the gate) and then follow the right hedge northwards to a cross-path (518 421) (9.5m), recognised by a stile on the right. Don't cross but look three-quarters left and a tree should be visible. Head just to the right of this tree (which is in the next field) and this should bring you to a gate. Cross into the next field. Now head a quarter-right, keeping to the right of the tree, to reach a gate close to the bottom right corner of the field. Pass through and cross a cattle track into the next field, where the right hedge is followed, to a walkers' gate just left of the bottom right field corner. Pass through and go straight across to a gate which gives access to a footbridge marking the border with Wales (510 424).

5: Beyond, ascend on a path through a small patch of woodland. At the top, pass through a walkers' gate into a field and go straight ahead just north-of-West keeping to the left of a pond and to the right of Wolvesacre Hall's farm buildings to reach a stile. Cross and emerge on a byway (507 426) (10.3m). Turn right along the byway. When it meets a track junction, turn left over a stream crossing back from Wales into England, but Cheshire this time not Shropshire. Follow the byway all the way to meet a lane at a corner. Follow the lane to the right for 80 yds to a sharp right turn (509 435) and take a signed footpath off left. Go half-right towards farm buildings to a stile. Cross another stile close by and then follow a right hedge to a stile. Cross, go half-left to a stile and continue half-left towards a black and white house to find a stile onto an access lane. Cross and go straight on past a pond and on through two farm gates. Take the second path off left, opposite a black and white house (511 441). Go a quarter-right to a stile, then just right of straight ahead to a stile. Go straight across a small field to take a stile and then follow a right hedge to a stile by the second gate on the right. Beyond, meet an enclosed track and join the Bishop Bennet Way (509 444) (11.6m). Follow the track to the right to shortly meet a B-road. Turn left briefly and then turn right on a signed bridleway. Follow along a left, then right boundary, to a disused railway line which is crossed on a bridge. Beyond, follow right boundaries and then enter a field where the left boundary is followed until just before power lines. Here, diverge from the left hedge by heading a quarter-right towards a lone barn to reach a stile onto a surfaced bridleway track; alternatively the left hedge can be followed to the surfaced track. Turn right to meet a lane opposite the Bell o' th' Hill pub (523 455) (12.8m).

Stage 26
Bell o' th' Hill to Tarporley

VIA: Bickerton Hill, Peckforton Hills and Beeston Castle
DISTANCE: 14.9m [396.3m]
ASCENT: 1420ft DESCENT: 1450ft
EXPLORER: 257 (Crewe), 267 (Northwich & Delamere Forest)
LANDRANGER: 117 (Chester & Wrexham)

Today's route is a very satisfying day's walking mainly along the Sandstone Trail to Tarporley. On this stage we were accompanied by a well-behaved brown Labrador dog called Twix and two close family members (also well behaved!). The route quickly picks up the Sandstone Trail following it to the bottom of Larkton Hill. A more direct route is taken to the Iron Age hill fort of Maiden Castle and the ridge is then followed to the fine viewpoint on Bickerton Hill. After descending to the road, the Sandstone Trail is followed as it ascends to Raw Head, the highest point on the trail at nearly 740ft. After descending, a more direct route is taken to the edge of Higher Burwardsley village nestling in the Peckforton Hills. Beyond, the Sandstone Trail is again followed past Beeston Castle (café). After crossing the Shropshire Union Canal, the trail is left for paths into Tarporley. The directions might seem complicated, but the Sandstone Trail is well signed using a 'S' embedded within the footpath or bridleway arrow. Moreover, paths in Cheshire are usually also well-marked, so route finding is much easier than it might appear. Tarporley is a small picturesque town with facilities and accommodation for travellers.

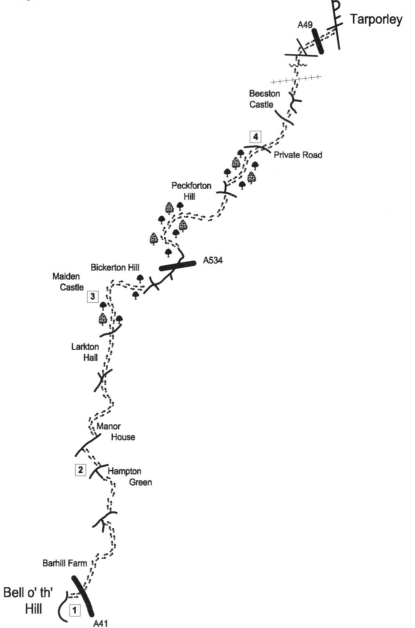

Tarporley

A49

Beeston
Castle

4

Private Road

Peckforton
Hill

Bickerton Hill

A534

Maiden
Castle

3

Larkton
Hall

Manor
House

2

Hampton
Green

Barhill Farm

Bell o' th'
Hill

1

A41

1: From the lane in Bell o' th' Hill (SJ 523 455) turn left for 230 yds, northwards, to a surfaced track off right (523 457) which passes under the A41 and continues east-of-North. When it ends, go through a walkers' gate into a field and head half-right on a track towards the church. Turn left in the field, before the church, on a trodden path to a stile and join the Sandstone Trail. Cross, turn right along the right boundary to a stile. Go across the next field to the diagonally opposite corner (far left). Go through walkers' gates, then follow a right fence until swapping sides at a walkers' gate and at the next walkers' gate meet a farm track at Barhill Farm (526 467). Turn right along the surfaced track and then its grassy continuation to a stile. Over, gently ascend along a left hedge to a walkers' gate onto a track. Turn left to follow a right edge to a walkers' gate. Through, go a quarter-right to a waymark post and continue to the top right of the field then turn right into a strip of land to a walkers' gate. Turn left along the left edge to a walkers' gate. Through, go half-left to a marker post and continue in the same direction to a walkers' gate. Cross and go left to a walkers' gate onto a lane (523 480) Turn right to a T-junction (2m). Turn right here for 130 yds and then turn left on a track to a stile. Cross, go half-right across a field to a field turn, then follow the left hedge until it turns, at which point go straight ahead to a stile. In the next field, follow the right hedge to a stile at the bottom and cross a footbridge into a field, where the left edge is followed to a footbridge. Beyond, follow a left edge. Ignore a farm crossing of the ditch to cross the ditch on a new footbridge and then follow the ditch back to the farm crossing. Now turn right on a cut path to a stile with a footbridge, and then go half-right up the hill to a stile. Over, turn left and follow left edges to a lane by Middle House Farm and turn right to shortly reach a T-junction at Hampton Green (514 495) (3.4m).

2: Take the walkers' gate opposite. Follow the left field edge to a brief stretch on a gravel drive and take a stile into a small field. Go half-left to the next stile and continue half-left again to a stile in the top left corner. Then follow left edges across three fields to Shay Lane (508 499). Turn right for 230 yds and then turn left on a path, immediately after an imposing drive on the left. Follow the enclosed path to a walkers' gate. Beyond, follow a right edge to a walkers' gate, then go along a left edge to a horse track. Cross, follow a left edge until it bends sharp left, when go a quarter-left to the left of fencing and enter an enclosed path. Cross the horse track and continue straight on to a stile. Over, cross the field just right of straight ahead to a stile. Cross, then it's straight on ascending on a trodden path to a stile. Over, follow the right hedge along the top of a slope but towards the field end, veer left to reach and cross a stile onto Long Lane (505 514) (5m). Take the drive opposite but immediately turn right through a walkers' gate (temporarily leaving the Sandstone Trail). Go a quarter-right (west-of-North) to a lone tree and continue in the same direction to a walkers' gate in the field corner. Cross a farm track to the walkers' gate opposite, proceed a quarter-left (again west-of-North) to the field corner and out onto a lane (502 522). The path continues opposite right. Go straight across the field to cross the visible stile and reach a track round the wood edge. Turn right briefly, then branch left at a signed footpath fork and ascend to a house access drive. Go left, curving left at a waymark to a track passing the back of the house and reach a waymarked gate. Pass and turn right along the right fence for two sides to a wooden gate, with a good path beyond, which is taken. When this shortly meets a path, turn right and ascend to the ancient hill fort of Maiden Castle and rejoin the Sandstone Trail (6m).

3: From the castle, follow the Sandstone Trail signs on the ridge path which follows the top of the steep wooded slope on the left. Eventually turn right, as directed, for the summit of Bickerton Hill, with its very good view and Kitty's Stone with its 'poetic' compositions. Beyond, continue on the main track which descends. After passing through a gate, the track becomes surfaced and meets a lane (509 535). Turn left to very shortly reach a cross-roads (7m) and go straight across. Ignore a lane turn-off right to reach the main A534 road. Take the lane opposite left, following it as it curves left. At Chiflik Farm, go straight ahead through a walkers' gate and along an enclosed path. Beyond, follow the main track up and past Raw Head (8.1m) and continue along the high path, eventually dropping to meet a rough stony track. Turn right briefly and join a rough lane coming in from the left. Immediately after 'The Bungalow', turn off left on a path, temporarily leaving the Sandstone Trail (518 552). Follow a left boundary and ignoring a path off left after a short distance, reach a stile at the bottom of the field. Cross onto and follow a stony track to emerge at the end of a public road (526 559), having rejoined the Sandstone Trail a short distance before. Turn left on the lane for a few yards, then turn right on a path which follows a right wall and then a right edge to a lane (527 566) (10m). Turn left for 90 yds, then turn right on a lane. After 160 yds, take a walkers gate off right. Follow the right edge for two fields and then enter woods. Ignore a track off right, to stay on the Sandstone Trail, and continue to meet a stony track. Turn right and at a cross-track, go straight on to meet a lane which is a private road (533 584).

4: Turn right for 230 yds and just after Moathouse Farm on the left, take a walkers' gate on the left (11.5m). Go half-right through the field on a trodden path to a walkers' gate. Turn left along a left boundary to a footbridge and beyond, pass through the field on a cut path to the road; there are good views of Beeston Castle on the hill ahead. Turn left briefly then turn right on a path. This ascends in woodland to the castle wall and then follows it to a lane (540 590). Turn left, ignore a lane off right and follow the lane as it curves round Beeston Castle. Pass Castlegate Farm on the right and shortly afterwards take the walkers' gate on the right and take the track leftwards. Turn right over a stile and then left to follow the left edge up to a stile. Over, go a quarter-left to a marker post. Continue in the same direction to pass under the railway and from there follow a rough gravel path along a left fence, curving left to cross the Shropshire Union Canal (12.9m). Pass through a walkers' gate into a long field and go half-right, to eventually converge on and follow the left boundary onto Huxley Lane (541 607). Cross the lane to the path opposite and follow right edges to exit onto Pudding Lane (543 610) (13.5m). Leave the Sandstone Trail for good here by turning right for 80 yds and taking a footpath off left. Follow the left boundary, then in the next field go a quarter-left on a trodden path to a stile. Cross, go a quarter-left to a stile, passing a telegraph pole and the left hedge at a field turn on the way. Cross, go a quarter-left into a strip of land on the far side of the field and pass through a field gap. Then head three-quarters right to cross a stile by a gate onto a track. Take the stile opposite, follow the left hedge until it turns left and then take the cut path ahead to steps down to the A49 road (552 619) (14.4m). Cross with care to the ascending steps opposite. Cross the field entered parallel to the left edge and enter an urban passageway, marred by the amount of dog mess deposited. This soon emerges on Nantwich Road at the south end of Tarporley. Turn left, go straight across at a cross-road onto High Street, and continue for 340 yds through this charming town to a 'No Entry' street on the right called Park Road (554 625) (14.9m).

Stage 27
Tarporley to Barnton

VIA: Little Budworth Country Park, Sandiway and River Weaver
DISTANCE: 12.9m [409.2m]
ASCENT: 530ft   DESCENT: 790ft
EXPLORER: 267 (Northwich & Delamere Forest)
LANDRANGER: 117 (Chester & Wrexham), 118 (Stoke-on-Trent)

This is a day of typical gentle, undulating Cheshire countryside and we were pleased to be joined by friends and Twix. Starting from Tarporley, footpaths are taken across a golf course to the picturesque village of Eaton. Field paths and quiet lanes then lead across the woodland of Little Budworth Country Park. After crossing the A54 road, field paths, one of which is particularly wet, lead on across Newchurch Common where the lakes seen cover the old sand workings. The busy and fast A556 road is crossed at Sandiway. From here, a good byway and field paths, which cross the Stockport to Chester railway and the West Coast Main Line, are taken to reach Weaverham. After passing a couple of shops, the route takes to the River Weaver in a scene of utter tranquillity, with fields across the Weaver to the left and a large embankment to the right hiding all signs of previous industrial activity. In my view, this section is the highlight of the day. As Barnton is approached, the surroundings do get scruffier, but this is a relatively short section and doesn't spoil the overall impression. As you might imagine, Barnton is not exactly flush with places to stay, but there is a pub at the north-west end of the town which offers food and accommodation.

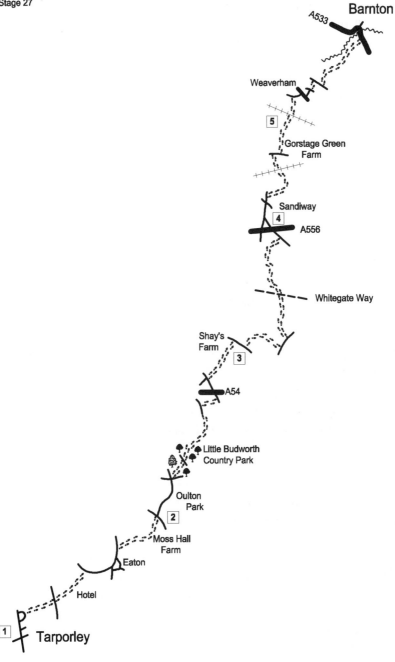

Barnton

A533

Weaverham

5

Gorstage Green
Farm

Sandiway

4

A556

Whitegate Way

Shay's
Farm

3

A54

Little Budworth
Country Park

Oulton
Park

2

Moss Hall
Farm

Eaton

Hotel

1

Tarporley

1: From the High Street in Tarporley (SJ 554 625) take the 'No Entry' street called Park Road off right. Follow the road as it curves to the left passing a school. At the next curve left in Park Road, turn right on a signed well-walked field path which follows a left boundary to a minor road (561 628). Turn left for 80 yds and then take an unsigned unsurfaced road off right. After a short distance the way appears blocked by the entry to a house. Look for a path signed off right which meets a surfaced drive after a few yards. Turn left along this for a few yards, but then turn left to meet a surfaced track after a few yards. Turn right on this and follow it keeping left of the hotel buildings. Ignore an access drive on the left to shortly reach a signpost. Follow the sign direction to 'Sapling Lane' and make for the clump of trees visible to the left of a mound (with a structure on top). On reaching them, join a descending concrete path, but soon leave it to remain close to the left boundary and reach a stile onto an enclosed track, which shortly meets Sapling Lane (568 634) (1.1m). Turn right towards the small village of Eaton. When a road is met, turn left on the 'major' road through the village. Beyond, pass the now closed Red Lion on the left and then Chapel House on the right. Immediately after Chapel House, take a footpath off right which enters a field. Follow the left boundary and in the next field take a cut path a quarter-right to a stile. Beyond, follow a cut path, just left of straight ahead, to Moss Hall Farm (581 640). Here turn left to circle round the outside of the farm buildings and then carry on along a field edge to a stile. Cross and go straight across the field on a faintly trodden path. Cross the next field in the same north-easterly direction, towards a cottage, to reach Dogmore Lane (584 643) (2.4m).

2: Take the lane opposite left and follow it to a T-junction, passing to the left of Oulton Park (of motor racing fame). At the T-junction cross and take the bridleway path diagonally-right, signed 'Delamere Loop', through the woods of Little Budworth Country Park to Coach Road. The track continues in the same direction opposite left and continues to the edge of the wood (587 661). Here the track widens as it turns right and becomes the access track to the houses passed. The track curves left and descends to a direction sign at a track T-junction. Turn right here to stay with the byway. Ascend, curve left and the track becomes a public road. Continue north along the lane to take a signed path off right immediately after the last house on the right (590 667). This quickly enters a field following a left boundary across two fields and then continues along a right boundary in the following field to meet a byway (594

667). Turn left and follow this to the A54 main road (4.4m). Take Longstone Lane opposite. Proceed for quarter of a mile to a lane on the left and take a track off right (591 672) which leads into a field. Follow the left boundary across two fields to reach a small wooded gully. Cross this and ascend to enter a field where the right boundary is followed to a stile. Go straight ahead with a house to the right, cross a gravelly track and enter an enclosed grassy track which reaches the surfaced access drive of Shay's Farm. Turn left on this and follow it to Shay's Lane (597 677) (5.2m).

3: Turn right for 250 yds and then take the access drive off left to Chaise Farm. Keep to the right of the house, to take a very short grassy track to the right of a holly hedge, and pass through a gate. Descend by the left hedge and keeping left of straight ahead, cross the stream then turn right beside it. The path gets progressively boggier and in wet conditions becomes very unpleasant. Reach a stile, cross and continue to flog through the bog beside the stream. Cross another stile arrangement and turn left to ascend to the top hedge, where it is drier, and turn right along this looking for a stile on the left. Cross with a sigh of relief into a field. Go just left of straight ahead to a stile and follow the right boundary in the following field to emerge on a minor road (605 676). Note the alternative to the Chaise farm path is to continue following Shay's Lane to a T-junction with a minor road and turn left on this to reach (605 676). Turn left for 80 yds and then take a surfaced byway off left (6m). Pass to the right of Coach Road Farm and continue for a short distance to a fork. Go left here (right goes to Totties Hall) and shortly beyond, ignore a grassy track off left, to continue northwards on the surfaced byway. Proceed to a gate ahead and continue ahead on a track to a walkers' gate. Carry straight on as directed to a gate onto a path along the right hedge and meet the Whitegate Way (604 686), which is a multi-user track along a disused railway line. Take the footpath opposite left. Turn left to take the anti-clockwise path round a flash to a track (604 690). Turn left on the track but after 300 yds turn off right through a barrier onto a track (602 691) (7m). The track picks up and follows a left hedge with a flash to the right. After joining a track coming in from the left, it continues past Daleford Farm. Shortly beyond, the byway turns sharp left, and then shortly after, turns sharp right as it passes to the left of a caravan site. Finally, the byway turns sharp right to shortly reach Dalefords Lane (606 699). Proceed left with care up Dalefords Lane to the even busier main A556 trunk road at Sandiway (8.2m).

4: Cross to School Lane opposite and after 210 yds, when it meets Weaverham Road, turn right. Continue along this road to a staggered crossroad and go straight across. After a further 170 yds, turn right through a gate onto a well-walked north-of-East byway (606 714). When the track becomes unenclosed follow left boundaries, all the time maintaining the north-of-East direction. Eventually the path curves left along the left boundary and then enters an enclosed area, where it turns sharp right and continues as an enclosed grassy track heading towards Moss Farm above. However, after 120 yds turn left over a stile onto a field path which converges on and follows the left boundary to a stile. Beyond, ascend a steep flight of steps up to the railway line through Delamere (615 721). Cross and descend the steep flight of steps on the other side to a stile at the bottom. Turn sharp left for a few yards to another stile and then go half-left to a telegraph pole with a footbridge stile in a dip beyond. Go just right of straight ahead in the next field to a stile and then just left of straight ahead in the next field; beware of the (mainly) hidden planking just over this stile. Now follow the left hedge to the bottom of the field and out onto Hodge Lane (612 726) (10m). Turn right for 110 yds and then turn left on the access drive to Gorstage Green Farm. When the farm buildings are reached, turn left through the farmyard area and at the end of the farm building on the right, turn right, as signed, down the side of this. At the end of the building, go through a walkers' gate onto a short, muddy concrete farm track which leads to two gates. Pass into the field on the left; the stile is to the right of the white gate. Follow the right field boundary. At the end of the field, cross a stile onto a bridge over the West Coast Main Line (617 731).

5: Go straight ahead for a few yards along an overgrown path, cross over a wide track and continue into a field where the well walked path along the right boundary is taken. This curves left to enter the next field. Again follow the trodden path across the field which converges on the left boundary, becomes a track and reaches a street at the south end of Weaverham. Take Elm Road opposite right and on reaching a green on the right, cross it half-right to a road. Turn right, pass a small row of shops on the right and continue to meet a B-road (623 736) (11m). Take Wood Lane opposite right. Pass up this and at its end, continue straight ahead on a tarmac footpath to reach a minor road. Cross and follow the road to the right; a large grass verge can be taken to shortcut a left bend. Descend and take a footpath off left opposite a cottage on the right (628 737). This quickly joins a track. The track soon curves left and is left here to go half-right. Soon reach a footbridge followed by a walkers' gate and go on to join a track from a disused factory. A lovely, peaceful track close to the River Weaver on the left now follows. Eventually, the track passes to the left of sewage works and becomes distinctly less lovely. The path turns to cross an iron bridge and descends by steps to the Weaver. It then turns right to pass the works opposite and emerge on the main A533 road (642 748). Turn left and immediately cross the River Weaver. Continue to shortly cross the swing bridge over the Barnton Cut, with its footway on the left, and almost immediately after reach a busy T-junction which denotes the end of the stage (642 750) (12.9m).

Stage 28
Barnton to Glazebrook

VIA: Great Budworth, Arley Park, Lymm and Warburton Bridge
DISTANCE: 14.9m [424.1m]
ASCENT: 570ft   DESCENT: 550ft
EXPLORER: 267 (Northwich & Delamere Forest), 276 (Bolton)
LANDRANGER: 118 (Stoke-on-Trent), 109 (Manchester)

This is an easy walking stage through some delightful and interesting parts of rural Cheshire and is the final day in this county. Greater Manchester awaits in the succeeding stage. The route follows the Trent & Mersey Canal and field paths to Marbury Country Park, where we and Twix were joined by members of the East Cheshire Ramblers. From here, a path to the west of Budworth Mere and then a lane lead to historic and picturesque Great Budworth village. More field paths follow leading to an excellent path northwards to Arley and a further northwards track and path lead over the M6 to a lane. The lane goes parallel to the M6 and would be idyllic if it weren't for the noise. The noise gets considerably quieter after leaving the lane for field paths which lead to a crossing of the M56 motorway (more noise but not as much!). A short section of a main road with a pavement follows and then a delightful much-used path past the extensive lake of Lymm Dam. A path known as 'The Dingle' is then entered through a decorative metal arch which has had a crown and date (2012) added to commemorate the Queen's diamond jubilee. The centre of Lymm, with its many historic buildings, lies at the other end of The Dingle.

The route now takes to the Trans Pennine Trail along Lymm's old railway line as far as Heatley. Here our rambling friends left us by turning south whilst our route turned north, crossing briefly into Greater Manchester. After passing through the village of Warburton, the Manchester Ship Canal is crossed on Warburton Bridge; it's free to pedestrians and the canal marks a re-entry into Cheshire. To my mind, the Manchester Ship Canal marks a complete change in the landscape. South of the canal, it's lush farmland and rolling countryside, while to the north the farmland seems less fertile as the hills and moorland take over. After the Ship Canal the route soon crosses the A57 road and a path and quiet lane then lead past the Bikers' Church which offers a monthly service, particularly aimed at those on motorbikes. A further path and quiet lanes lead shortly to the end of the stage at Glazebrook. There is a nearby country hotel offering accommodation, and this is preferable to using the poor railway service to get into Manchester or Warrington.

4

M56

A50

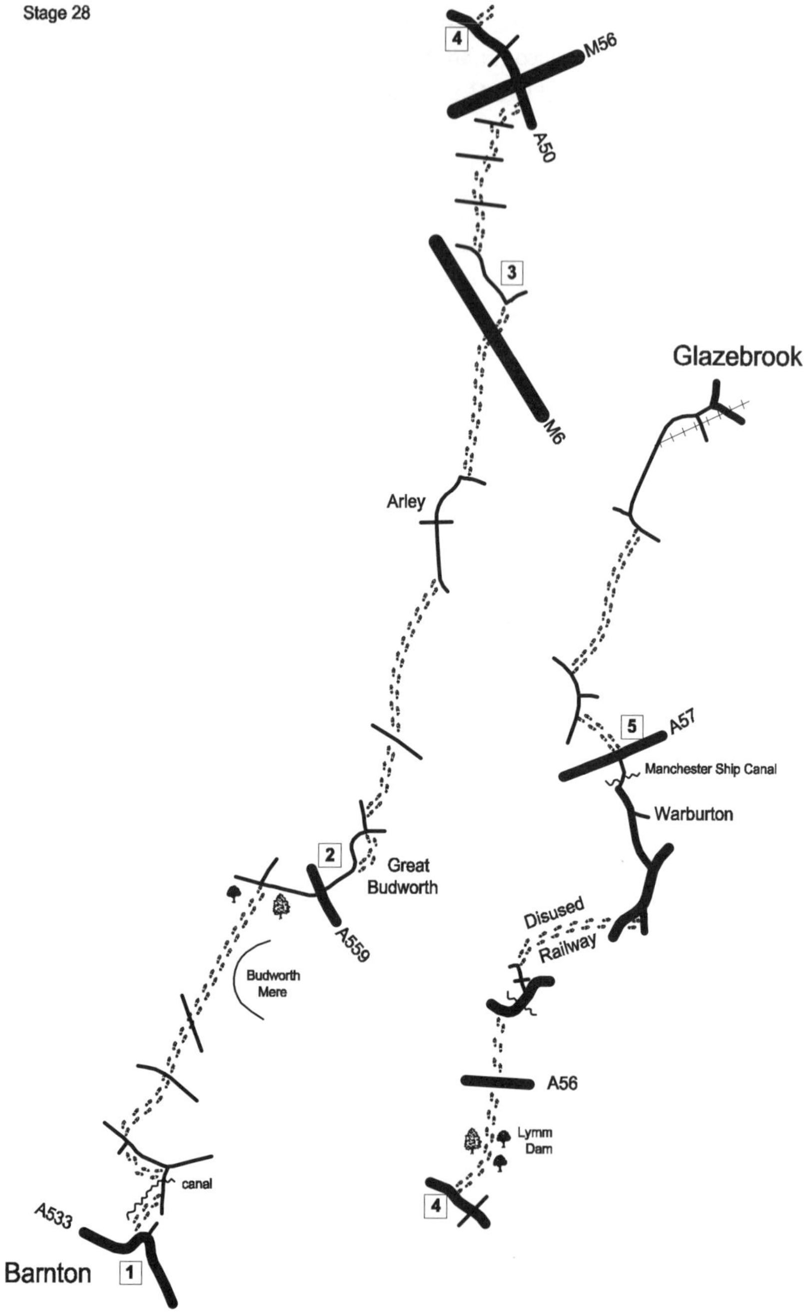

3

Glazebrook

M6

Arley

5 A57

Manchester Ship Canal

Warburton

2 Great
Budworth

A559

Disused
Railway

Budworth
Mere

A56

Lymm
Dam

canal

4

A533

Barnton 1

1: From the T-junction at Winnington Bridge (SJ 642 750), take the ascending surfaced path opposite right up to the Trent & Mersey Canal. Turn right on the canal towpath and leave immediately before the next bridge to join a road. Turn left to cross the canal and immediately turn left on a path beside the canal. After 25 yds and just before the first telegraph pole, turn right on a trodden path. Follow the path, keeping right at a path fork to reach steps up to Hough Lane. Turn left. Ignore a turn-off left to carry on towards Cogshall, but just afterwards turn right through a walkers' gate onto a footpath (640 756) (0.6m). Follow this well-walked field path, which follows a left boundary and then a right boundary, before turning a quarter-right to emerge on Cogshall Lane (643 761). Take the excellent path opposite, following it down across two fields to a short patch of wood. At its end, pass through a walkers' gate and follow the left hedge out on to a minor road (647 765) (1.3m). Turn left for 60 yds, then take a signed path off right. Go slightly left of straight ahead along a lightly trodden path to reach a walkers' gate in the right corner. Keep close to the left boundary in the next long field, with views of Budworth Mere to the right. Pass through a walkers' gate and keep to the left boundary on a slight embankment, until reaching a trodden path diagonal-right which leads to a walkers' gate into woodland. Follow the good path through the wood onto Budworth Lane (655 774). Turn right, cross over the main A559 road and continue into scenic Great Budworth village (2.7m).

2: When the road in the village turns sharp left, continue straight on along a cobbled lane (School Lane). Having passed the school, the lane passes through a walkers' gate and continues as a path which turns left after 110 yds to soon emerge at a lane junction (666 778). Go straight across into Heath Lane and after 190 yds take a footpath off right (3m). Follow the right boundary briefly to a crossing point and then the right edge round two sides. Cross a track into a field then follow the left edge to Budworth Heath Lane (667 785). Take the concrete farm track opposite. When the concrete ends, continue on a field path along a right boundary and then pass through a piece of woodland to enter a field. Here, follow the right edge to meet a track and go straight on, northwards, along this. When this meets an estate road, turn left along this through the grounds of Arley Park. On reaching a lane (673 809) (5m), go straight across on Back Lane; Arley Hall is on the right. After a third of a mile turn left off Back Lane on a track, signed 'The Firs' and 'Public Footpath' (675 813). Ignore a track turn-off left and shortly after, when the track turns left (to the Firs), go straight on through a walkers' gate into a field. Follow the left boundary to a kissing gate and footbridge on the left. Beyond, turn right on a path between a fence on the left and a ditch on the right, coming to a stile with regimented trees beyond. Go half-left over rough ground (no path but not far) to a stile to the right of visible farm buildings and to the left of a copse. Cross, ascend steps to a wide farm access drive and turn right to cross over the M6 and shortly reach Moss Lane (679 825) (6.2m).

3: Turn left for just over half a mile. Moss Lane would be delightful if it wasn't for the motorway noise, so concentrate on the good views of open Cheshire landscape to the right. After passing a large farm on the right, ignore the path off right immediately after it and continue for another 200 yds to a stile at a signed path off right (674 832). Go slightly left of straight ahead, across the field, to emerge via a large hedge gap onto Moss Lane (673 835). The path continues opposite through a hedge gap and crosses a short field straight ahead on a path to a visible stile. The large field that follows is rough mainly untrodden pasture. Go a quarter-left to a stile just to the right of the buildings ahead. Cross and follow the trodden path down the short left hedge onto Swineyard Lane (673 838). Turn right briefly and then left on a signed path which is fenced on the left. This emerges on a lane at Rowlinson's Green. Turn right briefly and then turn off left over a stile onto a rough path. This passes alongside the woodland on the right into a field where the right boundary is followed. After the end of the wood, enter the field ahead right and follow the left boundary round two sides to a gate; the second side runs parallel to the M56. Pass through the gate onto a short track which exits onto the main A50 road (678 845) (7.7m). Cross to the pavement opposite and turn left crossing the M56. Continue on the A50 passing Broadheyes Lane and then the Primrose Hill Nurseries both on the right; on a clear day Winter Hill and its transmitter, an early destination of stage 30, can be seen half-right. Just before a double bend sign, take the signed footpath off right (673 848) (8.1m) onto a much-walked and loved path which is taken all the way into Lymm.

4: Follow the trodden path slightly left of straight ahead to a stile and go half-right in the next field to emerge on a grassy track. Turn left briefly, cross a stile and enter a large field where the right hedge is followed. A beautiful deciduous wood is then entered. Here follow the obvious path, keeping left on reaching a fork after some duckboards. Eventually, stately Crossfield

Bridge on the right is reached. Don't cross but carry straight on keeping to the main path. Take the waterside option right when signed, which passes alongside the west edge of lovely Lymm Dam and comes out on the main A56 road (681 870) (9.6m). Take the signed path opposite, called 'The Dingle', now distinguished by its commemorative arch. Descend and follow the surfaced path to the A6144 road which also serves as Lymm's high street. Turn right along the main road, pass to the left of the ancient cross marking the centre of Lymm, cross over the canal and a few yards later when the main road turns sharp right, go left on humped Dane Bank Road. At its end, go opposite right onto Lymmhay Road and when it curves left, carry straight on along a dirt track to very shortly meet an excellent disused railway track which is now the multi-user Trans Pennine Trail (683 877) (10.1m). Turn right on this. Cross Reddish Lane and then Birchbrook Road (the A6144) opposite left. Chaise Meadow road is crossed very shortly and the next crossing point is Mill Lane (703 882) (11.4m). Leave the Trans Pennine Trail here by turning left on the B-road to the A6144 road. Turn right on the main road to cross the River Bollin, crossing (briefly) into Greater Manchester. Seventy yards beyond, turn left onto Townfield Lane (a B-road) and follow the road northwards through Warburton village. Continue up and over the toll bridge which crosses the Manchester Ship Canal (695 902) (12.8m) and back into Cheshire. Beyond continue to the main A57 road and cross by the traffic lights.

5: Go right for a few yards then take the footpath off left over a stile (692 905) Go straight ahead and then veer right to meet Brook Farm's gravel access drive which is followed leftwards to Chapel Lane (690 906). Turn right, pass the Bikers Church on the left, and at a T-junction shortly afterwards turn left. Follow the road to just after a sharp left bend and then take a wide, well-trodden signed path off right (689 910) (13.6m) through a large field. After a footbridge the path continues to the same high standard to a lane. Turn left for 170 yds, then turn right. Ignore the first lane turn off right to continue on to a B-road at a T-junction (694 926) with Glazebrook Station just to the right (14.9m).

Stage 29
Glazebrook to Horwich

VIA:	Glazebrook Trail and Lilford Park
DISTANCE:	14.4m [438.5m]
ASCENT:	630ft DESCENT: 350ft
EXPLORER:	276 (Bolton)
LANDRANGER:	109 (Manchester)

This stage crosses Greater Manchester to be close to its northern extremity by the end of the stage. The route is surprisingly rural, considering it threads its way through the towns in the north of Greater Manchester, and came as a pleasant surprise to the two friends joining us. The Glazebrook Trail loosely follows the brook of that name for a few miles through farmland. Soon after crossing the A580 road, the Trail turns west as did our friends. The end-to-end route, however, continues northwards skirting to the east of Leigh so as to arrive in and pass through its Lilford Park. From here, paths and a disused railway line lead on to Dangerous Corner. Further paths in the green corridor between Hindley and Westhoughton lead via tracks northwards to the A6 road. Horwich Station, close to Bolton Wanderers football ground, can then be reached via a quiet road and a good byway. A Premier Inn is adjacent to the station although Horwich does have a relatively good railway service into Manchester.

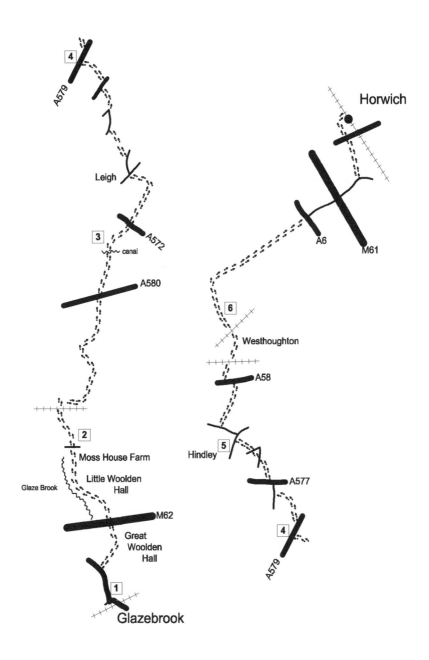

1: From the T-junction at the B-road (SJ 694 926) in Glazebrook, turn left for 800 yds and turn right on unsurfaced Woolden Road (693 933). Follow the access track to shortly cross the Glaze Brook into Greater Manchester and 120 yds further on, turn left on the Timberland Glazebrook Trail which loosely follows the Glaze Brook. Follow the track past Great Woolden Hall on the left. Curve right and then left as directed past its buildings onto a track which is followed over the M62 motorway (692 938) (0.9m). Beyond, descend and almost immediately turn left off the track through a signed walkers' gate. Go parallel to the motorway towards woodland and enter it far right. Turn right to a footbridge followed by steps up into a field. Go slightly left of straight ahead across the field, aiming to the left of Keeper's Cottage, and cross a stile onto its access drive (689 939) which is now followed towards Little Woolden Hall directly ahead. When the access track to Little Woolden Hall is met (1.5m), turn right on this. The track curves left, keeping to the right of the farmhouse and continues on into the farmyard. Here go half-right to continue on a farm track which meets the Glaze Brook (at last!). The Glaze Brook can now be closely followed until woodland is met. Don't enter but branch right along a ditch, keeping to its right until shortly reaching a crossing point at a waymark. Cross and almost immediately cross another ditch and turn left along it on a clear path. When the path crosses the ditch, go straight ahead as directed on a track towards a barn. The track passes to the right of the barn and Moss House Farm to reach a lane (678 961) (2.8m).

2: The path continues opposite right up the left side of a field and out onto an access lane. Go straight ahead to pass to the right of Light Oaks Hall and under the railway (676 969) (3.3m). Beyond, turn right parallel to the railway for 200 yds and then at a sign turn three-quarters left on a trodden path leading to a stile. Cross and traverse a small patch of woodland. Beyond, curve left on a better path to a track T-junction and turn left on a good track. When this shortly reaches another track T-junction, turn left on a fenced farm access road which comes alongside the Glaze Brook. Don't take the bridge across the brook (676 980) but continue ahead on the track which curves right to Hawk Hurst Farm. Pass to the right of the farm and its buildings to reach and cross a stile. Follow the left field boundary as it quickly curves left to a stile. Cross and follow the left hedge to a substantial footbridge. Cross a tributary of the Glaze Brook and continue straight ahead, before turning half-right to the field corner (the right of way actually follows the field boundary round two sides).

Exit the field in the corner via steps and a stile onto the main A580 trunk road (called the East Lancs Road) (677 986) (4.7m). Cross to the stile opposite, follow the right hedge until it turns right, then go half-right to a stile and cross onto a track. Cross to the track straight ahead. At the end of the field take the track straight ahead, leaving the Glazebrook Trail. Initially the track follows the left hedge northwards but soon swings right and then left. Keep heading towards a large building (part of a school) to reach a bridge over the Leigh branch of the Bridgewater Canal (676 996) (5.4m).

3: Cross the canal and continue on a good track alongside Bedford High School on the right. Ignore a turn-off left to continue by the school. Pass a school entrance to the left and right to reach the main A572 road (678 998). Cross to the enclosed track opposite (to the left of No. 311) and follow this into (open access) scrubland. Take the grassy path half-left just inside the entrance, following it to meet a gravel track along the edge of trees. Turn left to a minor road (SD 675 004); note the change from the SJ to the SD 100 x 100 km square. Cross opposite left towards a 'No Through Road' sign to reach Green Lane. Turn right up Green Lane for 200 yds and take a signed track off left before the first house on the left. Keep on the main track which curves gently right to a track junction (671 007). Turn right to go north passing between a fence left and a ditch right. Continue on the main track to reach a disused railway which is being converted into a guided busway between Leigh and Manchester. Cross this and at the footpath junction just beyond, enter the field ahead right and follow the left hedge on a good path with allotments over the hedge. At a cross-track, turn left and shortly reach the amenities of Lilford Park. Go half-right towards the slides to reach a surfaced drive and turn left to exit via the gates of its main entrance (665 010) (7m). Turn right on Elmridge to a T-junction and turn right. When the road bears left, carry straight on along an 'Unsuitable for Motor Vehicles' track. A fork is soon reached. Branch left here along Old Hall Mill Lane and follow it to meet a B-road (662 018). Cross and turn right for 180 yds and then take a track off left to Jubilee Park 'the home of Pennington FC' (662 019). Follow the track to its ground, then turn right on a gravel track which quickly curves left. When the gravel track ends, carry straight on (just to the left of scrubland) to pick up a short gravel track leading to the main A579 road (659 020) (7.9m).

4: Take the path opposite, and immediately go ahead right, over a rickety stile, giving access to an enclosed track in a poorly state. At its end, continue a quarter-right on a trodden path to a 'stile', which is officially straight ahead but so wet and in such a poor state, that people have clearly opted to cross two boundaries just to the right in order to access the large field ahead. Follow the left hedge in this large field with views of Winter Hill half-right. Bend left with the hedge until a telegraph pole. Here turn three-quarters right to a prominent path up an embankment carrying a disused railway line. Cross the line, and maintaining the same direction, very shortly reach another disused line, now a wide level track. Follow this left (ignoring a turn off right) to reach a minor road (650 027). Turn right to shortly meet the main A577 road at a junction called Dangerous Corner (649 030). Turn left for a few yards and then take a signed path off right. Descend to a footbridge and beyond go up the field by the left hedge. When the path goes up the embankment of yet another disused railway line, don't ascend but turn left to a small tunnel. Pass through and follow a good track on the other side to a substantial footbridge. Cross and continue on the main track to Coupland Road. Go right briefly, then turn half-left to pass round the back of a children's play area to a back-of-houses gravel track, which is followed to the right. Cross Penswick Road. Ignore a branch left shortly afterwards and continue to emerge at the end of Levengreave Close. Turn half-right to take the surfaced path to the right of No. 9 and re-meet Coupland Road. Take a walkers' access opposite left into scrubland (645 035) and follow the trodden path half-left towards a farmhouse. On reaching its grounds, the path circles round its perimeter to the right to reach its access drive. Turn right on this following the track out onto Hindley Road (641 039) (9.7m).

5: Turn right for a short distance and at the Alexandra pub (which does B&B), turn left into Alder Lane. After 390 yds, turn right on a signed track (638 041) down the side of Number 92. Follow the track, pass to the right of a house then enter the field ahead right. Go straight down the field to a footbridge. Beyond, go straight ahead to join and follow an ascending gravel track on a golf course. Cross a stile to the right of the track when indicated and follow the path between a fence right and a hedge left, and then just a hedge on the left. Pass through a walkers' gate and continue straight ahead to very shortly emerge on the main A58 road (641 052) (10.7m). Turn left for 200 yds then take unsurfaced Old Fold Road off to the right (640 052) and follow the track up, crossing over the Manchester to Wigan railway line. Ignore a signed track off right and carry on for a short distance. Just after the track curves right, turn left over a stile and follow the left fence. At the bottom of the field, cross a stile on the left onto a short enclosed path. At its end, cross a field on a trodden path to a crossing point of the Bolton to Wigan railway (640 059). Beyond, cross a field half-left and continue half-left in the following field to a waymark at the left field edge, signing the way to a sunken path to the right of a ditch. Follow this to a ditch crossing point and then follow between the fence on the left and the ditch on the right to steps up to a good farm access track called Jack's Lane (636 061) (11.5m).

6: Turn right and shortly reach Wilson's Farm. Follow the track through the farm and ignore a turn-off right and left to keep straight on. Cross a disused railway and carry on towards Taylor's Farm ahead. As the farm is approached, turn off right on a path which follows the left fence until it turns left. Then head a quarter-right to cross a stile and turn left on a track which passes to the left of Radcliffe House Farm. Keep to the main track, called Dodd Lane which, just beyond the farm, bends sharp right and then curves left. Eventually pass through a gate to reach a cross-track (639 077). Go straight on to shortly pass an industrial area (including a vehicle dismantler) and reach Chorley Road which is the A6 main road (642 079) (13m). Go right briefly, then turn left on Lostock Road. This crosses the M61 motorway and 180 yds beyond take a restricted byway off left (647 084) (13.5m) signed to 'Barnton Fold'. Follow this surfaced farm access and after nearly half a mile, pass to the left of the farm. The byway then becomes unsurfaced, curves left and then almost immediately curves right to pass under a dual carriageway main road. Just beyond, turn half-right alongside a left hedge/fence, with views of Horwich's railway station and Bolton Wanderers ground close by on the right. At the end of the fence, continue in the same direction to a waymark at the railway line, then turn left along the line to a footbridge over the railway (641 093). Beyond, turn right for Horwich Parkway Station (644 092) (14.4m); a Premier Inn is adjacent to the station.

Stage 30
Horwich to Billinge

VIA: Winter Hill, Great Hill and Witton Country Park
DISTANCE: 15.4m [453.9m]
ASCENT: 2330ft   DESCENT: 2070ft
EXPLORER: 276 (Bolton), 287 (West Pennine Moors)
LANDRANGER: 109 (Manchester), 103 (Blackburn)

Following our final rest day, we set off for the northern half of our journey of practically six weeks continuous walking. In retrospect it was a mistake not to include a rest day further north, as my feet would have benefited from a chance to recover from blisters I got in the very hot weather that hit us in the Scottish Borders area. The torrential wet weather we had experienced in the southern half of the walk revealed that our lightweight, but solid looking leather boots, were not waterproof and so we splashed out on some Sealskinz socks which claim to be waterproof and breathable. They cost an arm and a leg and I have to say I was sceptical about the claims. However, I can report that they really do work and when the boots were wet on the inside, these socks kept our feet dry. They are a pain to wash and get dry whilst you're out on the road, so wearing a liner sock with them is recommended and then they just need drying off at the end of the day.

This stage's walk soon crosses out of Greater Manchester into Lancashire as it climbs out of Horwich onto the bleak moors of Winter Hill (1,498 ft) with its television transmitter. After a couple of flattish days it is good to be in the hills again! On Winter Hill, we observed a man running after us (definitely a first). This proved to be a long-retired friend who had omitted to tell us he was joining in. A short steep descent and then longer ascent, much of it now paved, leads to the summit of Great Hill (1,238 ft) with its welcome wind shelter. By this time the friend decided he had had enough and would jog back! From Great Hill, the route descends past the ruins of Pimms Farm into the Tockholes Plantations and keeps east of the Roddlesworth Reservoirs. The route continues via tracks and paths northwards, picking up one branch of the Witton Weavers Way after passing under the M65. Urban paths lead past Cherry Tree Station on the Preston to Blackburn line, and soon after paths descend into Witton Park where the River Darwen is crossed. A delightful path through a thin strip of woodland follows, ascending to the base of Billinge Hill. Originally I had planned to go to the top of the hill, but trees prevent any sort of a view so, instead, paths are taken round its west side. A short distance to the east lies Beardwood, a suburb on the edge of Blackburn. Unfortunately, the nearby hotel appears to have closed its doors. It's therefore necessary to find either accommodation nearer to the centre of Blackburn or continue along the end to end route to use the available accommodation in Mellor village.

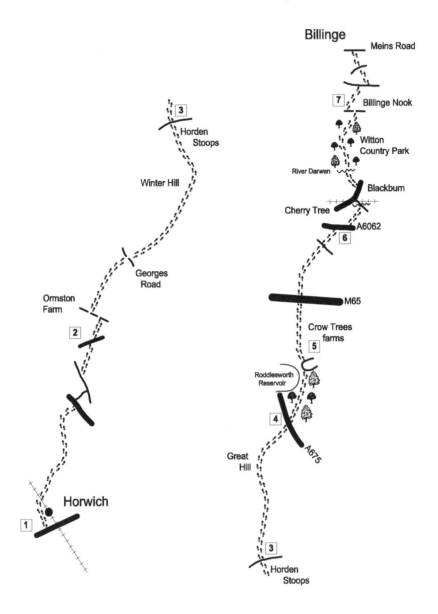

1: From Horwich station (SD 644 092), return to the footbridge over the railway. Don't cross but take the trodden path which goes half-right to a fence encircling the woodland covering Red Moss, a nature conservation area of wetland moss. Turn right on the sometimes boggy path along the fence to a footbridge. Beyond, continue on the clear path to reach a signed path T-junction. Go straight ahead (not signed) across a ditch and immediately meet a good wide gravel track. Turn right along the track. Ignore a track coming in from the left, curve right to pass a Waste Disposal Unit and proceed to two tall poles acting as a height barrier. Do not go through the poles but just as they are reached, turn left on a track. When this shortly forks, branch right (towards the factory building). Very shortly, fork right again at the next branch to stay on the main track and almost immediately, branch right again off the main track onto a more minor path. Follow this to a path junction (with wet reeds to the left) and turn right. The path surface improves, becoming stony then surfaced, and eventually a wide tarmac passageway which emerges on New Chorley Road (645 106) (1.1m). Cross, turn left briefly, then take Telford Street off right (to the left of No. 429) and meet Victoria Road. Cross, turn left and take the signed path off right in the gap between Nos. 193 and 195; after passing the garage, the path leaves top right. The scruffy path enters a golf course. Follow the left hedge to a signpost and turn left along a paved path to a road. Turn right briefly along Stocks Park Drive and then go left on a signed path (Grosvenor Way). When this branches after a short distance, take the right fork to shortly meet a tarmac path. Go straight across here onto a path which meets a street. Turn right briefly, then go left on a signed path which at its end descends steps to Church Street (643 115) (1.9m).

2: Turn right briefly and then take a tarmac footpath off left (to the right of Il Toro) which descends steeply and crosses a stream. Once across, turn right along the stream, following a good path to the left of the stream to a footbridge. Don't cross but turn left and ascend to emerge on a rough track (646 118). Take the footpath opposite, ignore a turn off right, and keep straight on to reach a wide track (645 121). Turn right and follow the track up. When the track forks, take the right branch (following the footpath signs). Ignore the next path signed right to stay on the main track. At the next path sign (at Wilderswood Grange) keep straight on along the track signed Georges Road. Shortly after this, at a fork, go left along a stream and shortly after reach a multi-way path and track junction (647 125). Go left here and on shortly reaching Ormston Farm on the left, turn right (645 127) (3m) through a gate to take a lovely grassy ascending track. At the top of the tree avenue, the path turns half-left to cross a field and reach Pike Cottage on Georges Road (649 131). Cross to the footpath opposite (to the right of Pike Cottage) and follow the excellent track on the slopes of Winter Hill to a path fork. Go left here and follow the track until it emerges on a service road, south of the main transmitter. Follow the lane left crossing out of Greater Manchester into Lancashire. Pass the main transmitter (661 145) (4.6m). Continue on the lane and when the lane bends left, cross a stile on the right but don't take the track down to Belmont. Instead turn left, to follow the top of the slope, on rough ground close to a fence on the left (or stick to the lane). Pass the trig column and then the last mast (658 150) and come to a steeply descending fence. Follow the path down the fence line and then descend more gently along the fence line to reach Rivington Road (655 159) (5.7m).

3: Take the footpath opposite. This goes north-ish following a wall and eventually becomes a flagged path, leading all the way to the summit of Great Hill (646 190) (7.9m), where there is a much needed four-sided wind break. From Great Hill turn right down the main track. After the initial plateau and descent, the land flattens out and there's a track fork. Go left to trees sheltering the ruins of Pimms farm (652 195). A good path continues from the last tree which gradually converges with the wall/fence on the right, then crosses it and continues along the boundary now to the left. Ignore a walkers' gate on the right to continue with the wall. The path bends right with the wall and is followed to the main A675 road (658 201) (9m).

4: Turn left briefly, then take a path off right, just before the Lancashire/Chorley sign. Follow the trodden path which follows the stream. It soon crosses a side stream and continues by the stream, rising above it to meet the main track. Turn left and start gently descending, parallel but above the stream, to meet an even more major track (659 210) (9.6m). Turn left over a stone bridge and immediately take a path off right through a kissing gate. The path follows the stream. Keep by the stream to a footbridge. Cross and continue by the stream, which is now on the opposite side, to reach a Roddlesworth Reservoir. Continue on the path a short distance to a footbridge, with ascending stone steps beyond, which are taken. Follow the path up to shortly meet a major track and turn left along the reservoir. As the track curves right, away from the reservoir, branch left along the reservoir wall to keep with the reservoir. When the dam is reached, carry straight on along an excellent track (signed 'Information Centre') and when a track is met, cross the track opposite left to a path. Soon, pass through a metal kissing gate and ascend straight up the field aiming to the right of the farm. On reaching a path signpost, turn left through a kissing gate and go just right of straight ahead to a stile onto an access track. Turn right and very shortly meet another access track. Turn left and almost immediately the track forks. Branch left, signed as a bridleway. When the track shortly reaches a cottage and starts to curve right, take the path straight on, down the left side of the cottage. Descend to meet a lane (658 229) (11m) and continue straight on along Chapels Lane for a short distance.

5: When the lane shortly turns sharp right to the church, turn left on an access track past Ivy Cottages. At a signed footpath fork, keep straight on along the access track. Go past a Private, 'footpath access only' sign at Higher Crow Trees Farm and continue to the gate ahead with an unmissable 'Shut & Fasten Gate' notice on it. Enter a field and follow the right boundary briefly to a stile on the right. Cross and turn left. Initially, follow the left boundary but then diverge to follow the wood edge northwards just inside the wood; the path runs parallel to a stream below on the right. When the path enters the wood, look for and take a footbridge over Sheep Bridge Brook (653 237). Beyond, aim to the left of a large wooden building above to reach a stile into a field. Then proceed up the field aiming for the right of a house. On reaching a track in front of the house, follow it into the farmyard of Higher Whitehalgh farm and out onto its access which is followed under the M65 motorway (652 242) (11.9m). Beyond, continue on the enclosed surfaced track for quarter of a mile and then take a gravel farm access drive off right (652 246) to Lower Whitehalgh Farm. Just as the farm is reached, turn left along a right wall and then turn left as directed across the field aiming for the barn of Fowler Fold just ahead. On reaching a hedge, turn right along the left hedge to a stile on the left. Cross, pass to the right of the farm, then cross a stile left onto Fowler's Fold access drive and follow it to Broken Stone Road (655 251). The path continues opposite following left boundaries, passing to the right of Horden Farm and leading into an enclosed track which is followed to the main A6062 road (659 257) (13m).

6: Go right for 100 yds and then take a signed urban footpath off left which is in a poor state. Initially it passes between a school on the right and houses on the left to emerge onto waste ground. Cross this ground to the right corner of the garden fencing straight ahead; get there by turning briefly right onto an embankment and then left along it. On reaching the fence corner, go straight ahead, keeping to the right of the fences, to emerge onto Rannoch Drive. Follow this to a T-junction and turn right briefly on Nook Lane to meet the more major Green Lane. Turn left and very shortly cross the Leeds-Liverpool Canal and then the railway at Cherry Tree Station (with its hourly service to Blackburn and Preston). Cross the road and continue on to very shortly meet the main A674 road (659 265). Turn right to a pedestrian crossing. Cross here, continue briefly along the main road and take the next street off left, Geddes Street, signed as a cycle route. When the street very shortly turns sharp right, leave the cycle route by carrying straight on to enter Witton Park. Descend on a good path to a tarmac road running through the park. Cross this opposite left to follow a track north through the car park area and reach a footbridge over the River Darwen (656 269) (14.1m). Beyond, almost immediately leave the surfaced cycle track for a path to the left of the cycle track. The ascending path through Crow Wood goes northwards following above and to the left of a stream. The stream is then crossed and the path follows above and to the right of the stream, continuing to emerge on a tarmac track just to the left of Billinge Nook house (654 279).

7: Go left over a cattle grid, then immediately turn right along the right boundary, ascending steeply up a bank to meet an old (wet) lane (or for a lesser gradient, follow the tarmac lane further and then turn off right onto the grassy old lane). Ascend up the lane to the right and then follow the right wall with Billinge Wood beyond until there's a stile on the right crossing the wall. Cross, turn left through a car parking area and follow its access track to Billinge End Road (654 283). Turn right and then almost immediately left on a signed path down the right side of a house onto a lane. For accommodation turn right, curving left to Meins Road at a fork, and turn right along Meins Road to meet Preston New Road (the A677); public transport runs past here. If you are being picked up, cross the lane opposite left and follow the right hedge down a field to Meins Road. This is a good pick-up point (654 285) as it is close to the end of the public road with plenty of parking, and it marks the end of the stage.

Stage 31
Billinge to Dunsop Bridge

VIA: Ribchester Bridge, Longridge Fell and Whitewell
DISTANCE: 16.4m [470.3m]
ASCENT: 1880ft **DESCENT:** 1960ft
EXPLORER: 287 (West Pennine Moors), OL41 (Forest of Bowland)
LANDRANGER: 103 (Blackburn)

This is a fairly long and strenuous day with many of the paths not well walked, so the route is not obvious. Today's stage continues northwards through rural Lancashire. After passing through the large village of Mellor which has a shop, the route takes paths north-eastwards to pick up the course of a Roman Road. This is followed northwards to a crossing of the River Ribble. From Ribchester Bridge, paths northwards lead into the Forest of Bowland, designated an area of outstanding natural beauty. The "Forest" is not a forest at all, its name derives from royal hunting areas. The Forest of Bowland is also known as the Bowland Fells, which is a more accurate description of this wild and windswept upland area. Among walkers, it is known for its peat bogs which are similar to those on the Kinder Plateau in the Dark Peak.

After crossing Longridge Fell, the route descends to cross the River Hodder at Doeford Bridge. The next objective is the small village of Whitewell, with its welcome but expensive inn being the only facility. We found the paths between these two points not well-signed and difficult to find. After Whitewell, the route is better walked and from Burholme Bridge, the path is largely beside the Hodder. Dunsop Bridge is a village in the heart of the Bowland Fells and has accommodation, toilets, car park and a tea-room.

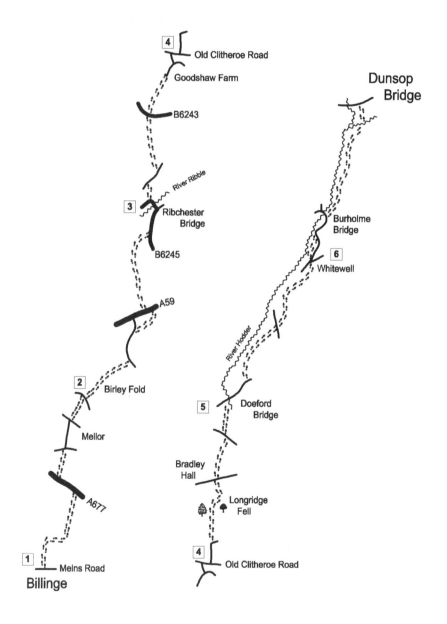

4 Old Clitheroe Road

Goodshaw Farm

B6243

River Ribble

Dunsop Bridge

3 Ribchester Bridge

B6245

Burholme Bridge

6 Whitewell

A59

River Hodder

Birley Fold

2

Mellor

5 Doeford Bridge

A677

Bradley Hall

Longridge Fell

1 Meins Road

Billinge

4 Old Clitheroe Road

1: From the pick-up point (SD 654 285), cross Meins Road to take the path opposite. Follow the path down to a stile. Cross, then follow the left boundary down the field, going straight ahead for a short distance, to a stile when the boundary turns left. Emerge on a farm access track and turn right. Ignore the first farm access drive left and continue briefly to the second drive off left (656 289). To get to this drive from the corner of Preston New Road and Meins Road, return up Meins Road for nearly a third of a mile, to take a farm access track off right (Carr Lane), and follow it to Stock's Farm where it turns half-left. Ignore the next track off right just after this farm and continue for 250 yds to an access drive off right to a residence (656 289) and the meeting of the two routes. Turn down this short access drive and just as the building is reached, cross a stile on the left. Cross the stream and proceed for a short distance along the stream, to a small wooden footbridge over it, leading into a field. Turn left down the short field to a stile and cross. Go straight ahead in the next long field, converging on the right boundary where a small copse of trees juts out. The edge of the field is then followed as it curves right to cross through a gap into the next field. Here, veer half-left to a stile, cross and follow the left boundary through a small belt of woodland into a field. Maintain the same direction, north, to exit between stone gateposts onto the A677 (655 295) (0.9m). Turn left for a quarter of a mile to take the second signed footpath off right. This follows parallel to the right boundary up a very long field. Escape at the end through a farmyard and go forward, keeping to the right of the farmhouse, to Mire Ash Brow road. Turn right briefly and then left up Church Lane passing the Post Office and church on the right of the road. At the T-junction at the top of Mellor village, go opposite right by the War Memorial along a track called Stoops Fold. Enter a field and take the trodden path that curves right, slightly ascending to a stile. Cross, follow the left boundary to a gate on the left and descend to the bottom right corner. Then follow the trodden path to very shortly pass through a small walkers' gate on the left and out onto a track. Cross to the stile opposite, follow the garden fence on the left and then go slightly right of straight ahead, aiming for a bungalow to reach a stile with steps down to Abbot Brow lane (653 315) (2.3m).

2: Take the access drive opposite. Keep to the right of the building and pass through two gates into a large field. Turn left descending to follow the left boundary. Soon, there is a stream to the left with the boundary fence just beyond. The path follows the stream all the way to Birley Fold. The track keeps right of its buildings, to pick up its surfaced access track which continues in the same north-easterly direction. Just after the drive curves right, cross a stile on the left, go half-right to the diagonal opposite corner and cross a 'stile' and plank bridge. Beyond, follow a left boundary to shortly reach a lane (Showley Road) (663 323). Turn left along the lane for half a mile to where it bears sharp left at Myre Edge Farm. Here, cross a stile on the right and then turn left on a track keeping to the left of the farm. When the track bends left, go straight ahead across a stile into a field and follow the right hedge to a stile. Cross, then go left and follow a right fence round two sides on an unpleasant path to reach the A59 (664 332) (3.7m). Turn left for 80 yds, then take a signed path off right (by Sunnyside) which follows the course of a Roman Road. This starts as a wide gravel track then follows right field boundaries to a track. Turn right briefly then turn off left down a farm track. At the farm (which resembles a scrap yard), keep to the right of the house and follow a (disgusting) track into the field ahead. Follow the right edge to a stile, cross, go a quarter-right to a stile, cross, go a quarter-right to a gate and meet a track. Turn left for a few yards then take a stile off right and follow right edges to a surfaced access track. Turn left and take the next signed footpath off right (658 348) (5m). Ascend the bank just right of straight ahead so as to be close to the left boundary, and keeping parallel to the left boundary descend to a footbridge. Beyond, keep by the left boundary to reach another footbridge. Ascend the bank to take a well-trodden path along its edge with good views of the River Ribble on the left. Exit via a stile into a car park. Go left on a path which emerges onto a B-road and follow it left to Ribchester Bridge where the River Ribble is crossed (662 357) (5.7m).

3: Over the bridge, go right very briefly, on the surfaced track along the Ribble and then turn off left on a signed path which goes straight across two fields west-northwest to Gallows Lane (660 358). Turn right for 360 yds and then take a signed footpath off left at Lower Dutton Cottage (661 361), which passes between the buildings into a small field. Take the trodden path which curves right and take the stile on the left. Follow to the left of the stream briefly to reach a footbridge. Over, go a quarter-right (north-westish) to a stile by a gate. Cross and continue in the same direction (aiming to the left of a large lone tree) to reach a stile. Beyond, go just left of straight ahead, aiming to the right of a phone mast on Duddel Hill, to find a stile and farm gate. Over, go just right of straight ahead, then go round to the right of the right barn and through the yard to a gate. Pass in front of the old farmhouse and out along its access track to meet a B-road (654 378) (7.4m) at a corner. Take the footpath opposite and cross the field east-of-North on a trodden path. Beyond, go half-right (continuing east-of-North) to pick up a trodden path to a fence. Turn left along it to a decrepit walkers' gate on the right out onto a track. Turn left, immediately cross a stream and almost immediately turn off right on a good path which ascends through the wood to a stile. Cross and turn left to follow the left wood boundary. Pass to the right of a barn to a stile to the right of a gate. Keep with the wood edge to a walkers' gate by a gate and take the ascending concrete track beyond, which passes into the yard of Goodshaw Farm. Cross the yard onto its access lane which is followed northwards to a T-junction. Turn left on Huntingdon Hall Lane to a T-junction with Old Clitheroe Road (656 395) (8.6m).

4: Turn right for 120 yds, then take a tarmac track off left (657 394) going west-of-North. When the track turns right, keep straight on along a path which crosses a stile onto open moorland. Beyond, follow the good path which keeps close to a right boundary to a stile. Cross and take the signed path half-right to a stile. Beyond, reach a cross path and continue opposite into the wood. Follow the path through and out of the wood to a stone stile over a wall (655 410) (9.6m); the trig point of Longridge Fell is visible to the right. Cross the wall and take the path straight ahead which soon descends half-right. When fairly close to the wall below, a small dip is reached. Turn left here and follow the dip to a gate. Beyond, go a quarter-left aiming to the left of a telegraph pole, to find a stile to the left of a stream. Cross and follow the stream down, crossing stiles as met, to emerge on a lane opposite Bradley Hall (653 417) (10.3m). Take the signed path opposite along an access drive, passing buildings until shortly there's a footpath sign off right. Pass between two buildings to a stile and beyond, follow a left edge to a stile on the left. Over, go half-right towards a far-off farm to find a stream crossing point. Beyond, aim to the left of the farm to find a stile. Continue half-right aiming for the left of the farm and exit onto a lane via a farm gate (654 425). Turn left for 190 yds then take a signed footpath off right through a gate onto a track. Soon pass a building and immediately after, turn off left through a gate. Follow the left edge down to a single plank footbridge on the left, then contour a field parallel to the River Hodder below, to find a stile onto a lane (650 431) (11.3m) just to the left of Doeford Bridge.

5: Turn right over the bridge, go up the hill and take a signed path off left, just after Doeford Bungalow on the left (652 435). Cross a cattle grid and follow the track until it bends left. Then go right over a stile and slightly left of straight ahead to get close to the Hodder (just after a fisherman's hut). Continue by the river over a stile and then through a kissing gate. Ford a stream (652 443) and follow an ascending track away from the river which curves right towards a small wood. On reaching the wood corner, cross a stile and follow a left fence north-east until it turns left, when go straight on along a small embankment to meet the end of Ing Wood with a stile by it onto a lane (658 452). Turn left for 140 yds (13m), then take a signed path right which loosely parallels the minor road on the left to Whitewell. In the field entered, diverge gently away from the left wall to find and pass through a tall kissing gate in the wall. Then follow the left fence to a gate. Cross and contour round a hill, curving right without losing height (while keeping just below a maintenance track). Pass an isolated waymarked stile and go a quarter-right, as directed (not losing height), to come beside a left wall. Shortly afterwards reach a tall kissing gate and pass through. Now follow the left wall for a few yards and then go through a farm gate on the left. Follow the left fence briefly and then turn three-quarters right down an improving descending track. Just after passing a house on the right, turn left off the track to find and follow a right boundary to a walkers' gate with steps beyond down to a road. Turn left and immediately right to a T-junction at the hamlet of Whitewell (659 469) (14.1m); the Inn at Whitewell is opposite.

6: Turn right and clamber over the left wall for a concessionary path that parallels the road. Follow the path to a footbridge. Cross into a field, turn right and follow the right boundary to the end of the field and exit onto a lane. Turn left to Burholme Bridge and just before the bridge, turn off right on a tarmac drive to a farm (658 479) (14.9m). Go through the farm, passing to the right of the farmhouse, and continue to a gate with a waymark where the path forks. Go straight on (left fork) keeping close to a left boundary and reach a gate. Go through two gates close together and continue by the left boundary. The path comes close to the Hodder and again keep close to the left boundary. Eventually, the access drive of Thorneyholme is reached. Follow this briefly until a sign directs the walker left along the Hodder to a bridge. Cross and follow the access drive to meet a lane in Dunsop Bridge (661 502) (16.4m). Turn left for the car park and right for Wood Lane Farm B&B.

Stage 32
Dunsop Bridge to Wray

VIA: Bowland Fells and Salter's Way
DISTANCE: 14.2m [484.5m]
ASCENT: 1520ft   DESCENT: 1720ft
EXPLORER: OL41 (Forest of Bowland)
LANDRANGER: 103 (Blackburn), 97 (Kendal & Morecambe)

This stage continues the traverse of the Bowland Fells to the delightful village of Wray at the northern end of the fells. It forms a splendid and memorable day's walking which was enjoyed by all who joined us. There are excellent views throughout, starting with the walk along the River Dunsop which gently ascends to where its two main sources combine. Here, the Whitendale River is followed along its east bank through Whitendale Farm and on across the open fells. Eventually the path turns away from the river and ascends to meet the Salter's Way. This is the old high level road from Hornby to Slaidburn which crosses Salter and Croasdale Fells. Now it is primarily a traffic free route for cyclists and walkers. With its good surface, it is possible to make good time along here and the ridge views are tremendous, with the three peaks in the Yorkshire Dales visible on a good day. The track is followed to where it becomes surfaced at High Salter Farm. From there, paths over rough pastures lead down into the gentler farmland surrounding Wray. Wray is known for its annual scarecrow festival held during late April and early May. It is a charming village which has the added attraction of being situated on the River Roeburn. It has an excellent tea room passed on the way into the village and the local pub claims to offer accommodation.

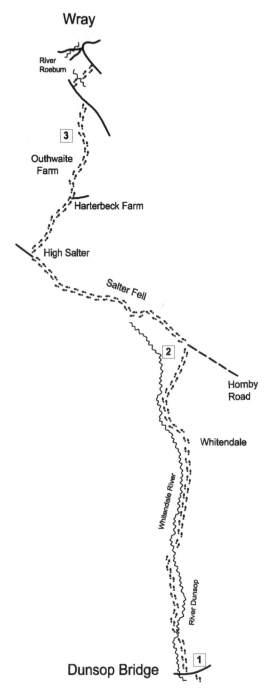

Wray

River Roeburn

3

Outhwaite Farm

Harterbeck Farm

High Salter

Salter Fell

2

Hornby Road

Whitendale

Whitendale River

River Dunsop

1

Dunsop Bridge

1: From meeting the minor road in Dunsop Bridge (SD 661 502) turn left to the River Dunsop. Don't cross but turn right, just after the tearoom, up a signed bridleway which starts as a surfaced track. After cottages on the right, go straight on beside the river to a footbridge and cross to the surfaced access track on the west side of the river (657 509). Turn right and follow this surfaced track to just after the rivers Brennard and Whitendale meet to form the Dunsop. The surfaced track crosses the Brennard River and almost immediately (just before a cattle grid) take a walkers' footbridge on the right crossing the Whitendale River (653 533) (2.4m). Having crossed, turn left on a good bridleway track. Near a stone hut the track leaves the river and curves right to negotiate a small side valley. Cross its side stream and beyond, ascend to a mesh bridge. Cross and ascend to meet a path (660 536) and turn left (ignoring foot bridges to the right). The path contours the hillside opposite Middle Knoll. Eventually (approaching Whitendale), the path meets a track. Turn left here, pass the farmhouse and continue a very short distance to Whitendale Farm's access lane (660 550) (3.9m). Turn right here and follow the track to a gate (ignoring a turn off left to Salter Fell) and take the track to the right of Whitendale River (ignore a track left which crosses the river). Follow the track which leaves the river to a marker post. Here go a quarter-right to a gate, in a gap between two sets of trees. The path continues straight on contouring and is always clear, although boggy in places, necessitating some detours. The path returns to and follows above the river. Eventually, a stream is forded and marker posts along the path lead upwards to a wide, gravel track (662 578) (5.9m) which is the Salter's Way.

2: Turn left and follow the Salter's Way, also called the Hornby Road, for nearly 5 miles to High Salter Farm where the track becomes a public road (608 626) (10.6m). Immediately after passing the farm, take a signed path off right through a gate. Follow the track and then the left wall to a ladder stile. Cross and turn right to follow the right wall to a ladder stile. Cross and go half-left to a stile. Over, go half-right to a wall and then follow the wall down to the left to a stile. Beyond, go straight ahead aiming for a farm to reach a waymarked gate. Pass through and go three-quarters right to a fence and follow the fence down (left) to a footbridge over Goodber Beck (612 634). Across, gently ascend half-left to a wall, which is followed to the right and shortly joins a very short farm track, which turns left to a lane at the end of the public road, with Harterbeck farm to the left (612 636) (11.3m). Turn right on the lane and immediately left over a cattle grid on a gravel farm track. Just before the next cattle grid, turn off right through a walkers' gate and follow right boundaries out onto open moorland. Keep with the right boundary, pass a barn and when the right boundary turns right, go a quarter-right to a wall gap crossing point. Beyond, maintain the same north-easterly direction to a lone tree and continue north-east to the left of a broken down wall. Cross a stile and continue along the left side of the broken down wall. Pass through a wall gap crossing point, go half-right to a wall and left along it to a gate. Pass through and follow the right wall to a gate into an enclosed track which continues along a right wall to the access drive of Outhwaite Farm (615 657) (12.8m).

3: The path continues opposite right and follows to the right of a ditch to a stile. Over, follow the left field edge to a stile in the wall and beyond, go half-right to a gate onto a lane (612 662) (13.2m). Turn left down the lane for a third of a mile and then take a signed footpath off right (609 667) opposite Alcocks Farm. Descend by the left fence to a footbridge across Hunt's Gill Beck. Beyond, ascend to the left on a good track which meets a lane (610 669). Go left for 760 yds to meet a minor road, turn left and cross the River Roeburn (605 675) (14.2m) to enter Wray village; there's an excellent tea shop on the right just before the river.

Stage 33
Wray to Barbon

VIA: Burton in Lonsdale, Leck Beck and Barbondale
DISTANCE: 15.7m [500.2m]
ASCENT: 1680ft   DESCENT: 1490ft
EXPLORER: OL41 (Forest of Bowland), OL2 (Yorkshire Dales S & W)
LANDRANGER: 97 (Kendal & Morecambe), 98 (Wensleydale)

This is a day of contrasts both in terms of the scenery and the counties encountered. From Wray, paths lead to Wennington still in Lancashire and on to the large village of Burton in Lonsdale in North Yorkshire. Burton has a pub which doesn't appear to be open at lunchtimes. It was a miserable morning, so the waterproof socks had their first outing and the hot drink and sandwich we got from the local shop was very welcome. Paths northward to the small village of Ireby see Lancashire re-entered. From there the hamlet of Leck is the next objective. It's mainly field paths up to this point, mostly not well-walked. Beyond Leck, there's a complete change of scenery as a moorland path above Leck Beck is taken. Although still in Lancashire, the landscape becomes typical Yorkshire Dales scenery at the point where Ease Gill, which flows into Leck Beck, is underground and this provides a crossing point into the large county of Cumbria. After passing Bullpot Farm, owned by a caving and potholing club and offering pre-booked bunkhouse accommodation, a good bridleway is taken down into Barbondale, where we were pleased to be joined by friends for the rest of the day. The walk along Barbondale to the village of Barbon is on a good and delightful track. Barbon is a charming village, which although small, possesses a shop, inn and accommodation.

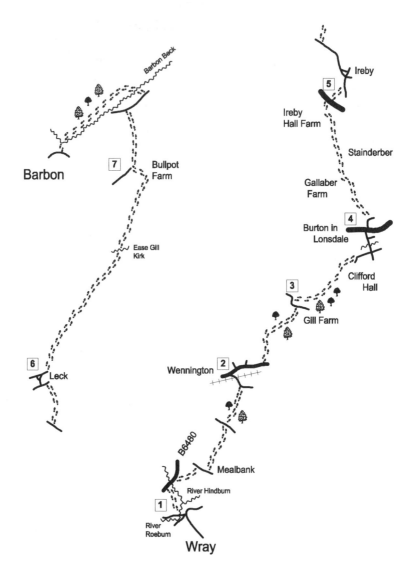

Barbon Beck

Barbon

7 Bullpot
Farm

Ease Gill
Kirk

6 Leck

Ireby

5

Ireby
Hall Farm

Stainderber

Gallaber
Farm

4 Burton in
Lonsdale

Clifford
Hall

3

Gill Farm

Wennington **2**

B6480

Mealbank

River Hindburn

1

River
Roeburn

Wray

1: Having crossed the River Roeburn in Wray (SD 605 675), turn right along the river on a good trodden path following it out onto the B-road from Wray (604 680). Turn right, cross the River Hindburn and 90 yds beyond, turn off right on a footpath (605 681). Keeping to the left of the trees, curve right uphill to a stile. Beyond, follow the tree line eastwards, towards the farm, to find and take a stile. Then follow a left field edge to stiles by Meal Bank Farm onto Agnes Ing Lane (609 679). Turn right for 160 yds, passing the farm, then take a signed footpath off left (611 679). In the field entered, go to a crossing point in the bottom right corner. In the succeeding field, go slightly right of straight ahead and at a waymark continue a short distance along the left edge to a gate (with a hidden waymark). Pass through and go just right of straight ahead to a stile. Cross and find the next stile in the top left field corner. Over, follow the left edge for three fields and then go slightly right of straight ahead, keeping right of buildings, to cross a 'lane' and take a signed path opposite (617 690) (1.7m). Now go slightly left of straight ahead, aiming for the middle of Coat Bank Coppice, to a waymarked gate into the wood. Follow the path through the wood and beyond, go half-right to a stile. Over, go a quarter-left towards Overends Farm and through a farm gate. Turn right as signed to the farm's access drive and turn left on this briefly. When it turns right, go straight on through a gate and continue half-right to a stile and gate onto a lane (618 697). Turn left descending, shortly cross over the railway line and meet the B-road from Wray (616 699) (2.4m).

2: Turn right to cross the River Wenning into Wennington village. Keep with the B-road and continue beyond the end of the village for another third of a mile, taking advantage of a gravel path to the right just beyond its last house. Just beyond Cravens Farm on the left, take a signed path off left (623 702). Follow a left wall to a stile and then a right hedge to a stile. Now go slightly right of straight ahead to cross a stream and then half-left to a stile in the wall. Beyond, go a quarter-left to find and follow a right edge to a gate gap. Through, head to a waymarked telegraph pole and then continue straight on, aiming to the left of Old Hutton farm, to a stile. Across, follow to the left of the farm boundary and then follow a right fence to a stile in the wall. Beyond, go straight on, without losing height, to a stile into the wood (630 710). It's very wet here. Cross the stream and then go left keeping above a very boggy area. When a stile is spotted a quarter-left away, make your way to it as best you can across the bog and after go straight on along the wood edge. When the wood edge turns, keep on in the same direction to a stile and maintain this direction to a footbridge. Then follow a right fence to a farm track and turn left on Gill Farm's access to Back Lane (635 712) (4m). Turn left and after 280 yds reach a left bend (633 714) (4m).

3: Go right here on a surfaced farm access drive serving Scalaber Farm and others. Ignoring turn offs left, keep right on the surfaced track which curves left to a track fork. Go right, pass through a walkers' gate and cross a small concrete yard to a farm gate. Then follow a short grass track to the right of a ditch to a stile. Now go south-of-East to a stile in the left field corner and beyond, go straight ahead to a stile in the top right corner (aiming for the left side of a wood) (640 713). Over, follow the right edge to a stile; Black Wood is to the right. Continue along a right edge to a gate and then another short right edge to a gate. Through, follow a track along the left hedge to a gate and continue on the track to meet a drive; the buildings of Clifford Hall are to the left. Cross the drive into a grassy track, between stone walls, and shortly meet a drive. Turn left and right round a pond then curve left onto a gravel path (not signed) which meets a drive. Turn left to follow the main track which soon curves right and descends. It meets other tracks but keep heading east with the River Greta below on the left. Eventually the track becomes a lane (651 719) and when it reaches a T-junction, turn left to cross the River Greta and continue to the main A687 road in the village of Burton in Lonsdale (651 722) (5.9m).

4: Its shop is on the main road to the right, but the stage goes up Manor Close opposite right. When the street bends right, briefly carry straight on to a stile. Cross and follow the left edge to a stile. Over, pass up the middle of the field, keeping left of a small copse, to a stile top right. Beyond, follow a right edge to a stile. Over, cross a field to a gate in the far left corner. Through, continue in the same direction, straight ahead northwards, to a stile. Over, cross Gallaber's farm drive (649 730) (6.4m) and continue across a field west-of-North to a stile in the top left corner. Across, go half-left to the field boundary and follow this to the right, along the hedge followed by a wall, to a farm track. Go through a gate on the left and follow the enclosed track until a waymark indicates to go straight on. Go through a gate on the left and follow the right wall until it turns, when go straight on northwards to a 'step' stile in a wall. Over, go a quarter-left to a gate in the far left field corner. Through, head half-left to a farm gate just beyond a stream, then follow a right field edge to a farm track. Follow this briefly but peel off left (towards Ireby Hall Farm), descending to a footbridge with a stile. Across, go half right to a stile and beyond, make for the right of the buildings and into a 'car' yard. Turn left and right to Ireby Hall's access drive and turn right on this to the main A65 trunk road (650 752) (8m).

5: Take the footpath opposite right and find a gate in the top right corner of the field. Through, follow a left wall to pass left of a bungalow and out on its access drive to a lane (654 753). Turn left towards Ireby village but after 100 yds, as its outskirts are reached, turn left onto a lane signed to 'Leck'. After nearly a third of a mile, the lane bends sharp left and shortly afterwards sharp right as it passes large Todgill Farm. Continue for a further 300 yds, pass the entrance drive to Leck Villa Farm and immediately after, take a signed path off right into a field (649 761) (8.8m). Go half-left to a step stile in a wall. Then go a quarter-right to take a gap stile in the far right corner. Now go straight ahead, north-westish, to a farm gate guarding a crossing of a stream (648 766). Beyond, continue in the same north-westish direction to shortly cross a track and then go north-of-West (left of straight ahead) to a ladder stile. Over, go ahead right to a gap stile and then a quarter-left through a field gap and straight on to a farm gate onto a lane (645 768) (9.4m). Turn left for 70 yds and take a lane off right. Shortly, keep right at a fork to very soon reach a T-junction.

6: Turn right up a 'No Through Road'. At its end it becomes a track curving left into a field. Follow the track, pass through a gate with a ladder stile and continue on the track to a gate gap; Leck Beck is to the left. Beyond the gap, continue on the track for a short distance, then turn off right to a large ladder stile. Having crossed, turn left along the left wall to a walkers' gate. Through, continue along left walls crossing ladder stiles as encountered. The wall direction soon swings round to north-east and this direction is maintained for a half-mile until the wall curves left (653 784). Here, go straight on, north-east, ascending to meet and follow a farm track. Pass to the right of a ruin (Anneside) and ignore a track off left afterwards. Eventually reach a walkers' gate (661 800) (11.8m) overlooking the headwaters of the beck. Pass through and turn right ascending. At a farm gate on the right, the path descends left down to the gill which is usually dry at this point (662 802); if the gill is in spate, there is a footbridge upstream at (675 805) with a direct path north-northwest and then west to Bullpot Farm. Assuming the usual dry crossing, take the ladder stile just across the gill and ascend to a wall on a trodden path. Then turn right and follow the track which follows a left wall to a gate onto a track at Bullpot Farm (663 814) (12.7m).

7: Turn left to shortly meet a bridleway/lane junction and turn right on the bridleway, signed 'Barbondale'. Follow the main track as it descends to Barbondale. It loosely follows the course of Aygill on the right and the track does a double bend when nearly down to a lane (654 826) (13.6m). Turn right on the lane for 360 yds, then turn off left, opposite a farm access drive, on a signed path which immediately crosses Barbon Beck by a footbridge (656 829). Over, turn left to join and follow a good bridleway track which runs close to the beck on its north side. The track enters a wood and reaches a fork. Fork left to stay close to the beck. Further on, ignore a turn off left crossing the beck. On exiting the wood, go straight ahead on a grass track to a surfaced drive. Cross and go a quarter-left to reach a grass track. Turn left on this and then cross the drive onto grass to cut another corner of the drive off. When the drive is met again, the church should be visible on the left. Turn left on the drive (632 826), cross over the beck and continue to shortly meet a lane; the church is on the right. Turn right a short distance for Barbon's inn, marking the end of this stage (630 825) (15.7m).

Stage 34
Barbon to Carlingill Bridge

VIA: Middleton Fell, The Dales Way and River Lune
DISTANCE: 16.1m [516.3m]
ASCENT: 2640ft   DESCENT: 2370ft
EXPLORER: OL2 (Yorkshire Dales S&W), OL19 (Howgill Fells)
LANDRANGER: 97 (Kendal & Morecambe), 98 (Wensleydale)

Barbon is overshadowed by Middleton Fell to its north-east which rises to 1,999ft at its summit of Calf Top. This is a top class walk with a good path up and it is this that the end-to-end route takes. From the summit, an equally good path continues in a great arc which eventually descends to the Lune Valley. Incredibly, the Yorkshire Dales National Park lies just to the east of this wonderful fell. Having reached the Lune Valley, a Roman Road called Jordan Lane and then a bridleway, lead to the crossing of the River Rawthey, a tributary of the Lune, at Middleton Bridge; the National Park *is* entered here. It's a short distance to join the Dales Way which follows the course of the River Lune northwards. However, when the Dales Way turns west to cross the river at Crook of Lune Bridge, the end to end route continues northwards along the valley sides, past the wonderfully named Midgehole, to emerge on the Roman Road of Fairmile Road. This lane is then followed to the end of the stage at Carlingill Bridge which crosses Carlin Gill.

Carlin Gill marks the half-way point of the walk and the completion of the equivalent of two Pennine Ways. It is also where the National Park is left. Unfortunately, there is no accommodation at Carlin Gill. There is accommodation earlier on the Dales Way section, otherwise it's necessary to get to Tebay to the north. Here the best option is negotiating a pick-up with your host. Failing that, the end-to-end route for the next stage will take you into Tebay, but it involves ascending Blease Fell and traversing a ridge from there. Given that this is already a fairly long day, you may feel it's a step too far, although there are alternative low level paths to Tebay. Continuing on Fairmile Road, it's just less than two miles to the main A685 road which has a regular but infrequent bus service to Tebay.

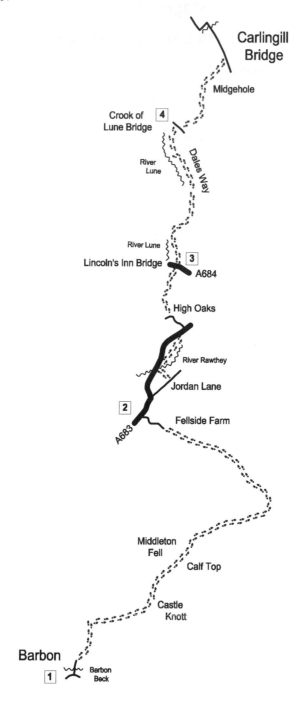

Carlingill
Bridge

Midgehole

Crook of [4]
Lune Bridge

River
Lune

Dales Way

River Lune

Lincoln's Inn Bridge [3]
A684

High Oaks

River Rawthey

Jordan Lane

[2] Fellside Farm

A683

Middleton
Fell

Calf Top

Castle
Knott

Barbon

[1] Barbon
Beck

1: From the inn at Barbon (SD 630 825), retrace the route to the church and turn left on the surfaced drive. Cross Barbon Beck and when the drive turns right (632 826) go straight on north-northeast. Pass down the right side of Ellers Wood and continue north to Eskholme Farm (634 833) on the left. Here turn right and climb steeply along an old field boundary to a gate leading out onto the open hillside. Follow the track up and at a mini ridge, turn right for a cairn on Eskholme Pike. Turn left here on a clear ascending grassy track making for the summit of Castle Knott (2.3m), before the final ascent on a clear track to the summit of Middleton Fell (664 856) (3.5m) with its trig point. By this time a wall on the right has been joined and this is followed from the summit. Eventually the traverse in the north-east direction finishes (674 872) (4.6m) and still following the wall to the right, the path and wall swing north-west. The clear path eventually diverges from the wall (662 883) (5.7m) and goes west-northwest. Keep left at track forks to reach Fellside Farm (636 889) (7.4m). The farm's zigzag access lane is followed, with a cut-off right used near its end, to reach the main A683 road (631 890) (7.8m).

2: Turn right briefly and then take Jordan Lane off on the right which is a Roman Road. After half a mile, turn left on a signed bridleway (633 898) which crosses a disused railway line and descends to meet the main A683 road (630 897). Turn right, very shortly cross the River Rawthey and then immediately take a footpath off right. Go half-left to a stile in the field corner. Beyond, the path follows left edges. When the edge turns left, go straight on descending the bank to a footbridge. Beyond, follow the right fence to the main A683 road (629 905) (9m). Turn right for a quarter of a mile then take a lane off left (630 909) (9.3m). After 360 yds, turn right on the surfaced access drive to the buildings of High Oaks. Just before The Oaks, turn left briefly, signed the 'Dales Way'; the well signed and walked Dales Way will now be followed to Crook of Lune Bridge. On reaching the next sign, turn right as directed for Lincoln's Inn Bridge and follow a track into a field. Follow the right edge round two sides, then follow a track along a left edge to enter an enclosed track and reach a gate into a farm. Follow the track through the farm and out onto its access drive, but go straight ahead through a gate into a field. Head half-left to a fence and then turn right along it to a stile where the boundary side is swapped. However, the right boundary is only briefly followed before the trodden path drops to and follows the River Lune to the main A684 road at Lincoln's Inn Bridge (632 923) (10.5m).

3: Turn right briefly then turn off left on a path signed to 'Low Branthwaite'. Follow the farm track alongside the Lune to a ladder stile. Cross, turn right alongside a stream to a footbridge. Over, go half-left to pass under Lune Viaduct, continue on an ascending grass track to a sign and turn right as directed. At the top of the slope, go a quarter-left to a stile in the left edge. Cross and follow the track along the right edge to a ladder stile. Over, cross the drive of Low Branthwaite (634 932) to take a ladder stile opposite left. Follow the trodden path to a field gap and go left at a sign just beyond. Descend by the left wall to a walkers' gate into an enclosed ascending track to a walkers' gate. Beyond, go a quarter-left to a gap stile in a wall then follow a right edge to a ladder stile. Over, go slightly left of straight ahead to come to the left of an old stone hut and enter a brief enclosed track. Then go ahead to a wall which the path follows to its left. It becomes a farm track. Follow the Dales Way sign left to a gap stile in a wall. Over, turn right along the left edge to a sign for 'Hole House' and then go left along a right wall to a gate. Through, go straight over the hill towards Hole House and left on its drive (630 945) (12m). Branch left as directed under an arch connecting cottages and reach a walkers' gate. Take the path beyond to a footbridge and over, go left on a path above the stream. On reaching the bank of the River Lune, turn right on the path which closely follows the river. Eventually, after spotting buildings above on the right, leave the river at a sign off right. Follow the path to a farm gate and through, follow the trodden track which soon follows a right edge to a gate onto a lane (621 962) (13.6m).

4: Turn left for 60 yds and then leave the Dales Way by taking the footpath off right, which runs parallel to the east side of the Lune but is not well walked and difficult to find in places. Start off by the river but soon ascend to follow the right fence and pass through a gate. Go straight ahead along the field edge (don't lose height) to a wall and look on the left for a stile in the fence. Cross and follow the line of trees for a short distance, then descend left to cross a dry stream. Keep on in the same direction to pass through a gate in the top right of the field (although the right of way follows to the right of the old wall line up the field then turns right along the left edge to the gate). Through, keep on in the same direction keeping to the left of Brunt Sike's walled boundary to reach a small walkers' gate with a sign. Pass along a good path between planted trees, which keeps to the left of Mire Head house. Cross a wall stile, and keeping close to the right field boundary, approach Low

Wilkinson. Go through a (signed) gate into its yard and pass down the yard to the left of the house to a (signed) gate. Beyond, go slightly left of straight ahead on a track to reach a walkers' gate. The path descends to a footbridge and then ascends left to come alongside a fence which is followed for a short distance. The path now branches right across a field. Midgehole is ahead and deserted (625 978) (14.8m). Pass behind it and continue on a grassy track to pass through a gate to open countryside. Take the path up to the telegraph pole and continue beyond on a grassy path up to Fairmile Road, branching left where possible to delay joining the road for as long as possible. Having reached the road, turn left and use the good verge to walk the mile or so to the end of the stage at Carlingill Bridge (625 997) (16.1m). The halfway point of the end-to-end walk has been reached!

Stage35
Carlingill Bridge to Bolton (on Eden)

VIA: Blease Fell (Howgills), Orton and Maulds Meaburn
DISTANCE: 18.1m [534.4m]
ASCENT: 1980ft   DESCENT: 2180ft
EXPLORER: OL19 (Howgill Fells)
LANDRANGER: 97 (Kendal & Morecambe), 91 (Appleby-in-Westmorland)

The western side of the Howgill Fells remains less popular than the fells north of Sedbergh. Nevertheless they are worth walking. As a prelude to the end-to-end walk, I had been up to this area a number of times trying out various routes. I have flogged up steep slopes, where I thought that I was on the summit bypass, and I have followed ridges which proved to be mainly bog hopping; you get there in the end but the getting is not an experience you want to remember or repeat. Thus I was pleased with the route I finally settled on which involves ascending to the summit of Blease Fell at 1,540 ft, either by an old mining track or by just doing a full frontal on the hill from Carlingill Bridge; the latter saves half a mile on the given mileage. On the day, despite being mid-May, it was a miserable, wet, cold (2 degrees would you believe), blowy day and one of our hosts had to be bribed to get out of the car to take a picture of us setting off! Fortunately, the rain had given up by the time we got to Orton and remained fair for the remainder of the day.

There's also a change in the grid square from SD to NY in reaching the top of Blease Fell. Squares in the southern half of the country start with the letter S, while those in the north start with N, so the progress northwards has been officially noted! From the top of Blease Fell, there's a lovely grassy track along the ridge with fine views which gradually descends into the village of Tebay. After joining the Lune and crossing it at Raisgill Bridge, paths lead to the picturesque village of Orton which has a shop, an inn and a tea room where there are handmade chocolates; I love chocolate but have no problem resisting these with their eye watering price tags! Orton is on the edge of limestone country and paths northwards lead across the eastern side of Crosby Ravensworth Fell at around the 1,000 ft level. On the fell, Wainwright's Coast to Coast route is crossed and we were amused to see the walkers here hurriedly consulting their guides to see if they'd gone wrong as it's assumed that any walkers met *must* be coast to coasters! Crosby Ravensworth village is charming as are most of the villages in this area.

Lyvennet Beck is followed to reach Maulds Meaburn village, where its houses are arranged around a large area of common land, with the beck running through the middle of it. The beck is left temporarily and then rejoined, crossing it near Barnskew Farm. The beck is crossed again on stepping stones near High Whitber, with a hard-to-find path leading into the village of King's Meaburn. Finally, a good track and field path lead into Bolton situated on the River Eden. Of the places passed through, there's accommodation and food in Tebay, Orton, Crosby Ravensworth and Bolton.

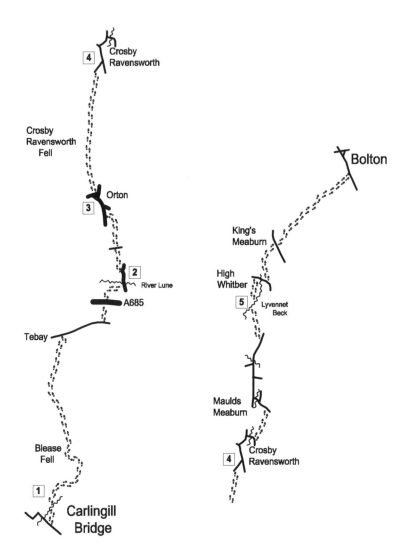

1: From Carlingill Bridge (SD 625 997), follow Carlin Gill to the right on its south side because of erosion on the north side, and observe that across the gill there are two paths contouring Blease Fell opposite. The old miners' track, that is to be joined and followed, is the upper path to the right. Ford to the north side of the gill as soon as possible and certainly before Weasel Gill flows down into Carlin Gill. Follow and ascend to the right of a wall and when it turns left to contour the hillside, ascend the hill steeply to a grassy ledge. Turn right on the old quarry track or continue straight up to the summit of Blease Fell. Assuming the miners' track, gently ascend the hillside on a clear grassy ledge. The track follows the general line of a tributary of Weasel Gill (Grains Gill), below on the right. Towards the top, the track becomes a path continuing straight ahead (still following above Grains Gill) to meet a track at the col between Blease Fell and Archer Moss. Turn left and follow the track up Blease Fell. The track passes just to the left of the summit (NY 624 004) (1m). Continue on the track, which becomes a wonderful grassy ridge track, and stay with the ridge for as long as possible, gradually descending northwards until finally meeting the access to High Woodend (620 042). Turn right and follow its access as it curves left to meet a minor road (619 045) (3.8m) in Tebay village. Turn right and follow the lane for just over three-quarters of a mile, then take a signed path off left after Row End on the left. Cross the field to the bottom right corner to exit onto the main A685 road. Turn right briefly to take a signed footpath opposite (631 053) and in the field entered go half-right to a gate at the furthest left of the field. Then follow the left edge to emerge on a B-road at Raisgill Bridge (635 057) (5.1m).

2: Turn left, cross the River Lune and 150 yds beyond, take the footpath off left through a gate signed for 'Orton'; this is the second path off left. Go three-quarters right as indicated, then aim to the left of the building to find a step stile in the wall. Now head north to a gate in the fence and through, curve left to the left wall. The wall is then followed to the right to a gap stile onto a lane (633 066). The path continues opposite over a step stile in the wall by the right end of the trees. Over, go half-left past the end of the trees and continue north-west to a hard-to-spot step stile in a wall. Beyond, go half-left to a telegraph pole and continue in the same direction to a step stile near the right end of the wall. Cross, proceed half-right to two gates in the bottom right corner of the field. Go through the left gate and follow to the right of a stream to a footbridge (629 074) over Chapel Beck. Over, cross a track, go through a gate and go half-right aiming just to the right of lone trees. Continue to a wall, then turn left down a right wall to a B-road (625 076) (6.6m) south of Orton. Turn right and follow the road into Orton ignoring a turn-off right. In the village keep left to pass its inn and later the chocolate shop and general stores.

3: Just beyond the stores, when the B-road turns sharp left, turn right briefly and then take a track off left (622 083) signed 'Crosby Ravensworth'; the path direction for the next mile is predominantly west-of-North. Enter the church grounds, keep left of the church and look for a stile in its left wall. Across, go half-right to a gap stile in the wall. Through, follow to the right of an old hedge line (parallel to the right wall) to a ditch crossing, then go a quarter-left to a stone stile. Over, head just left of straight ahead to a stile and then follow the right wall until it turns, at which point keep straight ahead to cross a stone stile. Now go ahead to join and follow a right wall to a stone stile and beyond, go just left of straight ahead to a gap stile (or use the gate field gap). Through, proceed just left of straight ahead to a gate gap, then on to a gap stile and ahead to a farm gate. Through, go straight ahead to join a right wall. In the next field, keep with the right wall to find a gap stile to the left of the top right field corner. Through, go just left of straight ahead to pass between a left wall and a kiln and on to a stone step stile (converge on the left wall if stuck) (617 100) (8.2m). The path direction now changes to north. Take the good and lovely moorland path ahead. Soon after crossing a track, a large cairn marking the Coast to Coast route is reached. Go half-right here as directed. On shortly meeting a track, turn left to a path fork marker and go half-right (there should be a wall and gate just ahead) to a step stile (618 109) (8.8m). Over, immediately pass through a gate on the right and turn left along the left fence. Descend, gently diverging from the left edge towards a gate (just right of the left corner) at the bottom. Beyond, follow the track to the next gate. Through, leave the track to go east-of-North, aiming for the left of Crosby Lodge. Pass through a gate and take the left path going straight on, just east-of-North, to a stone stile. Over, head half-left to a stile and a footbridge (to the left of the visible footbridge) (621 127) (10m). Ascend a quarter-left to a track. Don't pass through the gate opposite, but turn to follow the left fence northwards to a gate and continue along the left fence to a double gate. Through, continue in the same northwards direction into a narrow strip of land, pass through a gate at its end and go straight ahead to meet a lane. Turn right and shortly reach a lane T-junction (621 140) (10.8m).

4: Turn left through the small village of Crosby Ravensworth keeping to the 'major' road signed to Maulds Meaburn. Pass the church and continue for 110 yds to a lane off right signed to Bankhead (622 149). Almost immediately cross Lyvennet Beck, and after a few yards turn off left on a signed path which follows the beck through a garden gate into a long field. Follow the left edge but then curve right to a gap stile. In the following field, follow the right edge to a gap stile then follow the trodden path (east-northeast) a quarter-left away from the beck, towards trees, to find a gate in the top corner. Through, pass under a bridge and take the track beyond to join Flass's access drive. When it reaches a lane, turn left and follow the 'major' road, curving left to reach a substantial stone bridge over Lyvennet Beck. Cross and turn right (signed for Morland and Penrith) through the delightful village of Maulds Meaburn (12.5m) with its houses arranged around its large green. There are no facilities in the village. Proceed north along the King's Meaburn road. Cross the beck at Dairy Bridge (624 173) and 350 yds beyond, there is a footpath off right parallel to the road to get walkers off the road. However, it only extends to one field and has nothing otherwise to recommend it, so sticking with the road is preferable. After this 'path' re-joins the road, 80 yds later take a path off left signed 'Barnskew' (625 181) (13.7m). In the field entered, follow the right edge to a stile, then follow the left field edge to a stile on the left, with a subsequent short steep descent to a visible stile on the right. Beyond, and in the wood, go close to the left boundary (with the beck beyond on the left) to find a waymark. Continue along the left edge to a stile on the left and a footbridge over the beck to a concrete farm track. Turn right to Barnskew Farm (621 188) (14.2m).

5: Pass through the farm and do not cross the beck. Instead, turn off left to a stile just before the beck crossing. Over, the path ascends half-right in woodland then becomes a good level track/path. When it descends right, look for a stile straight ahead. Beyond, head to the left of a lone tree then go ahead towards Turnbank farm to pick up a left fence. Pass through three waymarked gates in quick succession then enter a field and converge on the right edge, fording a side stream to a stile in the furthest right corner. Cross, turn left to a footbridge and then walk along the beck, crossing stiles as encountered, and eventually reach a rough lane (619 201) (15.1m). Turn right, immediately cross Lyvennet Beck by stepping stones, and continue past High

Whitber Farm for a short distance to where the lane swings sharp right. Here, turn left on a signed path (622 201). Go half-left along a right fence to a footbridge then half-left to a farm gate. Through, go three-quarters right to the top left field corner and beyond, follow the left boundary to a farm track which is taken. Pass through double gates, and continue on the track turning left and right through a farmyard, to escape onto a lane at King's Meaburn (622 210) (16m); the White Horse Inn is to the left, otherwise there are no facilities. Turn right for 80 yds then turn off left on a bridleway signed for 'Burwain Hall'. After nearly half a mile, ignore a turn-off right to Stockenber (626 214) and continue straight on through a gate on the enclosed track. Follow the track through two gates into a field, going half-right to the opposite hedge, and then turning right along it to a gate in the top left field corner. Through, follow the right hedge line, then turn just left of straight ahead, across a short marshy stretch to a stile. Over, follow the left edge north-east for two fields then a right side for one field to a gap stile. Then head just left of straight ahead to a stile and beyond, a quarter-right to a stile. Then turn parallel to the right edge to reach a gate and through, go half-left, crossing a ditch by a stone bridge to a stile. Now follow the left edge down a field to a stile onto a track. Turn left on the track which soon turns right and follow it out to a lane on the outskirts of Bolton village (640 229) (17.8m). Turn left and then first right to shortly meet a road in the centre of the village (638 233) (18.1m).

Stage 36
Bolton (on Eden) to Melmerby

VIA: Milburn and Hanging Walls of Mark Anthony
DISTANCE: 11.5m [545.9m]
ASCENT: 700ft   DESCENT: 560ft
EXPLORER: OL19 (Howgill Fells), OL31 (North Pennines)
LANDRANGER: 91 (Appleby-in-Westmorland)

After the length of the previous stage, this stage is much shorter and is through predominantly lush farmland around the Eden Valley, with good views eastwards of the Pennine Hills. The scenery was enhanced by it being a pleasantly sunny and warm day in complete contrast to what had gone before. In fact this was the start of a week of blistering heat when we had cause to wish for cool dry weather. I had worries about whether the paths would be there, in this relatively quiet area of Cumbria, but in fact all the paths we wanted were present and this situation held until we got north of Hadrian's Wall.

Our hostess accompanied us beside the River Eden and we then continued to Kirkby Thore. Just outside this sizable village, there is a large gypsum factory and the route passes through this, on the way to Milburn village which is pleasantly situated around a village green. We had more company from here for the rest of the stage. A path northwards leads past the Hanging Walls of Mark Anthony. These are three low cultivation terraces although there seems to be some dispute as to their age and their exact location. There are various lumps which could qualify and it has to be said that what we identified as the terraces is not particularly exciting. The route continues north-west to Townhead, where the route takes to quiet lanes, before a footpath can be taken into Melmerby. Melmerby is a charming village in the foothills of the North Pennines and has a tea room, accommodation and the local pub does food.

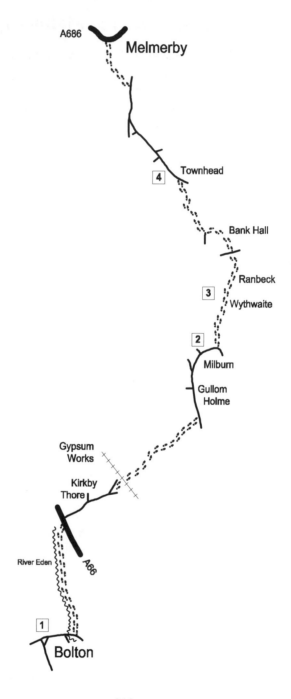

1: From the T-junction in Bolton (NY 638 233) turn right through the village to Bolton Bridge. Cross the River Eden and immediately take the footpath left along the east bank of the Eden. The path keeps very close to the river in a long field until the Eden curves left when the path carries straight on, aiming to the right of a copse of trees. Pass through a gate onto a concrete farm track and turn left along it. The track turns right passing to the left of a farm and out onto the main A66 road (636 253) (1.5m). Turn left for 110 yds then take the minor road off right into Kirkby Thore. Follow the road through the village, ignoring the turn-off left (unless you want its shop), and having passed the entrance to the hall on the right continue for another 70 yds to take surfaced Fell Lane on the left (642 257). Follow the lane to the gypsum factory and just after the barrier, follow the footpath sign onto an enclosed grassy path passing to the right of the works. The path continues across a factory driveway (all well signed), goes over a railway bridge, then crosses a railway line to a ladder stile. In the field entered, follow the right edge to a stile on the right. Over, follow a left edge to the corner, then turn right along the left edge to a stile on the left. Cross, follow the right fence for two fields then cross a drive to a step stile opposite. Now follow the left wall to a waymarked gate and through, turn left to follow the left edge onto a track. Turn right to shortly reach a lane (659 276) (3.8m). Turn left and ignoring all turn-offs left, follow the lane just west-of-North through Gullom Holme into Milburn village (655 293) (5m) where there is an attractive rectangular green with houses clustered around it.

2: Cross the green to the back left corner, passing to the left of the school and turn left onto a wide track. Shortly, there's a track branch. Take the left branch and almost immediately turn up half-right to a gate. In the field entered, follow the left edge until it turns, then go straight ahead to a stile. The next stile is ahead left followed by a quarter-right to a stile onto a track. Turn right and follow the track as it turns left and right. At the next left turn, don't turn left but go through the waymarked gate ahead (656 302). Cross the field a quarter-left to a stile and then head half-right to the next stile. Then it's half-right to a stile followed by half-left to a stile. Cross the next field three-quarters right to a double gate into open access land. Go northwards, crossing a stream on a track and then go three-quarters left to the right end of the trees. When the tree line is reached, turn right along the line looking for a substantial footbridge over Crowdundle Beck (656 313); the beck marks the old boundary between Westmorland and Cumberland. Over, go half-right to a waymarked gate and exit the open access land into a field. Go just right of straight ahead to a gate (aim just to the right of buildings of Wythwaite ahead), then go a quarter-left to a gate with a fingerpost sign. Pass to the left of Wythwaite and take its access drive (654 317) (6.6m).

3: When the drive swings right, cultivation terraces are visible straight ahead. Pass through two gates and immediately after the second, go right on a bridleway. Follow signs directing walkers around Ranbeck farm to a waymarked gate into a field. Go parallel to the right edge to a waymarked gate, then go just right of straight ahead to a waymarked gate in the top right corner. Beyond, converge on and follow the right wall to reach a walkers' gate onto a good track. Turn left and at Kirkland Hall (651 326), turn right on a path signed to 'Bank Hall'. Descend to a footbridge over the beck and enter a field. Go a quarter-left to converge on and follow the left fence to a stone stile in the far left corner. Now go half-left, aiming to the left of Bank Hall's farm buildings, to find a stile. Cross and go just right of straight ahead to a farm gate. Beyond, go straight ahead then turn right *through* a barn to a concrete access track, which is followed to the left until the start of the public road (643 330) (8m). Here, turn off right on a track signed as the 'Public Way to Townhead'. The clear track follows a left wall, then a right wall for two fields before curving right uphill along a right fence and entering an enclosed track that leads to a lane at Townhead (635 341) (8.9m).

4: Turn left and proceed north-west to a T-junction (628 347). Here turn right to take the lane labelled as 'Unsuitable for Heavy Goods Vehicles'. Follow the lane north-west for three-quarters of a mile to a T-junction (620 355) (10.2m). Turn right for 530 yds and near the top of the hill take a signed path off left (619 359). Cross the first field half-right to a step stile adjacent to a gate (waymark) and in the next field, continue in the same north-northwest direction aiming to the right of trees. Pass down the right side of the trees to a waymarked stile onto an enclosed track which is followed until two gates are reached. Go through the right gate as directed, then follow a left wall for a short distance before branching half-right to a ladder stile onto a lane, and turn left to meet the main A686 road at the west end of Melmerby village (613 372) (11.5m).

Stage 37
Melmerby to Castle Carrock

VIA: Busk, Croglin and Cumrew
DISTANCE: 14.9m [560.8m]
ASCENT: 1620ft   DESCENT: 1700ft
EXPLORER: OL31 (North Pennines), OL5 (NE Lakes), 315 (Carlisle)
LANDRANGER: 91 (Appleby-in-Westmorland), 86 (Haltwhistle & Bewcastle)

This stage is along the foothills of the North Pennines to Castle Carrock and is an excellent and scenic walk. It uses paths, tracks and lanes to link together hamlets, substantial farms and small quiet villages. Unsurprisingly, there are no facilities on the journey in this quiet area of Cumbria. The weather was really 'hotting' up and it was wall to wall sunshine. After passing through the village of Gamblesby and then the hamlet of Unthank, paths lead on to the farming settlements at Busk, Haresceugh, Outhwaite, Scale Houses and Davygill. After a short section on a quiet B-road into the village of Croglin, a track is taken to Townhead (different from yesterday's Townhead!), followed by a path to rejoin the B6413 road. After passing through the village of Cumrew, a track leads to the hamlet of Albyfield and paths onward to a track along the east side of Castle Carrock's Reservoir. The village is a short distance away and has accommodation and a pub serving food.

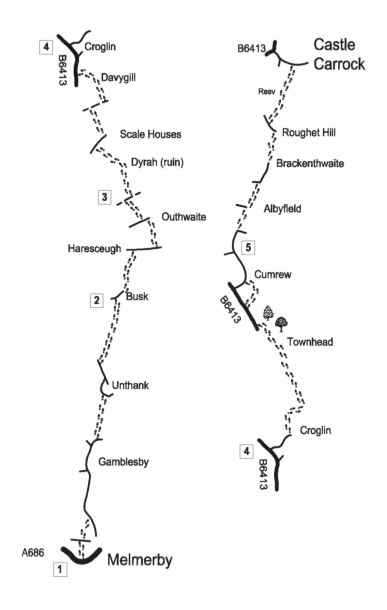

1: From emerging on the main road in Melemerby (NY 613 372), turn right for a few yards and look for a wooden door, in the wall on the left, signed to the village hall. Ascend on a well used path and exit by a door onto a lane. Turn right for a few yards, then turn left on a path signed to Todhills (613 374). In the field entered find a stile in the top right corner, then go half-right to a gate gap. Beyond, go straight ahead in the same direction to a stile, cross and go a quarter-left to the wall corner. Follow the left wall which turns left out onto a lane (614 379). Turn left and follow the lane northwards to and through the lovely village of Gamblesby (1.5m). Keep on the 'major' road beyond the village and when the road turns right, turn off left on a path signed to 'Unthank' (609 399). It's enclosed to a kissing gate into a field, which is crossed a quarter-right to a wall. Go left along the wall to find a stone step stile on the right. Cross and turn left along the left wall to a gate onto a farm track which is then followed out onto a lane. Turn right briefly to a T-junction (610 405) and turn left through the hamlet of Unthank. At the next T-junction turn left, ascend and at the top, take the second signed path off right (608 410) (2.5m), which starts as a track to a waymarked gate into a field. In the field, follow the left edge to a footbridge, cross and pass through a kissing gate. In the field entered, go a quarter-right to a stone step stile (left of the gate), then head a quarter-right to a stile and cross an access track to a stone stile. Proceed half-right to a waymarked gate then follow the left wall to a waymark. Here turn right to continue in the field along the left edge to a waymarked gate on the left. Through, follow the left edge and then go straight ahead out onto the lane at Busk Farm (610 421) (3.3m).

2: Turn right along the lane to its end at a gate and beyond, go a quarter-right up a grass track taking the second stile off left (not waymarked) (610 423). Follow a right wall to a stile, then go north towards Haresceugh farm, gently diverging from the right wall and descending towards an old tree line. Follow this tree line and continue in the same direction to join and follow a left wall down to meet a path. Go left and look for a waymarked stile on the right. Beyond, go ahead across a short stretch of rough ground to a stile onto a track (610 426). The path continues over a stile opposite and beyond, follow a left edge up the field to a gate onto a track which is followed out to a lane at Haresceugh (610 429). Turn right for 110 yds and then take the path on the left signed to 'Outhwaite and Croglan'. In the field entered, converge on and follow the left edge to the field corner. Turn right here to still follow the left edge, looking for a stile on the left into woodland. In the wood, go straight ahead on a trodden path which leads to a footbridge. Beyond, curve right and follow a right fence. When it becomes a wall, turn right on a steeply ascending path to meet a farm track and turn right on this ascending to a gate. Through, branch left onto the public road at Outhwaite (608 435) (4.3m). Go left briefly then turn right on a path signed to 'Scalehouses and Croglin'. Curve left briefly through the farmyard and then twist right to a gate with a marker post. Pass through and turn left by the left fence to a waymarked stile into the bottom left corner of the wood. Pass along the left edge of the wood to a stone stile on the left into a field and turn right to a stile by a gate. Through, follow a right boundary of a broken-down wall to a stile and beyond, follow a right fence going ahead to cross a ladder stile. After, follow the right wall to a ladder stile onto a track (602 439).

3: Cross to the enclosed track opposite, signed to 'Croglin Bridge' and when it finishes, turn right as directed through a gate into a field and follow the left wall to a step stile. Cross and turn right to follow the right wall to a waymarked step stile onto a farm track. Turn right as directed and follow the track to a waymarked gate. Beyond, go ahead north-northwest to a wall gap and continue in this direction to a stile. Over, head half-right to curve left round the bottom of Dyrah Hill to a waymarked gate. Pass to the right of Dyrah Farm's ruins (597 446) (5.4m) and on to a waymarked gate. Through, go a quarter-left to a gap stile then just left of straight ahead to a gap stile. Now head half-left to a (wonky) stile onto a farm track and turn right to follow it to a lane junction at the small hamlet of Scale Houses (588 451) (6m). Turn right briefly to a sign pointing left to 'Croglin Bridge'. Pass through a gate and turn left along a left edge to a stile. Beyond, follow a left wall, but then go a quarter-right to maintain height, and reach a step stile (to the right of a gate) onto a track. The path continues opposite and in the field entered, go half-right to a gap stile. Through, go three-quarters left to a wicket gate onto a wide track named Clint Lane (585 458). Turn right, pass through a gate and take the next gate on the left (waymarked). Follow the left wall on a lovely path above Dike Beck on the right. Keep by the left wall (losing the beck) to pass through a gate and keep with the left wall, ignoring a ladder stile on the left. The path becomes a track leading to the back of Davygill farm and here follow signs to go straight ahead to reach a waymarked gate (the left of two). Through, the path follows to the right of the beck passing a waymark post then descends to a footbridge over the beck. Beyond, turn right for a stile into a wood. Cross a footbridge and turn left along the right side of the beck. At the end of the wood, the path crosses the beck again and reaches a gate. Beyond, follow a right edge to shortly emerge on a B-road (577 465) (7.5m).

4: Turn right for Croglin. After half a mile, at the Robin Hood pub, turn right on a 'No Through Road' (574 472) and follow the lane through the village of Croglin. Keep going beyond the village and at just over a quarter of a mile from the B-road, the end of the lane is reached at Town Head Farm. Just before the farm, turn left on a wide ascending gravel track (576 475) (just after passing a path sign off left). The track climbs to a track T-junction (8.5m) and the route continues opposite right. Follow the enclosed track to a gate and subsequently follow the left fence. When the main track goes right, go left on a grassy track beside a left fence, to a waymarked gate onto a wonderful track between walls. Eventually the enclosed track descends and turns left to run above a beck on the right and meet a lane. Turn right briefly, cross the beck and immediately turn right, cross a small patch of grass and a track to take the path signed to 'Foul Sike' (562 491) (9.9m). In the field entered, go a quarter-right to the right fence and follow this along a wood edge passing through stiles and gates as met. In the field entered at the end of the wood, follow the left edge to a farm track but don't take it, instead turn left through a gate, then follow the left edge westwards to a double gate out onto the B-road (554 499) (10.6m). Turn right for a quarter mile and then take a path off right (551 502) signed to 'St Mary's Church'. Follow the farm track for 50 yds to a kissing gate off left, then follow the right wall through a kissing gate and walkers' gate into the church grounds. Exit via the church gates at the front onto a lane. Turn right and follow the lane through the small village of Cumrew for 700 yds.

5: When the lane bends sharp left (547 509) (11.5m), continue straight on along an ascending surfaced lane, keeping left at branches to maintain a northerly direction. When the surfaced lane turns distinctly right (548 519), north-of-East to go to Turnberry House, go straight on northwards through a gate and follow a good track along a right wall and then enclosed, to meet a track and lane junction (548 523), with the buildings of Albyfield visible directly ahead. Go straight on along a track signed for 'Brackenthwaite'. Keep straight on through Albyfield's farm buildings and towards the end pass through a gate into a field following its right edge to a gate. Beyond, follow a dip in the field, curving right to a signed gate onto a lane. Turn right to the lane end at Brackenthwaite farm (547 532) (13m). At the farm, go straight on signed to the 'Reservoir'. Follow a right wall until a field is entered to the right of a farm building. Cross the field northwards to a farm gate and beyond, go straight across, just west-of-North to a waymarked gate. Through, follow a right fence to a gate onto a short track which meets a lane at Roughet Hill (546 536). Turn left for a third of a mile then, as the south end of Castle Carrock's Reservoir is approached, turn off right through a kissing gate for a path signed to 'Garth Foot' (543 540) (13.6m). Follow the stony track along the east side of the reservoir. After passing the entrance to Tottergill Holiday Farm, the track becomes grassy and is followed past the dam out onto a lane (547 553) (14.5m). Turn left to a T-junction in the centre of Castle Carrock village and turn right briefly for the B&B (542 555) (14.9m).

Stage 38
Castle Carrock to Roweltown

VIA: Brampton, Walton and Stapleton
DISTANCE: 16.5m [577.3m]
ASCENT: 890ft   DESCENT: 1090ft
EXPLORER: 315 (Carlisle), 324 (Liddesdale)
LANDRANGER: 86 (Haltwhistle & Bewcastle)

There's a definite feeling that Scotland is near in today's stage, although the border crossing is not until the next day. Brampton is reached through Gelt Woods which has Roman inscribed rocks; if they were there, we failed to spot them. It was turning out to be a very hot day, so we enjoyed the shade of the woods. Brampton, with its solid red sandstone buildings, has the feel of a border town. It is a fair-sized pleasant town, with a compact centre, having a good range of shops and coffee houses. It's a good place to stock up as it's two days to the much smaller town of Newcastleton and there's very little in-between. Hadrian's Wall lies to the north of Brampton and this is crossed at the small village of Walton. Walton has only a tea room (where we had to wait over an hour for a simple lunch) as its inn has closed. Cumbria, north of Walton, is a largely unvisited and unwalked area as people tend to concentrate on the Lake District and Hadrian's Wall. This is a pity because whilst not being dramatic, it is attractive farming country and deserves to be better known.

From Walton paths took us to Whitehill and then by path and lane to Nickie's Hill without problem. Roads then had to be taken. At Knorren Lodge, two chairs had been thoughtfully placed by the roadside and we gratefully used them for a much needed rest in shade. Afterwards the road is followed onwards to Kirkcambeck and then to Cracrop Farm, where there is unfortunately no longer B&B accommodation. We experienced path problems after this, with a path not do-able as shown on the map, but able to be picked up shortly afterwards. This was followed by paths passing through areas of plantation, where the trees had been felled but no provision left for walkers, who are clearly not expected to want to cross this forgotten area of Cumbria. Furthermore, the entry to one plantation was blocked by (negotiable) barbed wire; path problems have been reported and hopefully resolved. Bizarrely, considering the state of the paths, there is often a substantial bridge across streams and rivers! At Roweltown, the paths improved and after crossing the River Lyne, the river was followed to Low Luckens Organic Resource Centre. Accommodation is scarce and this is where we stayed at the end of a long day which saw my feet get horribly blistered. The centre is a non-profit making organisation promoting farming sustainability and countryside conservation, together with energy, water and waste management. Education is part of their remit and residential self-catering accommodation is available to the general public and groups.

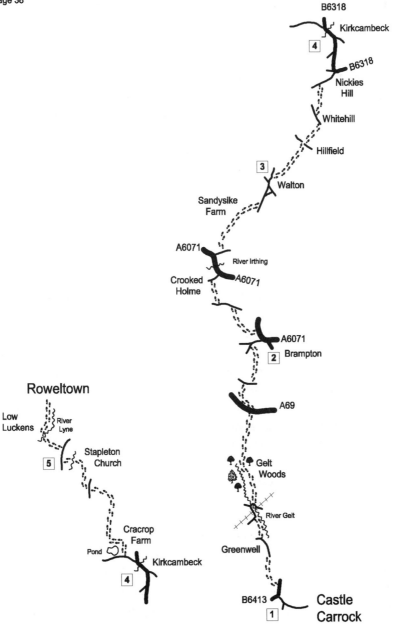

B6318

Kirkcambeck

4

B6318

Nickies
Hill

Whitehill

Hillfield

3

Walton

Sandysike
Farm

A6071

River Irthing

Crooked
Holme

A6071

A6071

2 Brampton

Roweltown

A69

Low
Luckens

River
Lyne

Stapleton
Church

5

Gelt
Woods

River Gelt

Cracrop
Farm

Pond

Kirkcambeck

4

Greenwell

B6413

1

**Castle
Carrock**

1: From the B&B in Castle Carrock (NY 542 555), carry on north along the B-road for 130 yds turning off on a track signed to Cowran (542 556). After 200 yds at a track T-junction, turn right and follow this north to meet a farm track. Turn left and follow the track through a waymarked gate, past buildings and through another waymarked gate onto a lane (ignore a bridleway branch off right down to the River Gelt). Shortly, when the lane curves left (536 566) (0.9m), turn right on a path signed to 'Middle Gelt'. After a short track, follow the trodden path which keeps left of the trees surrounding the River Gelt but reaches the river bank at the end of the field. Thereafter the path closely follows the river to reach a lane (533 572) (1.4m). Turn right, pass under the railway viaduct, almost immediately turn right (signed 'Talkin'), cross the river and immediately turn left on a path signed 'Gelt Woods'. Take the main track through the woods (ignoring turn offs right), ascend away from the river then descend back to the river, cross a side stream and ascend (still keeping to the main track). Just after a quarry area on the right, a path fork is reached. Here, go right (527 587) (2.6m) and following the main track, shortly reach another fork (signed) where the left fork is taken. Continue on the track northwards until a lane is met. Cross to the path opposite, and when it soon meets a lane, turn left under a bypass (530 597) (3.3m) then immediately left on a signed path which joins an access drive. When a lane is met, turn right and when the lane curves left, go straight on to a fingerpost (527 600) (3.7m). Take the path opposite signed to 'Elmfield'. Initially enclosed, when it enters a field, keep with the left hedge across several fields. As the path curves left to reach Greenhill road, look for a gap on the right onto an informal path past bungalows onto a street and Greenhill road is a few yards to the left; the route taken emerges on Greenhill road slightly closer to Brampton! Turn right on Greenhill road to meet Carlisle Road (526 610).

2: Turn right here, signed 'Town Centre' to shortly reach a major junction with the A-road to Longtown signed off left (528 611) (4.6m). The route turns left here but turn off right for the centre of Brampton, with its excellent range of shops and cafes (recommended but not included in the mileage). Take the main road to Longtown for 140 yds and take a path off left signed to 'Old Church Lane' (527 611). Follow the obvious path and when it gets to houses, follow the right fence to pick up the path again. Eventually the path crosses the stream it has been accompanying and continues to shortly emerge on Old Church Lane (521 614). Turn left and follow the lane west for 700 yds to a path off right signed to 'Crooked Holme' (515 616). Follow the right fence for two and a bit fields, then swap the boundary side and follow to a stile at the bottom of a descent. Over, go a quarter-left across a field, keeping to the right of houses, to emerge on the Roman Road of Stanegate (511 621). Turn right and follow the lane to the main A6071 road (6.1m). Turn left and cross the River Irthing on Irthing Bridge. After a further 500 yds, take the first road off right signed to 'Walton'. After 110 yds cross a stile on the left signed to 'Walton' (just before the field gate). Go half-right to a boundary, then turn right along this left boundary following it to three trees. From here, go a quarter-right to a stile. Over, go straight ahead to a kissing gate in the top left corner of the field (just to the right of the wood) and emerge on a track. Turn left to a waymarked gate off right onto a track to Sandysike. Having crossed a cattle grid, turn right along a track and after passing through two gates, the Hadrian's Wall Path national trail is joined. The trail follows a right fence to a road (522 643) (7.8m). Turn left and leave the trail to take the 'major' road through charming Walton village.

3: Close to the end of the village, look for a path off right onto a grassy track signed 'Hillfield' (522 646). Follow the left boundary to a stone stile. Cross, and go just right of straight ahead to cross three stiles and reach the edge of woodland. Continue forward along the wood edge, to find and follow a waymark half-right into the woodland and down to a footbridge over a stream (526 650). The path continues by ascending half-left to a stile. Over, turn left, loosely following the left boundary to a waymark pointing right. Cross the field half-right to a gate as directed. Don't pass through but turn left along the right field boundary to a walkers' gate. Continue straight ahead across a small field, cross Hillfield's access drive (Hillfield is to the right) and then cross a stile opposite. Now go half-right across the field to reach a walkers' kissing gate in the fence. Through, turn left, along left hedge boundaries to a field gate at the buildings of Whitehill. Here, go through the gate onto a farm track which curves right to meet the end of its access lane (537 659) (9.4m). Turn left. After passing a barn with a circular tower, turn right on a signed path (536 662). In the first field go three-quarters left to a stile, then half-right in the second field to a gate gap and half right in the final field to a gate onto the road from Walton (536 667). A lack of paths now means unavoidable road walking for nearly 3 miles. Turn right for a quarter mile to a T-junction with the B6318 road at Nickie's Hill. Here turn left signed

'Kirkcambeck'. Follow the B-road as it crosses Knorren Beck and ignore a lane off left then right. The B-road descends to cross Cam Beck and a short distance beyond, turn left on a lane signed for Stapleton (11.5m).

4: After 1 mile, just after passing Cracrop Cottage, pass a signed path off right to Whitegate pointing up the drive of Cracrop Farm. Continue for another 150 yds to take an unsigned track off right through double gates (519 697) (12.6m). The track passes to the right of a pool and shortly meets a farm track. Turn left here, the track soon turns right and ends at two gates. Go through a gate gap and go straight ahead, northwards, along a left field edge. When the edge turns left, go straight on to cross a stile. Descend just left of straight ahead (north-northwest) to a fence guarding a plank bridge and stile beyond. Pass up the right side of a (felled) plantation to a stile. In the field entered, follow the right fence to a footbridge and stile (516 707). Over, turn left along the left edge to join a farm track which can be followed along a left edge to a lane (509 706) (13.8m). Use the gate opposite left and go half-right across the field to a waymarked gate. In the next field follow the right boundary round two sides to the bottom left corner of the field, where there's a stile into the wood on the right. Descend on an old cart track which curves right to a footbridge. Across, ascend a field loosely following its left boundary. Turn left at the top of the field along the right boundary to a stone step stile into Stapleton Church (503 713). Pass to the left of the church and at a path fork in the churchyard, turn left looking for a waymarked stile on the right into a field. Follow the right edge south-of-West to a gate at the bottom. Through, follow signs to take a gate on the right and a stile on the left into another (dreadful) plantation. Follow the line of the beck on the left to find an old track down to a substantial footbridge. Over, turn right along the beck to a stile into a field, where the left edge is followed to a stile onto a road (494 711) (15.1m).

5: Turn right for 240 yds then turn left into a field on a signed bridleway (494 713). Follow the right boundary, pass through a signed gate and go half-left to cross a ditch (post waymark). Beyond, go just left of straight ahead to a waymarked post which leads onto a short descending track to a very elegant suspension bridge over the River Lyne (490 718) (15.7m). Cross and turn right along the river on a trodden path. Cross stiles and footbridges as encountered; the path closely follows the river. Eventually, the path rises and follows a left fence to reach a stile into a field. Cross and turn right along a right fence to a gate. The right of way follows the field edge round a loop of the river to the top left corner of the field, where a subsequent path diversion leads through a gate and along a left edge to a gate into Low Luckens. Follow the signs through the barn and turn right into the farmyard of Low Luckens Organic Resource Centre (494 727) (16.5m).

Stage 39
Roweltown to Newcastleton

VIA: Kershope Forest, Kershopefoot and disused railway line
DISTANCE: 11.9m [589.2m]
ASCENT: 1100ft   DESCENT: 1040ft
EXPLORER: 324 (Liddesdale)
LANDRANGER: 86 (Haltwhistle & Bewcastle), 79 (Hawick & Eskdale)

After nearly 600 miles, the route crosses into Scotland on this stage and there's still over 400 miles to do to reach John O'Groats! Again, it was an overwhelmingly hot day from the start and my feet seemed in the same jolly (awful) state as they were on the previous day. The route continues parallel to the river to Blacklyne Bridge. From here a bridleway north through The Hagg Farm to The Roan Farm leads on into an extensive plantation. The bridleway through the forest only lasts a couple of miles and is straightforward with signs; the forest tracks seem to correspond to those shown on the map. After a good half mile on a quiet B-road, the route takes a path across moorland and rough ground to Nookgate. Lane walking follows, until a rough footpath off left, leads into the hamlet of Kershopefoot and the post marking the border with Scotland. From here, the disused railway line, which is now a multi-user track, is followed to Mangerton Farm and then quiet lanes take over until Liddel Water is crossed, when the riverside path can be taken to shortly reach the centre of Newcastleton. Needless to say, there are no facilities during this stage.

Newcastleton is a small town with streets constructed on a grid pattern. The town has accommodation, eating places, an excellent tea room and shops, including a good and helpful hardware shop. We were more than fortunate in our choice of B&B. I was quietly expiring from the heat and my blisters, so that I wondered how I was going to manage over 20 miles to Hawick on the following day. This resulted in us being able to do 5 miles of the following stage in the cool of the evening without our sacks, with our hosts picking us up. This left us with a manageable 15 miles for the next day, which also promised exceptional heat and sun. The following day was made even better by a very early breakfast and we were walking by 7.30am before the heat really got going. The Newcastleton B&B is my choice for the best on the route.

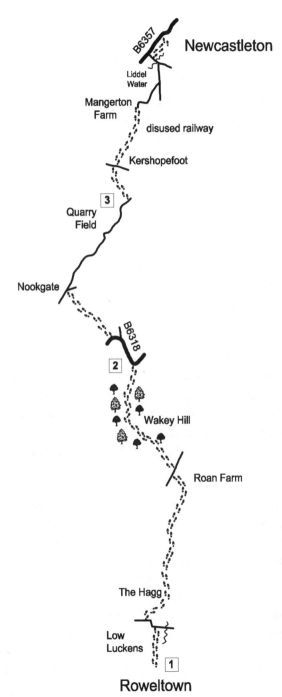

1: From Low Luckens (NY 494 727) continue on the track northwards through the farm and follow it all the way to Whiteholme farm. At Whiteholme, keep to the right side of the buildings to join a track, which soon drops beside the River Lyne and follows between the water and a left boundary, all the way to a lane at Blacklyne Bridge (496 734) (0.5m). Turn left for 400 yds and then take a bridleway off right signed to 'Russelgate' (493 736). Go up the access drive of The Hagg Farm, go through the middle of the farm buildings and enter a field. Turn left along the left boundary, curving right to cut its corner before curving left to re-meet the left boundary. In the field corner at the end of the second side, ford a stream and follow the left bank of a side stream which is forded to a walkers' gate. Beyond, go straight up the bank (right of the stream) to a rough field with a waymark at the bank top. Go a quarter-left to the top left field corner to find a waymark and a gap. In the field entered, follow the left edge around two sides to meet a farm track by a barn in the top right corner of the field. Turn left and follow the track past Roan Farm to a lane (493 751) (1.9m). Take the bridleway track opposite right, which passes through a gate and continues to a walkers' gate into Kershope Forest after 0.4 miles. In the forest, the bridleway continues west-northwest for 210 yds to meet a forestry track (486 756). Turn left here on a clockwise track which reaches a forestry track fork on the east side of Wakey Hill after 0.6 miles (483 760) (3m). Turn left here as directed and after a short distance reach a bridleway T-junction (481 762). Go right signed 'Ringing Flow'. The bridleway soon turns right and just afterwards ignore a forest track off right to carry straight on east-of-North. Stay on the main track ignoring tracks off right. Eventually, when close to the road, a track is met. Turn right for a few yards to meet a B-road (482 777) (4.1m).

2: Turn left along the B-road. Ignore the lane off right on a sharp left bend but 230 yds later at the next left bend, take a path off right signed to 'Nookgate' (476 785). In the field of rough ground entered, follow the right fence until it turns right when continue straight on in the same direction along an old boundary line. At the summit, turn half-left to a visible gate. Through, go a quarter-left to a left fence with a wood beyond the fence. The right of way follows the left fence down, but is so wet that stiles are provided to do some of this on the other side of the fence. After the path crosses back to the correct side of the fence, follow the left fence down to a wall gap and then follow a left wall veering right to a gate onto a lane. Turn left for a few yards to a T-junction at Nookgate (465 791) (5.6m). Turn right on a lane which goes north-northeastwards past tiny Stonegarthside and Bushfield. Continue beyond, crossing an unnamed sike on a hairpin bend (477 814) and later Coldwell Sike (480 816), then pass some housing originally connected with a now disused quarry. After these buildings at Quarry Field, turn off left on a path signed to 'Kershopefoot' (479 819) (7.8m) where the permissive route is taken to avoid wet feet.

3: Take the track and descend to a gate. Through, cross the marsh overflow and ascend on the track to a stile on the right into a field. Go half right to a kissing gate in the diagonal opposite corner. Beyond, go half-right to a stile at the end of a wood and then a quarter-right, aiming for the left of a house, to reach a stile. Then go a quarter-right to a stile near the bottom right corner. Over, go straight ahead for a few yards to a stile on the left. Curve round the edge of a tipping hole to meet a path and turn left to meet the unsurfaced disused railway track, then turn right to a lane (475 829) (8.5m) at Kershopefoot. A sign welcoming you to the Scottish Borders is just to the right and worthy of a picture. Take the unsurfaced track opposite marked 'Reivers Trail' to follow the disused railway line which ran through Newcastleton and on to Hawick. Just follow the track which eventually curves left to meet a lane at Mangerton Farm (480 856) (10.3m). Turn right to a lane T-junction and turn left here. The road curves left to cross Liddel Water on Holm Bridge and immediately after, turn right on a riverside path. The path becomes a road by the river. Continue by the river, until turning left after No. 13 (XIII) up George Street, to the entry on the right into a children's play area and recreation ground. Cross this half-right to emerge on Union Street and follow this to the left to reach the B-road through Newcastleton. Turn right and shortly reach Douglas Square in the centre of Newcastleton (483 875) (11.9m).

Stage 40
Newcastleton to Hawick

VIA: Hermitage Water and disused railway line
DISTANCE: 20.3m [609.5m]
ASCENT: 1830ft   DESCENT: 1800ft
EXPLORER: 324 (Liddesdale), 331 (Teviotdale South)
LANDRANGER: 79 (Hawick & Eskdale)

I had read that parts of the disused railway line between Newcastleton and Hawick could be walked and this seemed to be the most feasible route between these two towns. Not only was it a viable route, but it turned out to be a magnificent walk amidst beautiful surrounds, with the railway mostly a lovely grassy track overlooking a valley to the east, with hills beyond and overlooked by hills to the west. So although it's a high mileage stage, it's easy walking with no navigational problems; you can therefore expect to make good time into Hawick. On the day we walked, because it was another blisteringly hot cloudless day, we set off very early to benefit from the lower temperatures at the start of the day.

The old railway line can be picked up from the north end of Newcastleton and followed to where the railway reached Hermitage Viaduct across Hermitage Water. Alas, the viaduct has been removed, so it's necessary to take to the road to Hawick which follows Hermitage Water. Further along the road at Hermitage, there's a craft centre (refreshments) but then it's a case of continuing on this very quiet B-road until the old railway can be accessed at Whitrope Heritage Centre. The signed route does not immediately follow the actual line of the railway as Whitrope Tunnel is closed, and an alternative track over the tunnel has been constructed for walkers and cyclists. The track descends to join the disused line and proceeds through forest to the valley carrying the Lang Burn and the road to Hawick. The railway then runs parallel to the road and the burn until Shankend Viaduct is reached. This viaduct is still standing, although there are notices saying that one crosses it at one's own risk, and an alternative path has been provided. We crossed at our own risk, as you do if you opt for the viaduct.

Beyond, the disused line and road part as the railway follows Stilrig Burn. The road and railway come closer after Stobs Castle is passed. Shortly after, just before Barns Viaduct, the line comes to an abrupt end and field paths can then be taken to Acreknowe. We had hoped to rejoin the line here, but building work prevented further progress along the line. We therefore took to the road for a mile to get to the hamlet of Flex where a path can be taken to the southern outskirts of Hawick. It's then a good half mile to Hawick's centre. Hawick is a fair sized town and as one would imagine, has a range of shops and accommodation. It's a good place to stock up as the next place with shops is two days away.

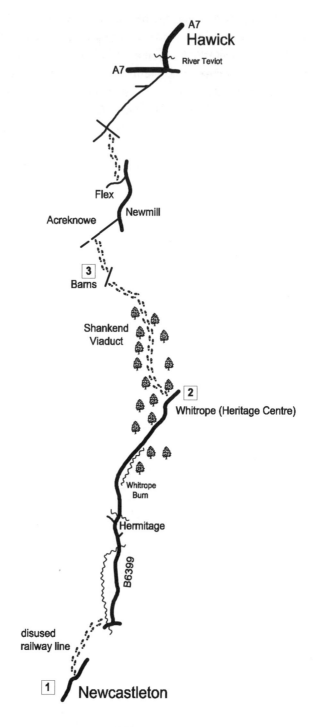

1: From Douglas Square in Newcastleton (NY 483 875) follow the B-road, north towards Hawick, to the north end of the town. Just beyond the last building on the right, cross Black Burn by a bridge and then branch half-left onto the old railway track. Follow the track to meet a farm road (to Roan Farm) (490 891). Cross opposite left and follow a wide access track. After the last house, cross a wooden barrier and continue on a trodden grassy path. Continue over the next wooden barrier, following the top of an embankment, until it starts to descend. Take the left of two paths and descend a quarter-left to an unfenced part of the farm access road to Redheugh. Turn right to shortly reach the B-road (495 896). Turn left and almost immediately cross Hermitage Water then reach a road fork. Here, go left on the B-road signed for 'Hawick' which follows Hermitage Water. Ignore a lane off right (507 942) (4.9m) and continue to the hamlet of Hermitage, where a lane off left is ignored (508 952) (5.6m); the craft centre is on the corner. Beyond, continue on the B-road crossing Hermitage Water by a graceful stone bridge. The road now parts from Hermitage Water, returning shortly to be beside its feeder burn, Whitrope Burn. Continue on the road which accompanies Whitrope Burn northwards and eventually pass under the disused railway line (NT 525 000) (9m); note the change from the NY square to NT. After a further third of a mile, turn left off the road at a Whitrope Heritage Centre notice by some re-laid track.

2: Cross the railway line and continue for a short distance on the gravel track turning off right at a signpost to 'Path to Summit & Tunnel Shafts'. Follow the excellent track which has been created over the Whitrope Tunnel, and then descends to meet a forest road which is followed to the right. Continue on, there is the odd sign to Hawick along the way. Ignore a forest road off right (528 035) (11.5m) and shortly afterwards, when the forest road curves left, go straight on through two walkers' gates and back onto a farmer's track at Langburnshiels. Continue on, pass a signal box then go through the grounds of a house. A signed diversion to going over the Shankend Viaduct is signed off half-right along its access drive. However, to cross the viaduct (522 059) (13.3m), take the grassy track left of straight ahead which leads onto the wide grassy track over the viaduct, with railings on both sides and a disclaimer from the railway company. Both routes meet up beyond the viaduct and the route continues uneventfully along the old railway track. After passing Stobs Castle, the track bends left to a gate into a field. Follow the track towards a ruined shed and then as it curves right gently ascending to a gate. Through, continue on the track which eventually curves left to a lane at Barns (504 096) (16.3m).

3: Turn right on the lane, cross a cattle grid and continue down the lane to cross under Barns Viaduct. Immediately after, turn left on a track looking for a gate with a walkers' gate on the other side of a viaduct arch. Take this and follow a line of telegraph poles until a farm track is met. Turn right on this, meet a track and turn right to double gates. Through, turn right on the track which quickly becomes a lane leading down to the B-road at Acreknowe (507 108) (17.3m). Turn left for just over a mile then turn left up the lane to Flex (504 124) (18.4m). Ascend, crossing over the disused railway and shortly after, at a waymark post on the left, turn right on a wide farm track (502 123). Follow waymarks left which direct walkers onto another farm track. Follow the ascending track through a long field to a kissing gate. In the next field, with Hawick now in view, follow the left fence to a walkers' gate. The path ahead passes along the right edge of woodland, eventually becoming a lane, which is followed down to a mini-roundabout (495 135) (19.5m) at the south-west end of Hawick. Turn right along Rosebank Road and after a third of a mile it joins the Loan. Proceed up the Loan to the road junction at the end of Drumlanrig Square and take the 'No Entry' road opposite, named Howegate. Howegate leads to a T-junction where the stage finishes (502 144) (20.3m). The end-to-end route continues left but for Hawick's High Street, turn right and immediately left.

Stage 41
Hawick to Yarrowford

VIA: Borders Abbeys Way and Yarrow Water
DISTANCE: 13.8m [623.3m]
ASCENT: 1720ft   DESCENT: 1520ft
EXPLORER: 331 (Teviotdale South), 338 (Galashiels, Selkirk & Melrose)
LANDRANGER: 79 (Hawick & Eskdale), 73 (Galashiels & Ettrick Forest)

This is an excellent day's walking. The Borders Abbeys Way (BAW) connects the abbeys of Kelso, Jedburgh, Melrose and Dryburgh. Between Jedburgh and Melrose, the route passes through Hawick and Selkirk. Thus, in moving north from Hawick, this trail was the natural choice. We set off early on what promised to be another blisteringly hot day once the early morning mist had cleared. Once out of Hawick, we found the route well marked and easy to follow. After passing through the Stirches area on the outskirts of Hawick, it ascends Drinkstone Hill and then passes through an area of forest before descending to cross Ale Water at Salenside. A convoluted, but signed route, across Woll Golf Course leads onto a lovely grass track labelled the Thief Road on the map and this meets a lane at Wollrig. Quiet lane walking follows until Hartwoodmyres Forest is entered, and beyond the path gently descends to Middlestead Farm.

The BAW turns eastwards here towards Selkirk while the end-to-end route turns westwards to reach a footbridge across Ettrick Water. Soon afterwards, a B-road is crossed at Gillkeeket to reach a good track named the Buccleuch County Ride. These are tracks provided by the Buccleuch Estate, principally for walkers and horse riders. The track is followed north-west and joins an estate road to North Lodge. Here, the estate road emerges on the main A708 road, which runs along Yarrow Water and then Ettrick Water, to Selkirk 5 miles away. The only accommodation nearby is Broadmeadows Youth Hostel which in 1931 was the first Scottish hostel to be opened. Nowadays, opening is limited to the summer and for this reason, the 0.4 mile to the hostel from the main road is not included in the mileage above. We had a very happy stay at the hostel, but be aware that you need to carry in all the food you need. If the hostel is closed, the nearest place with accommodation is Selkirk.

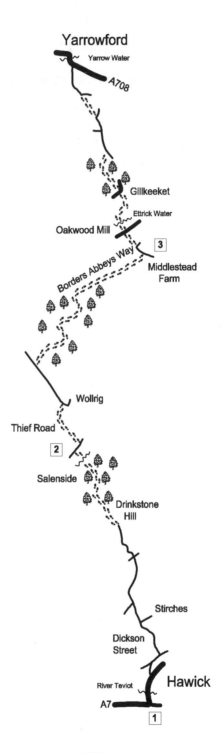

Yarrowford

Yarrow Water

A708

Gillkeeket

Ettrick Water

Oakwood Mill

3

Borders Abbeys Way

Middlestead
Farm

Wollrig

Thief Road

2

Salenside

Drinkstone
Hill

Stirches

Dickson
Street

River Teviot

A7

Hawick

1

1: From the T-junction at the end of Howegate (NT 502 144), turn left briefly to a roundabout with the A7 and branch right, signed Edinburgh. Cross the River Teviot and almost immediately turn off left onto Albert Road, signed for the Museum & Park. Follow this road for over a third of a mile as it curves right and ascends, then take the road off left, Dickson Street, to join the BAW; there's a BAW sign attached to the other side of a lamp post at this turn off. Dickson Street becomes Stirches Road and this is followed to the suburb of Stirches on the edge of Hawick. Continue to follow the ascending lane beyond Stirches, keeping to the 'major' road to reach a lane cross-road (494 175) (2.2m) and go straight across here. Near the entrance to Drinkstone Farm (492 180) on the left, the way continues as a track (unsurfaced). Continue to a track branch and fork left as directed (490 182). Follow the track as it turns half-right (as signed) to ascend round Drinkstone Hill. The track becomes a lovely grassy path continuing along the hillside to a gate. Through, the path continues along the left fence, still ascending, to a walkers' gate. Follow the direction sign and aim across the large field half-right to the near wood corner to find a gate left of the bottom right field corner. When the track enters the wood, follow the sign for the track ahead. Proceed along a good track with the trees well back so as not to be oppressive. On coming to a forest road (474 199) (4.4m), continue straight ahead close to the right edge of the forest. When the forestry road bends left, go straight on through a signed walkers' gate. The forest is left at a walkers' gate. Beyond, follow the left edge to a walkers' gate and turn right as directed. Go straight on (right) when a forestry road is met, pass Salenside, cross Ale Water on a bridge and very shortly afterwards meet a lane (464 211) (5.4m).

2: Turn right briefly and then go left over a stile. Follow the left edge to a ladder stile into Woll Golf Course. Go a quarter-left to a waymark, then left, then right at the next waymark to cross water and then immediately right. Go left at the next waymark to cross a fairway to the opposite side of the golf course. Turn left on a grassy track along the right fence of the golf course until it turns right, when go straight ahead (across the green) to reach and follow a right wall. When the wall ends, go straight ahead to a waymark and another right wall, which is followed to a ladder stile with a gate into a wood at the end of the golf course. The lovely grassy track that follows is the Thief Road. Follow this through the wood to a stile, then go half-right to a farm track and left on this. When the track turns right past houses, go straight on along a right fence curving right to a gate onto a farm track. Turn right and shortly meet a lane at Wollrig (454 226) (6.6m). Turn left along the lane for 1.3 miles turning off right at a BAW sign (439 239) (8m) onto a wide descending forest track. Keep on the main track (as directed) until a track fork signed left. Take this, cross a stream and almost immediately branch right at a BAW sign onto a grassy track. Turn right shortly (as signed) down a left fence and cross two stiles onto a farm track which is followed to the right, down through the farmyard of Middlestead farm (ignore a track off right), and out onto a lane (453 265) (10.2m).

3: Turn left signed Buccleuch County Ride, leaving the BAW. When the lane bends right, go straight on along an unsurfaced track which meets a B-road (444 267). Turn left briefly then turn off right at a sign to 'Gillkeeket'. Go straight down through the farmyard and curve right to a waymarked walkers' gate. Follow the enclosed grass track to a walkers' gate, cross a stile on the left and follow the path to a suspension bridge across Ettrick Water (442 269). Across, turn right on a grassy path along a left fence and when a farm road is met, turn left following it to a B-road at Gillkeeket (440 271) (11.2m). Go straight across on a short track which ascends to a track T-junction. Turn right on a delightful forest track which is part of the Buccleuch County Ride. At a cross-track, go straight on and keep straight on at other junctions. Ignore a purple sign left and go straight on past housing to the left. The track becomes a lane and at a T-junction, turn right for a few yards then left, to shortly meet a surfaced estate road (429 282). Turn left here on the lane for two thirds of a mile, ignoring a surfaced turn off left opposite a house (423 288), but shortly afterwards leaving the lane for a wide unsurfaced track left into woods (422 289) (13m). Follow the track to re-meet the (surfaced) lane and follow the lane to the left to exit at North Lodge onto the A-road along Yarrowford (414 299) (13.7m). Turn left and immediately cross over Yarrow Water that marks the end of the stage (413 300). Due to the limited time Broadmeadows is open, the 0.4 mile to the Youth Hostel is not included in the stage mileage. To reach the hostel from the stage end, immediately turn right off the main road, follow the road up for a short distance then turn right (just before the 'Broadmeadows House' sign) on a path signed 'Footpath to Hostel' and follow the path up to reach the hostel garden.

Stage 42
Yarrowford to Peebles

VIA: Minchmoor Road, Traquair and Kailzie Hill
DISTANCE: 15.8m [639.1m]
ASCENT: 2710ft   DESCENT: 2730ft
EXPLORER: 338 (Galashiels, Selkirk & Melrose), 337 (Peebles & Innerleithen)
LANDRANGER: 73 (Galashiels & Ettrick Forest)

This is a marvellous trek, with the old drove route of Minchmoor Road used, to meet the Southern Upland Way (SUW) national trail on Hare Law. From here, the SUW is taken along the ridge and down into the small village of Traquair. The direct route into Peebles is along the B-road but it looks deadly boring, so the SUW continues to be followed until the lane off to Glen House. The lane continues as a track to Birks cottage and beyond, the track gently ascends to contour Birks Hill. Only part of this track is shown on the map although it appears to be a well-used and established path. Eventually it reaches a bridle gate below Birkscairn Hill, and this gives access to the old drove road over Kailzie Hill into Peebles. From the bridle gate, Peebles can be seen in the distance but it is actually quite a tidy walk in. The drove route into the outskirts of the town is very well-walked and signed; it is an excellent ridge walk which gradually descends into Peebles. After a short stretch of road, Victoria Park can be used to reach the River Tweed and the town centre.

It was a hot day again when we did this route, but we set off very early so as to ascend the wonderful grassy track of Minchmoor Road before the heat got unbearable. We met a couple of people on the SUW section, but saw far more on the drove route into Peebles, including a Duke of Edinburgh expedition group sagging under the weight of their rucksacks! By the time we got to Peebles, the heat was bouncing off the tarmac and we were glad to retreat into one of the many cafes. Peebles is beautifully situated around the River Tweed and has the advantage of nice riverside walks. The town was very busy and we enjoyed listening to a piper, in traditional dress, playing a bagpipe on the steps of the Old Parish Church. Peebles has the appearance and feel of a prosperous town, and is quite a contrast to Hawick which appears more subdued. There is plenty of available accommodation and eating places in Peebles although we were fortunate in being hosted by friends.

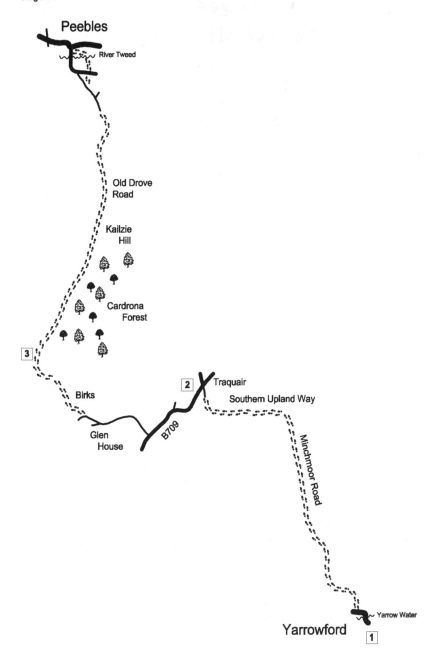

Peebles

River Tweed

Old Drove
Road

Kailzie
Hill

Cardrona
Forest

3

Birks

2 Traquair

Southern Upland Way

Glen
House

B709

Minchmoor Road

Yarrow Water

Yarrowford

1

1: The stage commences from the main A708 road on the north side of Yarrow Water (NT 413 300). Turn west along the main road for 0.4m, passing a turn off for vehicular access to the Youth Hostel, and take the next turn off right in tiny Yarrowford village (407 300) signed to 'Innerleithan via Minchmoor Road'. Pass the bright red village hall and go straight ahead into the forest, but soon turn right onto a forest track as the lane swings left. Almost immediately go left up wooden steps and then take the main track ahead; occasional Minchmoor signs can be spotted. The track soon runs alongside a left wall and comes to a waymarked gate. Through, turn left beside a left wall, with forest beyond it, and go straight on through a waymarked gate, still beside a left fence/wall with the wood beyond to another gate. Beyond, follow an enclosed track which shortly turns right (beside the left wall) to a walkers' gate. Through, go right as directed on a clear track. This splendid track continues through a waymarked gate alongside a broken down right wall, which it soon leaves to gently ascend the hillside above the treeline and eventually reaches the ridge, where it meets the excellently signed SUW national trail (379 328) (3.1m). Turn left along the SUW. The track down is well-walked and signed. The SUW crosses a forest road and later, at a path junction just after the Cheese Well spring, go straight on as directed. Look out for a pattern of large rings cut in the ground on the right; these are actually ovals but appear circular when viewed from the path. Cross another two forestry roads and then a bothy on the left on the descent from the ridge. On leaving the forest, an enclosed track is entered and is followed down to meet a B-road in Traquair (331 347) (6.6m).

2: Turn left along the B709 road for nearly a mile, then leave the SUW by taking the lane off right signed as a 'No Through Road' to Glen House and Estate (322 336). Follow the lane for just over a mile to the entrance to Glen House (306 336) (8.5m) and keep right here to stay on the lane. Beyond, at a Private No Through Road notice, turn right on an unsurfaced track signed to Peebles. Continue to a track fork and go straight on through a gate and turn left to follow the track to Birks up on the hillside. Pass to the left of Birks (295 338) (9.5m) on its access track and beyond, follow the grassy track beside a right wall. Go through a gate and very shortly after the track curves left away from the wall. Follow the track uphill, then continue on the track as it turns right to steeply ascend to the col; this highly visible track can be spotted by looking half-right when turning away from the right wall after Birks. At the col a wood is met (288 344) and here continue on the track following the waymark. This track, not shown on maps, ascends and then contours around the north side of Birks Hill eventually descending to a wood corner (278 341). Continue to follow the track which crosses a burn and carries on to reach a bridle gate (274 343) (11.1m).

3: Pass through and immediately meet the drove route down into Peebles. Turn right along the drove route, which is a clear track along the right fence with forest to the right. At the end of the forest, the path leaves the fence and curves left passing the west side of Kailzie Hill's summit. Beyond, a wide enclosed track is traversed which eventually reaches a gate. Here go straight on as signed along a right wall so as to go round the hill rather than over its top. Go through more gates, as met, following the obvious track down and eventually cross a stream (263 390) (14.5m). Beyond, follow the main track, curving right to ascend onto a good track which is followed ahead and becomes Glen Road on the outskirts of Peebles. Follow Glen Road past a Spar shop and shortly afterwards, just after passing the Tennis Club pavilion, turn right into Victoria Park on a tarmac path. Shortly take the first tarmac turn off left and on leaving the backs of houses, follow the path a quarter-left across the park to emerge on Kingsmeadow Road. Cross and go straight ahead a few yards, to cross the elegant walkers' footbridge over the River Tweed (254 402). Over, turn left on a tarmac path to a path fork. The end to end route continues straight on beside the Tweed to the road bridge (251 403) (15.8m), but for the centre of the town take the path half-right, cross a lane and ascend School Brae to meet Peebles main shopping street, with the Tourist Information Centre just to the right.

Stage 43
Peebles to Carlops

VIA:	**Drove route to West Linton and a Roman Road**
DISTANCE:	**15.7m [654.8m]**
ASCENT:	**2070ft** **DESCENT:** **1680ft**
EXPLORER:	**337 (Peebles), 336 (Biggar), 344 (Pentland Hills)**
LANDRANGER:	**73 (Galashiels & Ettrick Forest), 72 (Upper Clyde Valley)**

This is another very good day's walking, with the well-signed drove route to West Linton taken, followed by tracks to the stage end at Carlops. From Peebles, the route ascends to pass round Hamilton Hill and on past the farms of Nether Stewarton and the ruins of Upper Stewarton into the Cloich Forest. After traversing the forest, the route takes to the open hillside as it follows the Fingland Burn, before leaving it to go westwards and descend to near Romannobridge. Getting into West Linton is not straightforward if roads are to be avoided. The route taken here is to take a track towards Halmyre and then after a section of road, take a path following Lyne Water into the attractive small town of West Linton.

There are eating places and accommodation in the town. Again, it was a blisteringly hot day when we arrived and it was a relief to get out of the sun. Each significant town in the border area of Scotland has, from the early sixteenth century, run an annual Common Riding where the bounds of the town are ridden on horseback. On the day we were in West Linton, the junior ridings for children were taking place in a field just outside the town, involving races and games on horseback rather than the full riding of the bounds. However, the seriousness with which the training of these younger riders is regarded, can be gauged by the fact that after the games these riders paraded through the town behind a small pipe band in traditional dress and many visitors were there to watch. Whilst we were looking at this spectacle, we met another lady who was walking from Land's End to John O'Groats. However she had a husband in a camper van trailing behind to supply morning coffee, lunch, afternoon tea and to sort out somewhere to stay. I don't know how many miles she had walked, but he had covered 4,000 miles already in his van! On learning that she was planning to take to the A9 further north, we thought that there was little chance of us meeting up again.

When the day had cooled off slightly, we set off for Carlops, taking the Woodland Trust's path called the Catwalk (which is not as scary as its name suggests). Beyond a good track is joined. This is initially along the course of a Roman Road, but later is just a farm track which leads directly down into Carlops. Although only a small village, Carlops is on a main road and is only 15 miles from Edinburgh, so it has both an eating place and accommodation.

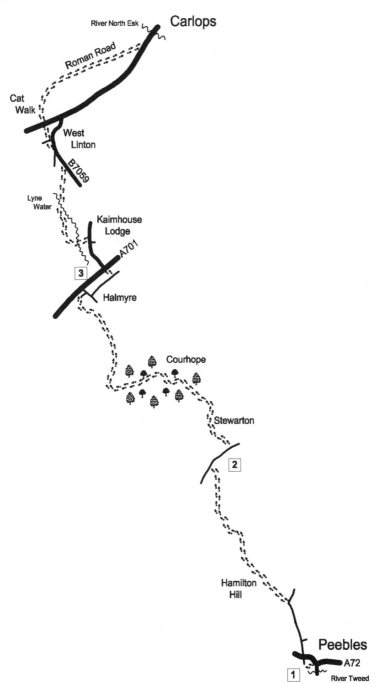

1: From the riverside path under Peebles road bridge (NT 251 403) continue westwards along the north side of the River Tweed for a short distance. At the far end of the car park (where you only have to pay on a Saturday) turn right and exit through the car park to ascend a short side street to the main road. Cross the main road to the street opposite (signed Rosetta) and ascend Young Street; ignore turn-offs left and right to keep straight on along this road. Eventually the edge of the town is reached and a speed derestriction sign is passed. Beyond, continue to a double bend sign and leave the lane at the right bend (244 146) (0.9m) to go straight on along an ascending gravel track, signed to the 'Meldons'. Follow the good track which beyond a farm is between walls, although these are sometimes hidden by foliage; there's a noticeable gradient. On reaching the hillside, the gradient lessens as the track contours round Hamilton Hill, keeping close to the right wall. The track continues with the right wall descending to a footbridge over a stream, then ascends on a between-fences path to a bridle gate. Beyond, the path continues between walls and then curves right. There's some rough walking which can be avoided by taking to a path the other side of the right wall. After a short distance, a bridle gate is reached. The path then turns left to follow a left wall up a field to a farm access drive from Upper Kidston. Turn right, signed 'West Linton' and follow the access drive out to meet a lane (225 448) (3.5m). Turn right for 530 yds and take the next track off left to Stewarton Farm (signed) (227 452).

2: Follow the access drive for over half a mile to a cross-track (220 455) and turn right as directed. Follow the track past the side of the house on the corner and after 400 yds, turn left at a sign. Pass through a gate and follow the track along the left wall to Upper Stewarton. Keep left of the ruin and pass through a gate. Beyond, go just left of straight ahead through a field to a bridle gate (216 461) (5m) onto a clear ascending path through forest. The path eventually drops to a forest track, turn right briefly as signed to meet a forest road and turn left as directed along a large clearing (with a house in the middle). Just before the forest road turns sharp left, turn off right as signed on a good descending path to a footbridge over a burn. Beyond, the path follows the burn to a bridle gate and then continues along a trodden path along the hillside to meet a track. Turn left here to a cross-track (by a seat) and go straight on as signed along a clear track. Ford a stream and continue on the obvious track ascending towards a small belt of wood. A gate gives access to a path through the wood (180 475) (8m) which gently ascends before beginning to descend. Beyond the wood, the clear track joins a more major track and descends to a cross-track. Go straight on along a lovely grassy path which emerges onto a lane. Immediately turn right through a bridle gate and follow the left field edge through a bridle gate onto a lane. Go straight on along Halmyre Loan to meet a lane (169 488) (9.3m). Turn right for 150 yds, then take the first left and follow this to the first track off left which shortly reaches the main A701 road (173 491).

3: Cross the A-road to the B-road opposite, signed to 'West Linton'. After two thirds of a mile, turn left on a track immediately after Kaimhouse Lodge on the left (165 499) (10.5m). On shortly meeting a track, turn right over a bridge to cross Lyne Water and then turn immediately right on a track. On reaching a track junction go half-right (north-west) towards Waulkmill. When the gravel track swings right into Waulkmill, go straight on. After the wood ends, turn right and follow the trodden path down to the west bank of Lyne Water. Lyne Water is followed to the left to reach a stone bridge (just beyond a water pipe). Cross and turn left over a footbridge following a well trodden path, which shortly leaves Lyne Water to follow a side burn, and then meet the B-road (156 509). Turn left for over half a mile and immediately after passing The Old Toll Tea House on the left, turn half-left into a park and follow its right edge to a lane. Turn right (past toilets) to re-meet the B-road and turn left for a short distance through this small town. Turn left into Upper Green and after a few yards enter a grassy area. Turn right up a tarmac path to steps up to the main A702 road (12.5m). Turn right for a few yards and then take the footpath off left signed for 'Carlops via Cat Walk & Roman Road'. After ascending steeply on wooden steps, the path contours in woodland above Lyne Water and is followed to meet a wide unsurfaced track (142 527) which is the Roman Road. Turn right and follow the track north-northeastwards, ignoring turn-offs left and right. Eventually, the track reaches Windy Gowl Farm and its access drive, north-eastwards is taken to reach the main A702 just south of Carlops (160 554) (15.2m). Turn left and follow the main road into the village centre where the River North Esk crosses the main road (161 562) (15.7m).

Stage 44
Carlops to Kirkliston

VIA: Pentland Hills, Ratho and disused railway line
DISTANCE: 15.7m [670.5m]
ASCENT: 940ft   DESCENT: 1890ft
EXPLORER: 344 (Pentland Hills), 350 (Edinburgh)
LANDRANGER: 65 (Falkirk & Linlithgow)

This is a day of contrasts, with the first half in moorland, as the Pentland Hills are crossed at a major crossing point called the Bore Stane. The second half of the walk threads its way northwards along the flat western edge of Edinburgh, ending a couple of miles (as the crow flies) south of the Forth Bridge. From Carlops, a footpath along a burn leads to Fairliehope farm. We had expected the path to be well-walked but this was not the case. However, from the farm there's a good track towards the North Esk Reservoir. Paths then take over with the path following the line of a burn from the reservoir to reach a col. A fairly unimpressive set of rocks named the Bore Stane marks the top of the pass, although they are to the left of the path and we didn't spot them! The path continues beyond, soon becoming a track descending past the entrance to Listonshiels Farm and through a narrow plantation to a lane. Lanes are then taken to the A70 and after a short section on this, a path round Kaimes Hill leads to the outskirts of Kirknewton village. A quiet lane and path are used to reach the village of Linburn on the main A71 road. Many of the buildings in the village are connected with the Scottish War Blinded institution which has been providing help for blind members of the armed forces since 1915.

There's now over 1.5 miles of road walking (sorry!) to the International Climbing Arena where you can get a lunch in a café and there is also entertainment since it overlooks climbing walls, with a Great Ape circuit above these, just under the roof. On the day we walked, it was again another scorching day and we were desperate to escape the heat, so we spent a long time at the climbing arena. The arena lies on the Union Canal and this is taken to Ratho. The village of Ratho Station, a good mile from Ratho, is the next objective and from there there's a short stretch beside the A8 road before a disused railway line is taken northwards; the solitude as soon as you get on

248

the line is in marked contrast to the busyness of the main road. There's B&B accommodation just beyond Kirkliston, but it's necessary to either eat in Kirkliston (limited!) or at the Bridge Inn in Ratho. On the day we were there, there was a nose to tail queue of traffic on the minor road outside the B&B due to a spillage closing the Forth Bridge. Suddenly we saw a car-size gap in the queue, occupied by a family of swans keeping pace with the crawling cars. There was dad manfully strutting out in the front, mum dutifully following behind and behind them there were five chicks, who must have been only a couple of days old, struggling to keep up. Fortunately dad decided he'd had enough of the traffic jam and soon lurched leftwards with his family onto a path to the disused railway line!

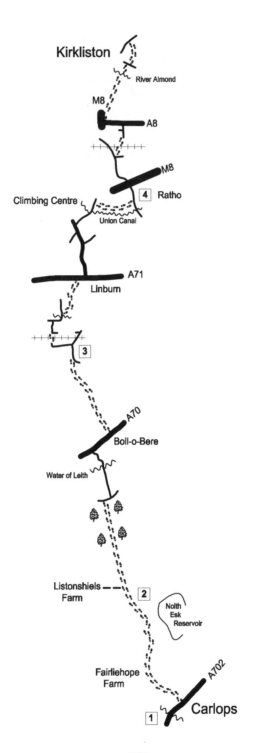

1: From the main road on the south side of the River North Esk (NT 161 562) take the track signed 'Buteland by the Borestane'; it is just before the last house on the left. Soon, cross a stream into Midlothian and then immediately turn right on a waymarked path through a kissing gate. On reaching a walkers' gate, go half-right beyond on a 'path' which follows above the line of the stream; this is rough walking at times. Keep going until a small metal plank bridge is spotted across the stream (157 565). Cross, ascend the field entered half-right and then contour to a kissing gate between the right fence and the stream below on the left. Beyond, follow a trodden path to a kissing gate onto a farm track. Turn right on an excellent track which keeps left of Fairliehope Farm. Beyond the farm, the track goes northwards and is followed to a sign 'Buteland'. Leave the track by going a quarter left through a gate. Continue a quarter left until a wood is seen ahead, when aim for its right side (152 582). Cross a gate or stile to reach the wood edge (1.7m) and then go half-left to a sign and join a track coming in from the left; the easier but slightly longer alternative is to ignore the sign off to Buteland in order to stay on the track to the cottages at the south-west end of the North Esk Reservoir. Then take the path up the west side of the reservoir which becomes the track joined. The track goes northwards to meet and follow a right wall to a gate. Beyond, go half-right uphill to a waymark post. The clear path then contours the hillside to a ladder stile. Continue on the path to the col summit at around 1316ft (144 598) (2.8m).

2: From the summit, go ahead on the path to shortly meet a track. Turn right and continue on the track for three quarters of a mile to meet a track (140 611) and turn left (right goes to King's Hill). Continue on to meet the access drive from Listonshiels Farm (136 621) (4.4m) and follow this to the right. It continues down through a narrow belt of trees to meet a lane (133 642). Turn right for 280 yds and then take the first lane off left (5.9m) and follow Haughhead Road down to the main A70 road (130 655). Turn right for 520 yds and then turn left at Boll-o-Bere house (immediately before the house and just before a bus stop) (7m). Pass down its drive to a gate straight ahead and onto an enclosed farm track. Pass through a gate and a gate shortly ahead and turn half-left along a ditch (with a sewage works on the left). The path soon crosses the ditch and turns left along a left hedge. When the path gets to a wood, continue along its left boundary to a stile and gate. Beyond, the path becomes a good farm track. Ignore a track off left and carry straight on until a cottage is reached on a right bend (123 668). Opposite to the cottage, go left on a very short track to a stile. Take the gravel track beyond to meet a track and turn right. Follow the track to a padlocked exit gate and use a walkers' gate on the right into a garden. Through, turn left briefly to another walkers' gate on the left and rejoin the track, now an access drive, which is followed to shortly meet a lane (123 672); alternatively at the cottage, continue on the track to meet the lane at (123 671). Turn left on the lane and take the first turn off left signed for 'Kirknewton' (8.2m).

3: Just after the 30 mph sign, turn right on a surfaced track which leads to a footbridge over the busy main line railway to Edinburgh. Beyond, follow the track to meet a lane and turn left. Keep with the main lane which passes Humbie Farm and swings right and then shortly after left. Descend to cross a burn and look for a gap in the wall on the right, almost immediately after, so as to take a well trodden path along the burn. When a tall wall on the left is spotted, leave the burn and join a track up the left side of the wall (away from the burn). At the top join a track which passes a row of garages ahead left and follow the track out onto the main A71 road (120 685) (9.6m). Turn right briefly to the road junction in Linburn and turn left on a pavemented B-road signed to the 'Climbing Arena'. As the B-road ascends, there's a view of the Forth Railway Bridge and the stanchions of the Road Bridge, an early objective of the following stage. Turn right off the B-road, when the Climbing Arena is signed, and follow its access road which crosses the Union Canal and then turns right into its car park. At the far end of the car park, branch left for the arena building but branch right and turn right down wooden steps for the Union Canal. Turn left on the towpath for three-quarters of a mile, leaving the canal just before the next bridge onto a pavemented road at Ratho (139 709).

4: The Bridge Inn is just over the bridge on the right but the stage turns left. Ignore a turn-off right and follow the road over the M8 motorway. Continue, pass the entrance to the Norton House Hotel on the right and take the next right into Harvest Wynd. Almost immediately turn off left on a tarmac path, which almost at once crosses the railway on a footbridge and descends into Station Road. Follow Station Road to the A8 (passing a small supermarket). Take the footbridge over the A8 (just to the right) and having crossed turn right, westwards, and follow the pavement for nearly half a mile to a footbridge over the M8 but don't take it (126 727). Instead continue on the pavement which goes *under* the footbridge ramp and becomes a path along a disused railway line. Just follow the line northwards. It crosses the River Almond (126 743) and shortly beyond it meets a lane; Kirkliston village is to the left. The disused line continues opposite as a tarmac path which crosses an estate road and continues straight ahead on a residential road. At its end, go round a barrier and back onto the railway line track. On shortly reaching a bridge, go straight on (left) signed for the Forth Bridge. Come off the line just before the next bridge, turning left at the top of the steps to very shortly meet a road with a B&B at Almondhill Cottages opposite (131 749) (15.7m).

Stage 45
Kirkliston to Carnock

VIA: Forth Bridge, Pittencrieff Park and disused railway line
DISTANCE: 14.5m [685m]
ASCENT: 1200ft   DESCENT: 1000ft
EXPLORER: 350 (Edinburgh), 367 (Dunfermline)
LANDRANGER: 65 (Falkirk & Linlithgow)

Today's stage continues the crossing of the highly populated area that stretches between Glasgow and Edinburgh, named the Central Belt. The highlight of the day is definitely the crossing of the Firth of Forth on the Forth Road Bridge, which is reached quite speedily by using the available cycle paths. The cycle route to the bridge is well-signed. The bridge is busy but has a dedicated lane for walkers and cyclists and on a clear day gives good views, particularly of the more impressive scenery ahead. On the day we walked, the weather had turned and it was cool and misty − after the roasting we experienced over the previous days, this turn in the weather was greeted with great happiness! Beyond the bridge, the route skirts round to the west of Rosyth. There is large road construction activity in this area due to the building of a new bridge across the Forth to run alongside the existing bridge. This may involve changes to the road layout, so you should note that the description here relates to the state at the end of May 2012. North of Rosyth, Grange Road is followed into attractive Pittencrieff Park, on the western outskirts of Dunfermline and beyond, a disused railway line is taken to Carnock village where there is both a B&B and a village pub that serves food.

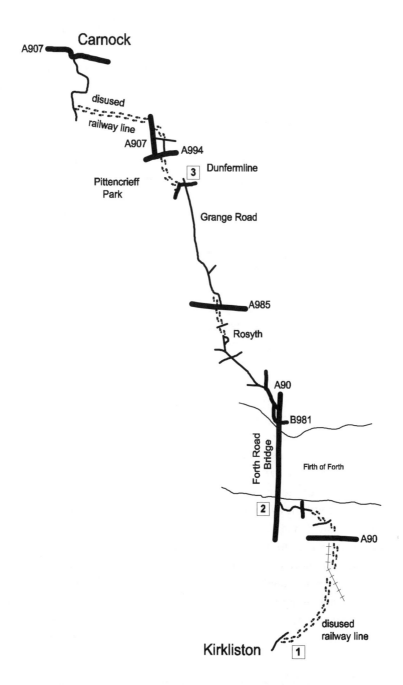

1: From Almondhill Cottages (NT 131 749), rejoin the disused railway line turning left to follow it towards the Forth Bridge. Follow the main track for nearly one and a half miles to a path fork off left (143 765) which is taken; the main track continues to shortly exit onto Standingstane Road. The path taken shortly reaches a cleared gravelly area. Cross this to the back left corner to pick up a gravel path. When this shortly ends, turn right under a railway bridge of a still operating railway and immediately turn left up wooden steps to a northwards path beside the railway line. When the path meets a tarmac track, go straight on (left) alongside the railway, soon passing under the A90 and then shortly after this take a ramp up onto Main Street (142 773) (2m); this lane carries Sustrans Cycle Route 1. Turn left, signed for 'Dunfermline', and after 340 yds turn right on a tarmac track at the Cycle Route 1 sign (139 772). Follow the cycle track to emerge on a road. Go left for a short distance, then turn off right (by a bus stop) as directed onto a tarmac cycle track. Shortly turn right as signed up the side of a school playing field to emerge in the school car park. Turn right to the road at the car park entrance. Turn right briefly to meet Rosebery Avenue. Turn left for a third of a mile to meet Kirkliston Road (129 779) (3m) and take the road opposite right (Viewforth Place). When Viewforth Place meets a road, take the road opposite right, following Hugh Russell Place until it curves right, when go straight on along a tarmac cycle track. Turn left as directed on a service road passing a car park entry and exit, then turn right on a tarmac track to very shortly reach the Forth Bridge Road. Turn right to cross the bridge which is now toll free for users.

2: Cross the Forth Bridge on its east side, admiring the expansive views with the railway bridge close by on the right. At the north end of the Bridge (5.2m), by the plaque commemorating the opening of the Bridge, turn right down steps to the road below, turn right, pass under the bridge and continue to a roundabout. Turn left signed for 'Rosyth & Rosyth Europarc'. At the next roundabout, go left again for the 'Rosyth Europarc' and then take the first road off right signed 'Local Traffic' (120 818), following this for over three quarters of a mile to a roundabout (109 826) (7m); fortunately there's a pavement all the way from the Bridge. Take the second exit (clockwise) into Hilton Road, which quickly curves left, and after 130 yds take the first right into Brankholme Lane. Turn left on a tarmac track immediately after No. 27, shortly cross a road and continue on a surfaced track. When the tarmac turns left, go straight on along a path and onto a tarmac pavement, left of railings, to meet a road. Go left briefly to find a gravel path on the right leading shortly to the main A985 road (104 836). Cross over onto a surfaced track opposite and follow this to meet a road. Turn left, shortly cross a ditch and enter a field on the right, and use it to keep parallel to and off the road which has no pavement. When the road can no longer be avoided, keep going north-northwest along this 'major' road, ignoring turn offs left and right. As the south-western corner of Dunfermline is approached, a pavement appears. Pass under a railway line and continue north-northwest to traffic lights at a cross-roads (092 869) (10.1m).

3: Turn left and when the road shortly bends left, go straight ahead through park gates into Pittencrieff Park (091 869). Follow the surfaced track to shortly reach a track T-junction. Go left and follow the track as it curves right. Go straight across at a cross-track and at the next two cross-tracks, so passing to the right of the Glen Pavilion. Continue just west-of-North, ignoring turn-offs, to exit the park onto the main A994 road (086 875). Go opposite right into Maitland Street and take the fourth road off left (Golfdrum St). Proceed down the street for 240 yds then take a tarmac path off right signed to 'Oakley'. Take the upper path, which quickly turns left, and follow it to the main A907 road running along the western edge of Dunfermline. Turn right for a short distance, to a cycle trail sign on the left, of a bicycle within a yellow diamond (081 881) (11.3m). Follow the short access road indicated into a car park, with a gate at the far end giving access to a surfaced track along a disused railway line. This is the disused railway line from Dunfermline to Alloa, now a multi-user route, which we observed to be well-used, particularly by cyclists. This excellent track is followed westwards for nearly two and a half miles. When power lines on the right come close and parallel to the railway line, leave the line just beyond the next bridge (043 883) (13.7m), by taking an exit left onto a lane. Turn left and follow the lane to the A907 road in the centre of Carnock village (043 890) (14.5m).

Stage 46
Carnock to Dollar

VIA: Steelend, Balgonar and Vicar's Bridge
DISTANCE: 12.5m [697.5m]
ASCENT: 1100ft DESCENT: 1280ft
EXPLORER: 367 (Dunfermline), 366 (Stirling & Ochil Hills W)
LANDRANGER: 65 (Falkirk & Linlithgow), 58 (Perth & Alloa)

This can be regarded as an interlude stage to reach Dollar. From here, a sequence of drove routes, old military roads and hill tracks can be taken northwards, up the middle of Scotland, to reach as far north as Oykel Bridge in Sutherland. This stage to Dollar uses available tracks and paths but road walking is necessary to link them. The first objective is the small village of Steelend which is reached from the farm access drive to Rhynd Farm. Steelend is just east of the large village of Saline and the now closed store adds to its general run-down air. A path contouring Saline Hill passes Killernie Farm and continues to Balgonar Bridge. Quiet lane walking westwards follows, until a good track north-of-East leads to Barnhill Farm's access drive. This and a lane are then followed to the main road at Whitegates. From here a path, track and lane lead down to Vicar's Bridge over the River Devon, and shortly afterwards farm tracks and field paths can be taken to the centre of Dollar.

Dollar is a pleasant town with streets down each side of the Dollar Burn. The town has shops, a tea room, Post Office, accommodation and eating places. Dollar marks the end of the low-lying section. The Ochil Hills rise up behind the town and are the first serious hills seen and undertaken since the Pentland Hills.

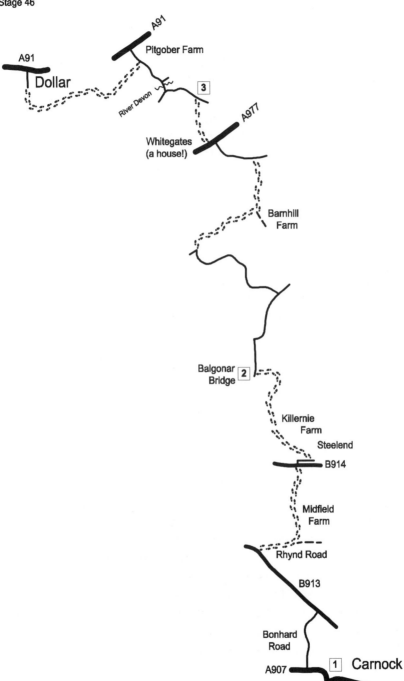

1: From the main road in Carnock (NT 043 890), follow the main road left for a quarter mile and turn off right onto Bonhard Road which is followed for half a mile to meet a B-road. Turn left for three quarters of a mile and then take a wide gravel track off right with a footpath sign to 'Saline' (035 911) (1.5m); the track (Rhynd Road) is immediately before the imposing turn-off right to Bandrum Children's Home. The track runs eastwards towards Rhynd Farm. However, turn first left off this after 390 yds to take the unsurfaced access track north through Midfield farm. At the farm, keep between the house on the right and a farm building on the left and carry straight on along an enclosed track. At its end, the track curves left round the edge of a wood following its left boundary and beyond, continues along a left boundary into an enclosed track leading down to a B-road at Steelend (039 922) (2.6m). Go straight across on Midfield Terrace turning right at the T-junction. Go right here, pass the houses and then what was the Steelend Stores. Turn left down a grassy track along the side of the stores, curving left round the back of the houses, diverging right to cross a ditch to the right fence and follow this leftwards to a kissing gate. Through, continue along the right fence to join a farm track. Pass ruins, follow the right edge and later pass the ruins of a castle. The track swings right to pass Killernie Farm. The farm's access track turns left (030 928), but continue straight ahead along the right boundaries of four fields to a wood. Again, keep with the right wall here and in the subsequent two fields, with the wall curving right, to emerge on a dirt track (028 937). Turn left to meet a minor road from Saline (4.6m).

2: Turn right, cross Balgonar Bridge, ignore a left turn off to Milton Farm and continue to follow the road to the next turn off left signed for 'Rivendell Kennel & Cattery' (024 949) (5.4m). Follow this twisting lane as it goes westwards, northwards and then westwards again, passing to the left of Rivendell. After Rivendell, the road bends right to go northwards again and when the road next bends left, leave it to go right through a bridle gate (000 955) (7.3m). Follow the excellent unsurfaced track and ignore a bridleway track signed off left for 'Rowmill Road'. Keep on the main track to meet a farm access road (011 963); Barnhill Farm is to the right. Turn left on the unsurfaced access drive. Ignore a track off right through a gate at what is labelled as Pitfar Farm on the map; Pitfar seems to have been knocked down and is being rebuilt. Continue on to meet a lane and turn left to the main A977 road (NS 997 973) (9.5m). Turn left for a short distance, then turn right into the drive of

Whitegates and follow its right boundary to go through a farm gate. Using a broken down right wall as a guide, follow this for about a quarter mile over uneven ground, to get to a good cart track leading to a (difficult) gate onto a lane (995 979) (10m).

3: Turn left for over half a mile to a T-junction and turn right, descending to shortly cross the River Devon by Vicar's Bridge (986 980) (10.6m). Over the bridge ignore a turn off right and follow the lane to Pitgober Farm on the left. Here, take a path off left signed to 'Dollar' (979 982). Follow the unsurfaced track which passes left of Pitgober House and pass through a gate/kissing gate onto an enclosed grass track that continues ahead alongside a right fence. Go through the gate to Linnbank Farm and curve right (as signed) to Westerton Farm. At Westerton, go left through a bridle gate into a field keeping to left edges, south-of-West, until a track is met. Go straight ahead (left) for a short distance to a walkers' gate off right which shortly meets a dirt track. Turn left for a short distance, then branch off right on a path to the right of a burn. The path becomes a street leading northwards alongside Dollar Burn into the small town of Dollar, reaching its centre when the main A91 road is met (963 980) (12.5m).

Stage 47
Dollar to Auchterarder

VIA: Drove routes to and from Glendevon
DISTANCE: 11.8m [709.3m]
ASCENT: 2020ft   DESCENT: 1880ft
EXPLORER: 366 (Stirling & Ochil Hills W), 368 (Crieff)
LANDRANGER: 58 (Perth & Alloa)

This is a splendid day's walking across the Ochil Hills. It starts with the ascent up through the National Trust for Scotland grounds of Dollar Glen. This is a delightful walk up the glen besides the tumbling Dollar Burn. Imposing Castle Campbell (now a hotel) is at the top of the glen with the Dollar Burn's feeders, wonderfully named the Burn of Sorrow and the Burn of Care, on either side of the castle. The drove route beyond follows the line of the Burn of Care northwards on a clear and well walked path to Glenquey Reservoir. After passing up the west side of the reservoir, the path contours Glenquey Hill before descending to the hamlet of Burnfoot. From there it's a short distance to a footbridge across the River Devon and the main road in Glendevon. There's a hotel here just to the right and we sought out morning coffee there after a rainy morning. They are obviously used to wet walkers and we were made to feel most welcome.

The next part of the drove route is a wonderful grassy track which follows Borland Glen northwards. It's a clear track which is followed to where the public road begins at Coulshill Farm. The lane is followed until a track off through Cloan Glen can be taken; this rejoins the lane further on. As the A9 main road is approached, the lane is left for the entry into Auchterarder from a pedestrian underpass of the main road. Auchterarder is a busy town used to tourists, as the famous Gleneagles golf course is nearby. As would be expected, it has shops, tea rooms, accommodation and eating places. We were unfortunate in our choice of accommodation as the ambience factor was minus 5 and suffice it to say that my companion got a worse breakfast the next morning than the caged bird situated in the eating room; not surprisingly, it does not feature in the accommodation listings!

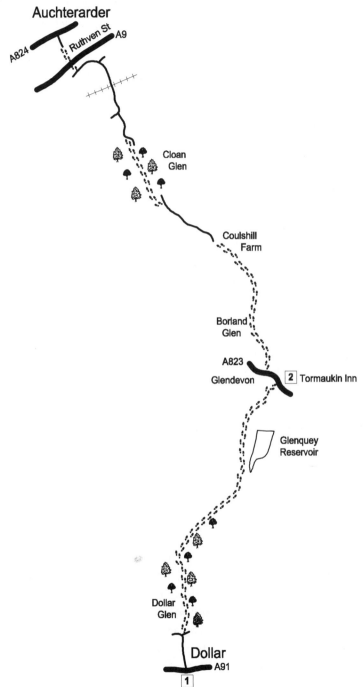

1: From the main road in Dollar (NS 963 980) take the road opposite, proceeding up East Burnside, still in the company of Dollar Burn, to a T-junction and take the signed path opposite. Follow the main path up through Dollar Glen, keeping to the right of the burn. The path eventually crosses the burn and climbs steeply via steps to Castle Campbell's access road; the fifteenth century castle is just to the left. Turn right on the access road and descend to cross a burn and ascend to a house (963 994) (1m). Here turn off left on a track by the house signed to 'Glen Devon'. Follow the good ascending track which enters a felled area of woodland. When a junction is reached go straight across, as waymarked, on a still ascending path. Follow the path to an exit from the wood and beyond the path is clear as it passes along the wood boundary. The path continues passing left of Glenquey Reservoir where it becomes a track. Beyond the end of the reservoir (3.6m), go straight on at a sign to the A823 road and shortly after go over a stile. Immediately after, turn left over a stile to leave the track and turn right along a right fence, following a grassy track which leads into a wood. In the wood, follow the grass track to a path junction and go right, signed 'A823'. Go straight ahead to a walkers' gate and descend the hillside towards the houses of Burnfoot to join a lane. Follow the lane right to shortly cross a bridge, then turn left on a path signed to the 'A823' and 'Auchterarder'. Follow the path to a stylish metal bridge over the River Devon and beyond follow the path out on to the A823 at Glendevon (NN 991 045) (5m).

2: The Tormaukin Inn is a short distance to the right, but the route turns left for 220 yds and then turns off right at the Auchterarder path sign (990 046). Go through a gate and follow the track to Glenfoot Farm. Here, go through the gate to the right of the garage (signed). Beyond, follow the track in the field which turns left then right, along a ditch, then joins a track along the right wall to a gate. Through, join a good track which is followed to the right. Go through a gate to continue on the track. The grass track gradually ascends, gently curving left to go round the hill on the left and reaches a col at 1,436 ft which is marked by a stile (988 074) (6.9m). Continue beyond on the grass track; there's a wind farm on the left with not a single blade turning when we passed – what a joy to be subsidising such an unproductive eyesore! The grassy track starts gently descending, meeting and following above a burn. The track crosses the burn, when opposite a wood on the left, and continues through awkward gates to become a lane at Coulshill Farm (979 092) (8.3m). Follow the lane for two-thirds of a mile to the start of a wood and take an unsurfaced track off left (973 101). Follow the attractive woodland track which follows to the right of Cloan Burn along Cloan Glen; where the burn crosses the track in quick succession, a path to the right is provided. When the track rejoins the lane (961 116) (10.2m), turn left and shortly cross the burn. Beyond, ignoring turn offs, reach a T-junction and turn right signed 'Auchterarder'. Pass under a railway bridge and continue to where the lane curves right (954 125), when go straight on along a 'No Through Road' (signed as 'Path to Auchterarder'). After 340 yds turn right on a surfaced underpass of the A9 main road. Beyond, turn left on a surfaced path which soon reaches the end of Ruthven Street. Turn right on this to reach Auchterarder's High Street, which is also the A824 road (and much quieter than the A9). Turn left briefly to be in the town centre (945 128) (11.8m).

Stage 48
Auchterarder to Crieff

VIA:	**Tullibardine and River Earn**
DISTANCE:	**12.1m [721.4m]**
ASCENT:	**530ft** **DESCENT:** **610ft**
EXPLORER:	**368 (Crieff)**
LANDRANGER:	**58 (Perth & Alloa)**

This stage is fairly low level as it crosses the farmland of Strathearn to reach Crieff. From Auchterarder, a track, minor roads and the disused railway line to Crieff are used to reach the hamlet of Tullibardine. From here, estate roads crossing the Strathallan Estate are used. These give a good view of its castle and emerge on a lane after passing a Parachute Club. Farm access tracks and lanes are then taken to the access drive to Strageath Hall, where a promoted and signed walking route from Muthill village to Crieff is joined; it may be 'promoted' but we found it a tad overgrown and rough walking in places. The route picks up the disused railway line to Crieff following it to the River Earn where the railway bridge has been removed. So the route into Crieff then follows the River Earn to Stuart Crystal just south of Crieff, which has a good coffee shop. After briefly taking to the main road, so as to cross the Earn on Crieff Bridge, a track and path along the west side of Crieff are taken to arrive close to the centre of this very pleasant, large town. Crieff has all the facilities that are associated with a town of this size. You should stock up here as it's two days to the next facilities at Kenmore and three days to those at Kinloch Rannoch.

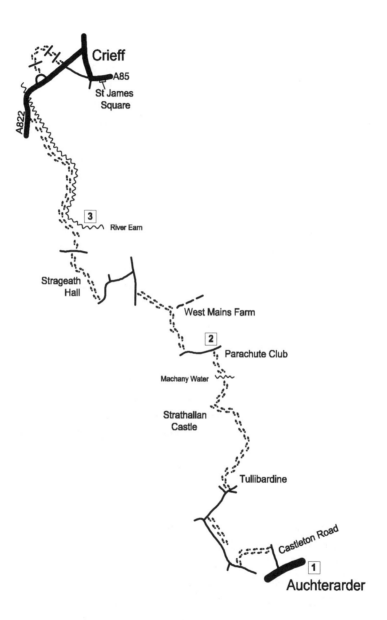

1: From the centre of Auchterarder (NN 945 128), continue left down its High Street and turn right down Castleton Road (941 127). After 350 yds, immediately after passing the last house on the left, take a wide surfaced track off left (940 129) and proceed west-southwest along the edge of the town for half a mile. The track then turns left on an enclosed path which crosses Glenorchil View and continues down to Tullibardine Road (933 124) (1m). Turn right and follow the road to a T-junction. Turn right into Easthill Road. After 680 yds and just past a depot on the right, go through a walkers' gate on the right, as signed, to join the track of the disused railway line from Crieff to Auchterarder. Follow this path which runs parallel to the road on the left. It crosses a farm access drive and continues to meet a road (919 136). Turn right, ignore a road off left signed to 'Muthill', and shortly afterwards reach a road junction in Tullibardine with an access drive off left to Strathallan Castle (925 142) (2.8m). Follow the main drive, going straight across at a cross-track. After passing to the right of a lake, with the castle behind, a track junction is reached (921 157). Turn right, away from the castle, and follow the surfaced track northwards to cross Machany Water. Beyond, continue for 340 yds to a track junction. Ignore the turn off left to keep on the main track, shortly pass the Scottish Parachute Club and continue to very soon meet a lane (918 163) (4.4m).

2: Turn left for a quarter of a mile and then take a dirt track access drive off right (914 163) servicing Whitehills and other farms. Follow the track and on reaching a house, turn left to farm buildings where there's a track T-junction. Turn right away from the farm (i.e. don't go left through the barrier into the farm). The track passes a ruined tower named Duke's Tower in the field on the right before reaching another track T-junction shortly after West Mains farm. Here turn left just after the bungalow (910 172). Ignore a turn off right to Auchinglen Farm in order to carry on westwards. Later, pass Parkhead farm and shortly afterwards reach a lane (895 176) (6.3m). Turn right. After 800 yds, just after the access drive to Strageath Mains, the lane curves sharp left. Continue for another 770 yds to a lane junction where go left signed for 'Muthill'. After 330 yds, at a path signed to 'Crieff', turn off right to Strageath Hall (883 177). Follow the farm access drive and at the house, turn left at a waymark onto a track which crosses a bridge over a stream. Beyond, continue for a short distance to a ruined railway bridge and go right through a signed bridle gate. Follow the sometimes overgrown railway line northwards to the

River Earn (881 187) (8.2m).

3: Turn left and follow the river bank. At a sign to 'Crieff', go right as directed, so avoiding Templemill. Later, after a kissing gate with a plaque about a shepherd's wading poles, keep along the left fence, leaving the river temporarily. Follow the waymarks provided; the path keeps fairly close to the river, although short cutting along the left field edge sometimes. Look for a sign right to a footbridge over a side stream. Eventually, follow a waymark up to a gravel path and follow this to a walkers' gate, where the path goes left through the car park of Stuart Crystal and out onto the main A822 road. Turn right to cross the river on the main road (857 209) (11m). Over the bridge, take the first street off left and follow Earnbank Road to a T-junction at its end. Turn left along a waymarked gravel track (signed 'Town Centre'). The track curves right to run northwards and crosses a lane. Beyond, it continues northwards briefly before curving right and ascending to Sauchie Road. Turn right briefly along Sauchie Road, then turn off left (sign) into Ryan Place, signed as a 'No Through Road', and go straight ahead on a signed footpath which ascends up steps to Carrington Terrace. Go straight across here into Drummawhandie Road which is followed to a cross-road with the main A822 road. Go straight across into Lodge Street and on shortly reaching a cross-road, go straight ahead on the A85 into the centre of Crieff marked by St James Square on the right (864 216) (12.1m).

Stage 49
Crieff to Amulree

VIA: Knock of Crieff, Monzie and Sma' Glen
DISTANCE: 12.6m [734m]
ASCENT: 1880ft   **DESCENT:** 1720ft
EXPLORER: 368 (Crieff), 379 (Dunkeld, Aberfeldy & Glen Almond)
LANDRANGER: 58 (Perth & Alloa), 52 (Pitlochry & Aberfeldy)

There's a definite feeling of entering Central Scotland on leaving Crieff and the principal feature of this particular stage is the walk up Sma' Glen, a narrow glen which the River Almond flows down. General Wade built a military road from Crieff to Aberfeldy which ran along the glen. While some of his route is now coincident with the main road to Aberfeldy, there are some good off-road sections which are used in this stage. To the back of Crieff, a hill called the Knock of Crieff is a local landmark and this is the first objective of the day; it has a panoramic view from the top. We spent quite a long time investigating whether the tiny village of Monzie could be directly reached from the Knock, but a plantation and wiring prevents this. So beyond the Knock, forest tracks are taken to the village of Gilmerton. Lane walking to Monzie follows and then tracks and field paths can be taken to what used to be the Foulford Inn; this was a much-used stop in past times, due to its situation on the Wade military road, and was also used by drovers on their way to the market in Crieff. It has closed its doors to travellers and now offers self-catering accommodation with the use of a golf course thrown in!

The best of the off-road sections of the military road is picked up just beyond the inn. It's a wonderful clear track, high above the main road. Eventually it descends to rejoin the main road which has to be followed to picturesque Newton Bridge. Here, the River Almond turns west and the main road to Aberfeldy continues north. Shortly after the bridge, the road is left for another off-road section of the military road. Again it's a track but boggier than the last section. After the road is briefly rejoined, the road is left just south of Corrymuckloch to follow the Wade road, now a path, to Amulree; annoyingly the exit onto the road on the line of the path is blocked and it's necessary to reach a lane via the village hall.

Amulree is tiny and I had planned to stay at the hotel marked on the map. Alas, the hotel has long closed its doors although you can patronise a new teashop which has opened there. So a pick-up from here is required. If you want the facilities of a town, then Aberfeldy or Crieff are the obvious choices. However, there are a couple of B&Bs in Sma' Glen which are much nearer. The day we did this stage, it was the start of the Jubilee Weekend to mark the Queen's sixty years on the throne. Several people came to join us and also walked some of the stages. During the weekend, we got rather used to people in cars screeching to a halt with offers of drinks and food. This also included our B&B hosts for the following night who we had stayed with on a reccie in the previous year.

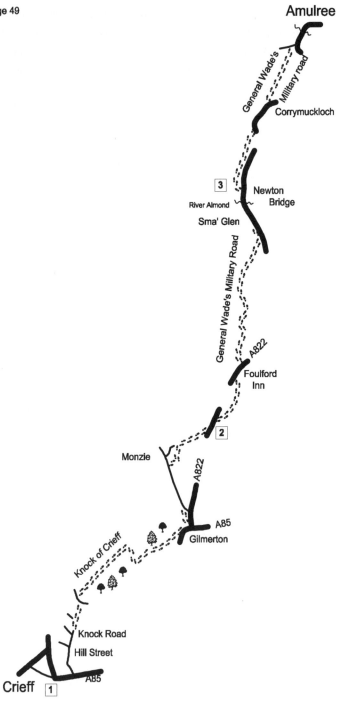

Stage 49

Amulree

General Wade's Military road

Corrymuckloch

3

River Almond

Newton
Bridge

Sma' Glen

General Wade's Military Road

A822

Foulford
Inn

2

A822

Monzie

A85

Gilmerton

Knock of Crieff

Knock Road

Hill Street

Crieff **1**

A85

1: From St James Square in Crieff (NN 864 216), carry on up High Street and take the first street off left, Hill Street and ascend to a road off left. Briefly turn left along Victoria Terrace and then first right into Knock Road, signed to 'The Knock'. The road bends left becoming Drummond Terrace, but go straight on here to stay on Knock Road. At its end the road continues as an excellent track. Continue ascending to a walkers' gate. Pass through and follow the clear path along the right wall. At the field end, pass through a gate into the grounds of Crieff Hydro and up the road to the left to meet a road. Take the signed path opposite, following a wide track, to the viewfinder at the 793 ft summit of the Knock (868 229) (1m). From the viewfinder, continue on the major path away from the summit which descends slightly and ascends to meet a path. Turn right and descend along a left deer fence to a major track. Turn left and follow the track to a sign post off right to 'Gilmerton'. Follow the sign but then go immediately left on a waymarked track along a golf course edge to reach a bridle gate at a path junction. Go left on the track signed for 'Gilmerton' and follow the track to the main A85 road (885 235) (2.5m). Turn left and almost immediately turn left on the main A822 road, signed for 'Dunkeld'. Just after the derestriction sign, turn off left on a track which runs parallel to the A-road and emerges on the lane to Monzie. Turn left and shortly after the Monzie village sign, turn right on a track which curves left behind Monzie's church to meet a lane. Turn right on the lane which soon becomes unsurfaced and follow it north-east to meet the main A822 road (888 259) (4.4m).

2: Go through the gate opposite and follow the track to a farm gate. Pass through, turn left along the left wall and then the left fence to a gate onto a farm track. Turn right on the track, which soon turns left along a right boundary, and follow this until the track enters a field with the Foulford Inn close ahead. Turn half-left and exit onto the A-road via a farm gate. Turn right and just after the inn, turn off left on an access track signed 'Connachan Lodge' (898 268) (5.3m). Follow the track which crosses a burn then curves left and immediately after the bend, turn off right on a grass track which gently ascends the hillside ahead. Follow the track up as it twists left and through a gate to meet a track (with a 'Main Road' sign). Turn right and follow this wonderful track to the main road (904 296) (7.4m). Turn left to follow the main road along Sma' Glen with the River Almond on the right. On approaching Newton Bridge, a popular beauty spot, there is a path with seats overlooking the river and parking for cars. The River Almond is crossed at

Newton Bridge (888 315) (9.1m).

3: Continue on the main road beyond Newton Bridge, pass the double bend sign, follow the road as it bends right then left and just after the left bend, turn off left through a farm gate (889 318) (9.4m). Immediately cross a burn on an old stone bridge and follow the track which soon turns right. The route of the path/track is always obvious although this section of the Wade Military Road is initially boggy. Keep on along the track, which is always fairly close to the road, until a more major track is met. Turn right to shortly reach a gate and rejoin the main road (892 337) (10.7m). Turn left for 680 yds, cross a bridge, and pass through the next gate on the left (892 344). Go half-right aiming for the left side of the trees. Pass through a gate and follow the left fence to a gate. Go through a gate on the left and curve right along a right fence. When the track turns half-left to leave the wall, go straight on in the same direction, keeping left of the farm buildings, to reach the wall visible ahead. Follow to the left of this wall and cross a wire fence to pick up a good path ahead which steadily improves. Just before it meets more fencing, turn left on a track to a gate which leads past Amulree's Village Hall to a lane (898 363) (12.3m). Turn right to shortly meet the main A822 road and turn left for the now defunct Amulree Hotel on the left which makes a good pick-up point (900 367) (12.6m).

Stage 50
Amulree to Keltneyburn

VIA: Glen Quaich and Kenmore
DISTANCE: 15.3m [749.3m]
ASCENT: 1430ft   DESCENT: 1950ft
EXPLORER: 379 (Dunkeld, Aberfeldy & Glen Almond)
LANDRANGER: 52 (Pitlochry & Aberfeldy)

This is a fine walk starting by using a track on the north side of Loch Freuchie. This meets the lane from Amulree to Kenmore after passing Turrerich Farm. The lane can be left at Auchnacloich, for a track along the north side of the River Quaich, before the lane has to be rejoined again. The lane rises steeply to a high point of 1,750 ft and a notice at the Amulree end sums it up by stating that there's no through route to Kenmore in winter conditions. Although this remote lane has to be followed down into Kenmore, the superb views more than compensate for this. Kenmore is a beautifully situated village at the east end of picturesque Loch Tay. The River Tay is crossed at Kenmore and a walk on the north side of the river ensues, with an avenue of ancient trees particularly noteworthy. Thereafter, lanes are taken to cross the River Lyon and reach tiny Keltneyburn which has a couple of B&Bs.

When we walked, we initially tried a track on the south side of the River Tay, intending to cross the river on the bridge labelled Newhall Bridge on the map. The bridge, however, has been washed away leaving practically nothing of the original structure. Furthermore there's obviously no plan to reinstate it. Thus it would be good if the Ordnance Survey removed this non-existent feature from their maps. We then went to use the Chinese Bridge across the Tay shown at the back of Taymouth Castle, but found this closed and under scaffolding. It has been closed for a long time (since 2008) awaiting restoration and the wait goes on! So the River Tay *has* to be crossed in Kenmore to get on the north side of the river. For ourselves, a straightforward day turned out to be very long with a lot of extra mileage.

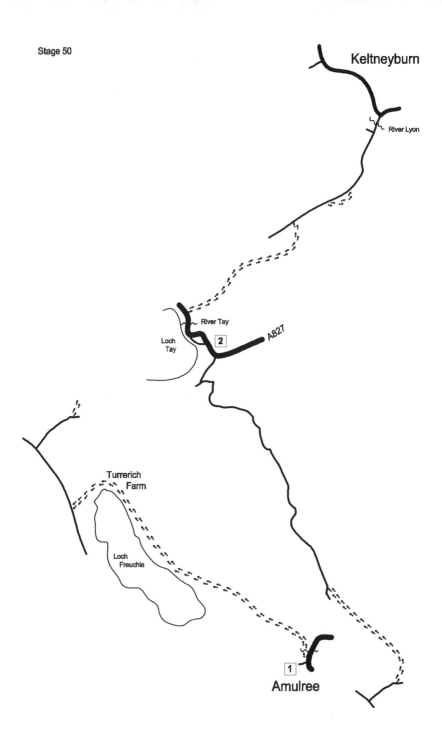

Keltneyburn

River Lyon

River Tay

A827

Loch
Tay

2

Turrerich
Farm

Loch
Freuchie

1

Amulree

1: At the end of the Amulree Hotel (NN 900 367) (and before the new bridge on the main road), turn left over the old bridge and immediately turn left on a (mainly level) unsurfaced access track. Follow this to Wester Kinloch and curve right at the barn to a waymarked gate, with the track continuing as a farm track beyond. Pass ruins and continue on the main track to Turrerich. The track turns left and right here to Turrerich's access drive, which is followed along the edge of Loch Freuchie to the lane from Amulree (852 384) (3.9m). Turn right along the lane for just over three quarters of a mile, turning off right on a lane signed to 'Shian School House' (843 393) which crosses the River Quaich. When the lane turns sharp right after a further 300 yds, carry straight on along an unsurfaced track, signed as footpath to 'Garrow'. Ignore a steep ascending track right and continue on the track to re-meet the lonely lane from Amulree to Kenmore (825 403) (6.4m). Turn right on the lane and ascend steeply to the col at 1,750 ft (808 419) (8m). Beyond, the lane crosses between hills before slowly starting to descend. Approaching Kenmore, the lane descends steeply on zigzags to meet a lane. Turn right briefly to the main A827 road at the east end of Loch Tay (775 452) (11.5m).

2: Turn left along the loch shoreline or the pavement and take the first lane off left, which follows the shoreline round to re-meet the A-road. Turn left over the bridge crossing the River Tay and immediately take the path off right signed to 'Comrie Bridge'. Keep to the main, very good track, which passes through a lovely avenue of trees. Turn left to a lane at a 'Drummond Hills' path sign (782 468) (13.1m) and turn right on the lane for half a mile. Turn right at a 'Riverside Path to Kenmore' sign and almost immediately left on a path which runs parallel with the lane. When this ends, take to the lane again following it to the right. Ignore a lane off left to Duneaves, cross the River Lyon on Comrie Bridge and almost immediately meet a B-road (786 487) (14.7m). Turn left for 0.6 mile to the road junction at Keltneyburn (778 492) (15.3m).

Stage 51
Keltneyburn to Kinloch Rannoch

VIA: Fortingall, Glenmore Bothy and Tempar Burn
DISTANCE: 13.7m [763m]
ASCENT: 2600ft   DESCENT: 2270ft
EXPLORER: 386 (Pitlochry), 378 (Ben Lawers & Glen Lyon)
LANDRANGER: 51 (Loch Tay)

This is a good day's walking. The small, pretty village of Fortingall is reached by a minor road which passes a church with an ancient yew tree reputed to be the oldest in Britain; its exact age is not known but is estimated to be 5,000 years old. From Fortingall, a good hill track, rising to 2,300 ft, over to Glenmore Bothy in Gleann Mor is taken. From the track there are excellent views of mighty Schiehallion (3,520 ft) to the right across the glen. Beyond the bothy, two burns needs to be forded; at the time we walked, water levels were low and these presented no problem. From here until a bothy is located at the start of the Tempar Burn path just over a mile away, there is no distinct path; this came as a surprise as the route over to Kinloch Rannoch is well known. This is the first of two occasions on the entire route when you need to go 'cross country'. The bothy you need to find blends so well into the scenery that it is hard to spot. So the verbal description given is aided by GPS readings that I took at the time. From the bothy there is a good path which becomes a good track. The track reaches a lane which is followed to Kinloch Rannoch on the east side of Loch Rannoch. This touristy village has a small supermarket, tea shop and hotel accommodation.

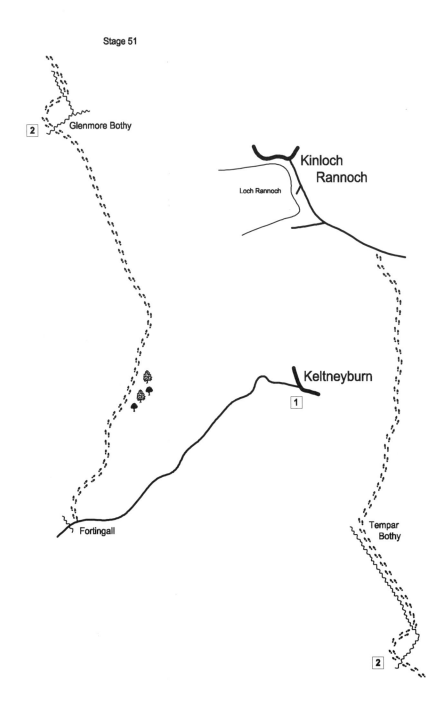

Glenmore Bothy

2

Kinloch
Rannoch

Loch Rannoch

Keltneyburn

1

Fortingall

Tempar
Bothy

2

1: From the road junction in Keltneyburn (NN 778 492), turn left on the minor road signed 'Fortingall'. In the village, pass the church with its yew tree and the hotel. Continue along the road but don't cross the burn, instead turn right on a track signed 'Balnald' (737 470) (3.1m). Follow the gravel track between buildings and continue on an ascending farm track to a T-junction (with a Lyon Estate notice). Turn right and follow the twisting wide track up, cross a cattle grid and continue to ascend (with a large wood on the right). Keep on the main track, go through a big deer gate (with a Lyon Estate notice) and continue ascending on the track. When clear of the wood, the track turns half-left (745 488) (4.6m) to ascend round Meall Crumach and eventually reaches a summit. Beyond, there's a short descent and ascent before the track descends past Glenmore Bothy (which you can only see by looking backwards) to the Allt Creag a' Mhadaidh (708 531) (8.3m); when the track down hits bog look for the track curving left.

2: Ford the allt where feasible and then follow the bank to the right to a side burn (Allt a' Choire Glais) and follow this to the left until a fording point is spotted; we forded easily just above the waterfall (707 536). Over, turn left and follow the bank for about thirty minutes to NN 69696 54289. Here turn right away from the allt and follow a small side burn north-east, past the ruins of shielings (NN 69686 54390); a shieling is a summer dwelling in the mountains for a shepherd. The course of the side burn leads to the well disguised Tempar Bothy (NN 69852 54543) (9.6m) at a height of around 1,970 ft. Turn left at the bothy onto a good path which soon becomes an excellent track leading down the hillside. The track loosely follows the Tempar Burn and as it descends, there are good views of Dunalastair Water. As the track gets nearer to the valley, the track turns back to the burn and follows it down to a lane (690 575) (11.8m) east of Kinloch Rannoch. Turn left for 1.4 miles to a fork (669 580). Fork right and soon get to a 'Welcome to Kinloch Rannoch' sign. Ignore a lane coming in on the left, cross a bridge, pass a small grocery store and continue to the B-road in Kinloch Rannoch (662 587) (13.7m).

Stage 52
Kinloch Rannoch to Dalwhinnie

VIA: Loch Garry, Dalnaspidal and Pass of Drumochter
DISTANCE: 20.3m [783.3m]
ASCENT: 1550ft   DESCENT: 1040ft
EXPLORER: 386 (Pitlochry), 393 (Ben Alder)
LANDRANGER: 42 (Loch Rannoch)

This is a long day but it's all easy walking and the navigation is straightforward so you can expect to make good time. Furthermore, about five miles into this stage marks the completion of the equivalent of three Pennine Ways – meaning there's only one more to complete. A path round the back of Kinloch Rannoch village leads to the road which closely hugs the north side of Loch Rannoch. This is taken to the start of the hill track northwards at Annat Farm. Once clear of the farm, the track is straightforward and climbs to a height of nearly 1,500 ft as it passes between Gualann Sheilach and Creag a' Mhadaidh before dropping down to the Allt Shallainn. Fortunately, there is a bridge across this fast flowing river. Beyond, vehicle tracks can be followed heading east-of-North which keep above the boggy plain to the right, before dropping down to follow the plain edge and reaching a good track at the south-west end of Loch Garry. On a good visibility day, the traffic that can be seen whizzing past the north end of the loch is on the A9.

The walk along the west side of Loch Garry is easy but unremarkable! Beyond the end of the loch, the track passes the entry to Dalnaspidal Lodge and crosses the railway line to Inverness. The busy A9 road is just ahead, but the walk takes to the off-road cycle route running parallel to the A9. Sometimes the cycle path is some distance from the road and at others it runs close to the A9. On the day we walked, the track was quite busy with cyclists although we saw no walkers. There's about six miles to do on this path and it's definitely not somewhere you will wish to linger. Probably the least lovely thing about this section is the incredible amount of rubbish that people have thrown from their vehicles, displaying a total lack of respect for their surroundings. On the way, there is a tea van in a layby opposite, but he had just packed up by the time we steamed past. The only other thing of note is a sign telling you that you are entering the Highlands of Scotland. I thought we'd already been in the highlands for some days! Just over a mile south of Dalwhinnie, the main road splits and the off-road cycle track terminates on the less major A-road which now needs to be followed into Dalwhinnie village. Dalwhinnie has a railway station and a distillery, but at over a thousand feet it is one of the coldest, least sunny villages in Britain and it certainly has a defeated air about it. The hotel has closed so it's necessary to organise a lift off and we stayed at Laggan although a B&B is passed on the cycle path.

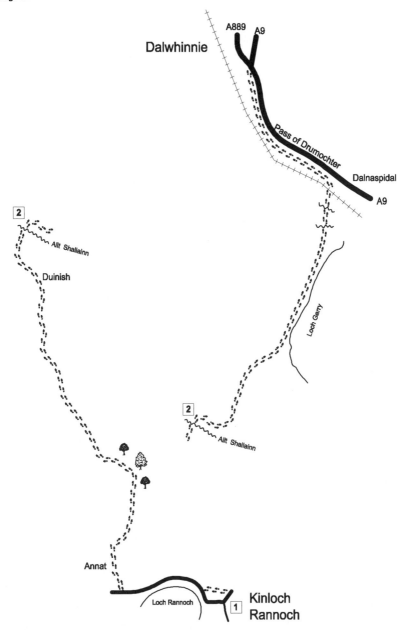

1: Turn right at the B846 road (NN 662 587) in Kinloch Rannoch village and just past the garage on the left, turn left on a track with a 'path to Loch Rannoch' sign. Follow the track through a gate to a path sign. Turn left here and follow an attractive path which keeps close to a left wall out onto the B-road. Turn right along the B-road which follows the north shore of Loch Rannoch. After passing an entry to Leargan on the right, get to an entry to Annat Farmhouse. Continue on the road for a few yards and turn right at a sign to 'Dalnaspidal via Loch Garry' (638 592) (1.7m). After a few yards, when it meets the Annat Farmhouse access track, turn left. At the farm, the track turns right to keep right of the farmhouse (signed). Go through a gate and then turn left beside a right wall. Continue along the right wall beyond a metal deer gate. At the next metal deer gate, don't go through but turn right through an unsigned wooden deer gate onto a between-walls track. This turns left, continuing between walls to a wooden deer gate onto the open hillside. Continue on the track to a track branch and fork right as directed. As a large wood is approached, the track swings left to follow the wood edge; ignore a track coming in on the left to stay with the wood edge. Beyond the wood, continue on the track which turns north-west to meet the more major track coming up from Craiganour Lodge (620 618) (4.3m). Turn right here (waymarked) and just follow the main track. Just before Duinish bothy, the track forks and go left here (right goes to the bothy). The track fords a small burn (a few times) before reaching a bridge across the Allt Shallainn (613 675) (8.4m).

2: Over, continue on the track, go over a plank bridge and ascend. When the track veers left (just after a small mound on the right), turn off right to pick up a quad bike grass track (which starts faintly at first). On the basis that if a quad bike doesn't sink, you won't either, follow this track as it heads eastwards before curving left to run north-northeast. Eventually the track drops to and follows the base of the slope to the left (north-northeast). Finally after fording a burn, the end of the Loch Garry track is reached (623 686) (9.4m). Follow the track along the entire west side of the loch. Beyond, continue to meet a track and turn left towards the A9. Cross the railway on a level crossing, ascend to meet the well signed cycle path (before the A9) and turn left (646 733) (12.8m). Shortly after, turn left at a T-junction and shortly after, keep straight on as signed when there's a farm access off left. Parts of the cycle path run along the old A9 road and are well away from the new main road, while at other times, such as when the Pass of Drumochter approaches, the cycle path is unpleasantly close to the current A9. However, the way ahead is always clear and the cycle path is followed until it meets the main A889 road into Dalwhinnie (639 829) (19.4m). Go left on this, following the road until the lane off left (signed 'Loch Ericht') just after the 40mph sign; this marks the stage end (637 842) (20.3m). Refreshment can be obtained from the garage on the left or at the distillery half a mile down the road. The hotel seems dead.

Stage 53
Dalwhinnie to Garva Bridge

VIA: Loch Ericht, Loch Pattack, Kinloch Laggan and Glen Shirra
DISTANCE: 20.9m [804.2m]
ASCENT: 1560ft   DESCENT: 1790ft
EXPLORER: 393 (Ben Alder), 401 (Loch Laggan)
LANDRANGER: 42 (Loch Rannoch), 35 (Kingussie)

The aim of this stage is to join the Wade military road to Fort Augustus at Garva Bridge. This 25 mile military road comes from Laggan and is a surfaced public road up to and just beyond Garva Bridge. There is parking at Garva Bridge making it a suitable pick-up point and finishing here, 7 miles from Laggan, makes the following stage to Fort Augustus manageable at just over 17 miles.

The original plan for this stage was to have a much shorter route to Garva Bridge by taking a drove route to Feagour from Dalwhinnie. However, a reccie in the previous year had revealed that not only was there no discernible route (and there is a sign to this effect at the start) but that the ground it passes over is just bog-land. This probably accounts for the fact that diagrams of where this route goes differ appreciably and I have viewed three versions! Therefore the stage takes to a longer route, but it's all easy walking on good tracks so you can expect to make good time. It's a lovely walk and because the underfoot conditions are good, there is plenty of time to savour the scenery as you go along. On the day we made excellent time to Garva Bridge, arriving well before the appointed pick-up time to take us to our (excellent) B&B in Laggan.

The route starts south-westwards along delightful Loch Ericht, following its western side until Ben Alder Lodge is reached. A track westwards then leads across to Loch Pattack, where the track turns north. After following the east side of the loch, the track follows the River Pattack north, before leaving it to descend on a forest track to Loch Laggan, and out onto a main road at Kinloch Laggan. This stretch has a number of bridges which carry vehicles but look distinctly dodgy outside the tyre area. So 'Tread on the Nails' became a familiar cry on this and subsequent stages! After a short stretch on the main road, a track off leads into the Cairngorms National Park. Part of this track along Glen Shirra has been 'upgraded' to take the traffic required for the new Beauly to Denny pylons to power the awful windfarms. I think of it as the uglification of Scotland. For the only time on the whole route, we found the access to the track blocked by a high padlocked deer gate which we had to climb over. Beyond, the track along Glen Shirra was straightforward and emerges on the lane from Laggan. The lane is now followed past Garvamore, where there used to be barracks and an inn, and on to Garva Bridge with the national park left just before the bridge.

Garva Bridge

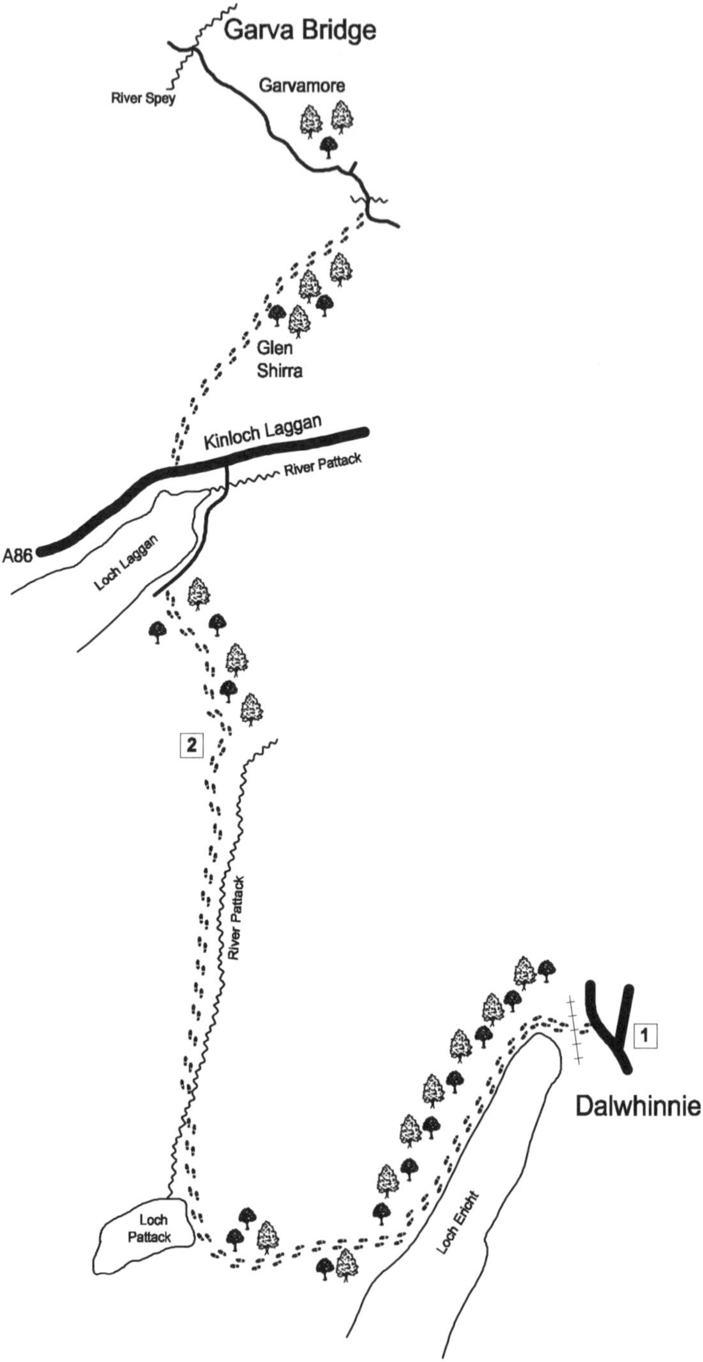

Garvamore

River Spey

Glen
Shirra

Kinloch Laggan

River Pattack

A86

Loch Laggan

2

River Pattack

1

Dalwhinnie

Loch
Pattack

Loch Ericht

1: Take the first track left after the '40 mph' sign for Dalwhinnie (NN 637 842). Pass under the railway line and take the first track right between stone gateposts. Follow this to meet a tarmac track (632 844) (0.5m) and turn left along this private road down the west side of Loch Ericht. After 3.6 miles, there's a short track alternative to the access drive (590 806) (4.1m). Branch left through a gate to follow along the loch side (or remain on the forest road). The track peters out and continues as a path which ascends to meet the upper forest road. Turn left and continue on the main track along the loch. Further on, a track fork is reached at Ben Alder Lodge (575 791) (5.4m). Fork right (path sign) and ascend to a gate with a track junction beyond. Turn right on the major track (do not take the one straight ahead) and follow this major track (initially) south-of-Westwards, ignoring turn offs, as it gradually curves right, round a hill. When Loch Pattack is reached, the main track turns left (545 790) (7.5m) but keep straight on here, northwards, on a grass track which passes to the right of Loch Pattack; in fact the direction is now northwards all the way to the main road at Kinloch Laggan. Beyond Loch Pattack, the track continues on the right side of the River Pattack to a substantial wooden bridge (544 812) (9m). Thereafter, the track stays on the left side of the river. Continue on the delightful track. After waterfalls, ignore a bridge over the river to stay on its left side. Continue on and the track leaves the river temporarily. At the next track branch (546 852) (11.7m), fork right along a wood edge. A side stream is soon crossed on a bridge and soon after this the track returns to the river. Continue to meet a more major forest track (548 865) (12.5m).

2: Here turn left to leave the river and follow the track round the edge of forest before it plunges into the forest, descending to a cross-track. Go straight across and descend to a surfaced estate road (535 889) (14.4m), with Loch Laggan just beyond. Turn right and follow this to an unusual wooden bridge over the River Pattack, then pass a lodge to reach the main A86 road at Kinloch Laggan (539 897) (15.1m). Turn left along the main road for half a mile, and then take an ascending track right (531 897) at a double bend (just before the 'adventure centre'). Ascend to a (padlocked) gate. Go through (or over!) and follow the construction road. When it forks, go straight on (left) on the lower road. When the construction road curves left, go straight on through a gate onto a nice grassy track. Follow this clear track to join another track and follow this to the right to meet General Wade's Military Road from

Laggan to Fort Augustus (553 932) (18.3m); it is a surfaced lane at this point. Turn left, cross the outflow from Loch Crunachdan and follow the lane westwards and north-westwards for just over 2.5 miles to the car park just before Garva Bridge (522 947), where from here a pick-up is required back to civilisation (20.9m).

Stage 54
Garva Bridge to Fort Augustus

VIA: Corrieyairack Pass
DISTANCE: 17.2m [821.4m]
ASCENT: 2200ft   DESCENT: 3110ft
EXPLORER: 401 (Loch Laggan), 400 (Loch Lochy for very small distance)
LANDRANGER: 35 (Kingussie), 34 (Fort Augustus)

Today's stage fulfilled a long held personal ambition to walk the Corrieyairack Pass. The track is straightforward and there are no navigational problems. From Garva Bridge the track remains surfaced until nearly Melgarve; there are views of the River Spey below to the left. From Melgarve there is a road closed sign, but this applies to motorists rather than walkers or cyclists! After Melgarve, the track starts ascending to the east of the Allt Yairack and after crossing it, the route ascends more steeply with the gradient eased by a staircase of zigzags. One can only admire the skill of the military road's positioning as it wends its way through the hills, keeping to the easiest gradients. The zigzags are so well hidden in the hillside that it's difficult to view more than a couple of the bends at any time and between the bends, there are sufficient level sections for horses pulling heavy wagons to stop and rest. A testimony to the brilliance of Wade's route is that this was later to be chosen to be the route for pylons bringing electricity to this area.

It is also the route used by the new Beauly to Denny pylons and there is much evidence of this on the descent, after having reached the summit of over 2,500,ft, which is the highest point on the end-to-end route. The track down has been ripped out and replaced with stones which are (literally) a pain to walk on. You will have plenty of time to contemplate the construction work going on as it's a straightforward but long descent. You may, therefore, find it helps to pass the time by singing the Balfour Beatty song which I have specially composed to commemorate what they are doing. It is to be sung with great feeling and rousingly to the tune Cwm Rhondda. So after three:

Guide me Mr Balfour Beatty
Over General Wade's green roads
Ripped out and full of sharp stones

Enough to make all walkers moan
(Chorus)
Balfour Beatty, Balfour Beatty
Will we ever get them back (get them back)
Will we ever get them back

On the descent, Loch Ness eventually comes into view although it's a long time getting nearer. Eventually, when near to the bottom of the descent, the pylon highway is turned off for a lovely grassy path down to a lane. Ironically, considering what's been done to the track, there's a notice at the bottom saying that the Wade road is a scheduled monument and anyone defacing it is subject to prosecution! It's necessary to follow the lane for a short distance before a track to a burial ground can be taken. Thereafter it's lane and road to reach the canal and the centre of the busy village of Fort Augustus. It is wonderfully situated around the locks of the Caledonian Canal which connect with the west end of Loch Ness. Fort Augustus looks to be thriving. As well as its picturesque situation which attracts a lot of tourists, it is also on the popular Great Glen Way national trail and is a good centre for bike trails. The main industry of the village is clearly tourism. Thus there is much accommodation and places to eat as well as a small supermarket and post office.

Finally you will see that the route goes on to Explorer map 400 (Loch Lochy) for a very small section. This amounts to about half a mile and given that the track is straightforward, in my view you can manage without this map.

Fort Augustus

A82

Loch Ness

2

Corrieyairack Pass
General Wade's Military
Road

Melgarve

1

River Spey

Garva
Bridge

1: From the drop-off point at Garva Bridge (NN 522 947), cross the River Spey and continue westwards on the tarred lane. Just before Melgarve the lane becomes an unsurfaced track. Beyond Melgarve (4m), the track steadily climbs but at a modest gradient following to the right of the Allt Yairack. On the approach to the zigzags, ignore a track branch right going to the right of a pylon. The track steepens when it reaches the zigzag staircase, even though the structure lessens the gradient of over 400 ft of ascent. After the summit of just over 2,500ft (415 986) (7.8m), the track descends to river crossings. Continue on the main track with its modest ups and downs. However, the track steeply descends on zigzags when crossing a side valley to cross a burn at the bottom (NH 369 052) (14m). Beyond, immediately meet a track and turn right, taking the track to the left of a mound. Continue on the major track to a track junction where to the right there's a 'Private, No Entry' notice and straight on through a gate is for construction road traffic. So, turn left here on a well-walked descending path alongside a right wall to meet a lane (373 072) (15.3m).

2: Turn right for just over a quarter mile and then take a track off left, signed 'Cill Chuimein Burial Ground' (377 074). Follow the track to a burial ground. Either use the step stile to enter its grounds, follow parallel to the left wall round two sides, to exit via a walkers' gate onto the end of a surfaced lane, or reach the end of the lane by following the track to the right around the outer perimeter of the burial ground. Follow the lane out to the main A82 road (374 084) (16.4m) on the edge of Fort Augustus and turn right along the A-road. After nearly half a mile, turn left down narrow Lovat Terrace. When it curves left, branch right on a between houses tarmac passage and when it emerges on a road, cross over to the 'No Entry' road beyond, which overlooks the Caledonian Canal. Turn right along the canal to the road bridge over the canal, marking the centre of Fort Augustus and the end of this stage (379 092) (17.2m).

Stage 55
Fort Augustus to Dundreggan

VIA: Wade Military Road and Torgyle Bridge
DISTANCE: 8m [829.4m]
ASCENT: 1360ft DESCENT: 1170ft
EXPLORER: 401 (Loch Laggan), 415 (Glen Affric)
LANDRANGER: 34 (Fort Augustus)

You may think you are very far north once you've reached Fort Augustus and indeed you are, but it's a sobering thought that there's still over 200 miles walking to get to John O'Groats! There's also a walker's dilemma in this and the stages to follow. The accommodation points mean that you either end up with a long walk, often over twenty miles, or have two rather short stages. Thus the choice from Fort Augustus is to either get to Tomich in one stretch, a distance of around twenty miles, or to split it into two short stages as accommodation is available in Dundreggan 8 miles from Fort Augustus. Having had several long stages in the preceding days, we opted for the two short stages, with the added bonus that in getting to Tomich in the following stage, we were able to incorporate a visit to the Plodda Falls which are well worth viewing.

From the Great Glen at Fort Augustus, the route follows Wade's Military Road as it clambers up the Inchnacardoch Forest. Unfortunately it all too soon joins the Pylon Highway and then the two routes are coincident until the Allt Phocaichain. The Wade route strikes off westwards to Glen Moriston after fording the allt, described as difficult when in spate. The e2e stays with the Pylon Highway, which takes a more direct route to Torgyle Bridge in Glen Moriston and has the significant advantage of a bridge across the allt, so diminishing the unwelcome prospect of wet feet; this bridge crossing is not shown on current maps. Torgyle Bridge is one of the few crossing points of the River Moriston. Beyond, there is a choice of accommodation which is remarkable as it's very isolated here. The recommendation is the B&B in Dundreggan, as there is a busy little café on the main road nearby, where you can get an early evening meal.

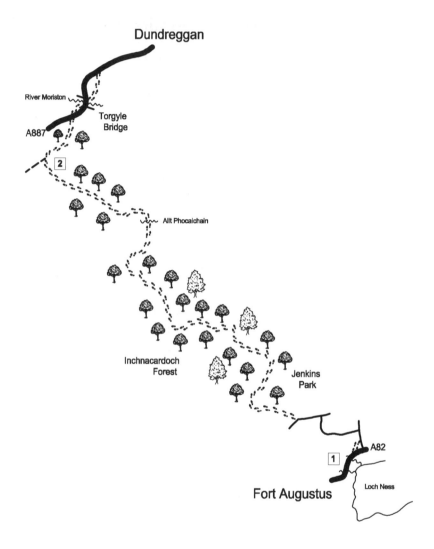

1: From the canal bridge in Fort Augustus (NH 379 092), follow the A82 towards Inverness, crossing the bridges over the canal and the River Oich. Pass the Tourist Information Centre and continue for a short distance to a sign off left for the Great Glen national trail and 'River Oich Forest Walks'. Follow the ascending tarmac path to meet a lane and turn left for a short distance, branching left (and leaving the national trail) on Church Road (just before the village hall). Follow this lane as it curves right to meet a lane. Turn left. When the lane is signed left to Auchterawe, keep straight on (signed 'Military Road'). The road soon becomes an unsurfaced track. Turn off right at a path signed 'Public Path to Glen Moriston by Old Military Road' (369 095) (0.9m). Follow the lovely snaking path which ascends to meet the Pylon Highway and turn right to reach a cross-track (with a bridge over the Allt na Fearna on the left). Go straight across here and follow the 'highway' along and to the right of the allt. The allt is crossed on a bridge (349 102) (2.5m) and the 'highway' then turns left towards the pylons. At the next 'highway' junction, go straight on (ignoring a left fork and a right turn off) slightly ascending. Shortly reach another cross-track and go straight on, eventually dropping to a bridge across the Allt Phocaichain. Continue on the main track, ignoring turn offs right, to reach a 'highway' T-junction (304 121) (6.4m).

2: Turn right and descend following the track out to the A887 road (308 127) (6.9m) in Glen Moriston. Go straight across on a short grass track to a gate. Don't go through but turn right and follow the grassy track along the left fence. When it shortly meets the main road, turn left over Torgyle Bridge and immediately turn off right on a track, which is followed to shortly re-meet the main road (7.3m). Turn right for nearly three-quarters of a mile to a path sign left with 'Public Right of Way to Tomich & Glen Affric'; note that the sign can only be seen in this direction! This is the path taken in the next stage and marks the end of this stage (316 140). However, for the accommodation and Redburn Café at Dundreggan (324 143), it is necessary to continue down the main road for just over half a mile (which is not counted in the stage mileage).

Stage 56
Dundreggan to Tomich

VIA: Drove track to Hilton Lodge and Plodda Falls
DISTANCE: 12.5m [841.9m]
ASCENT: 2120ft   DESCENT: 2140ft
EXPLORER: 415 (Glen Affric)
LANDRANGER: 34 (Fort Augustus), 25 (Glen Carron), 26 (Inverness)

The walk to Tomich is straightforward but not that exciting. The route is signed from the A-road. It ascends pleasantly on a path through woodland but soon joins the Pylon Highway through dour open moorland. The track follows close to the pylon line, ascending quite steeply with good views back to the descent from the Corrieyairack Pass. The track ascends less steeply to pass to the right of Loch na Beinne Baine. Beyond, the track starts descending gently towards forest and the Pylon Highway is departed from with a sigh of relief at a sign to 'Hilton'. Much pleasanter walking follows. Forest is soon entered and when Hilton is reached, there's a choice of proceeding directly to Tomich or indirectly via the Plodda Falls.

The falls are well worth seeing, particularly when in spate, and the diversion does not add significantly to the mileage. Good tracks then lead along Strathglass to the small village of Tomich with its hotel. Cannich, which is a further 4 miles down the valley, is a much larger touristy village, with a lot more facilities and would be a better place for a stage to end. However, it would result in an incredibly short following stage to Struy where there's nothing to do or see. For this reason, Tomich was chosen to end this particular stage.

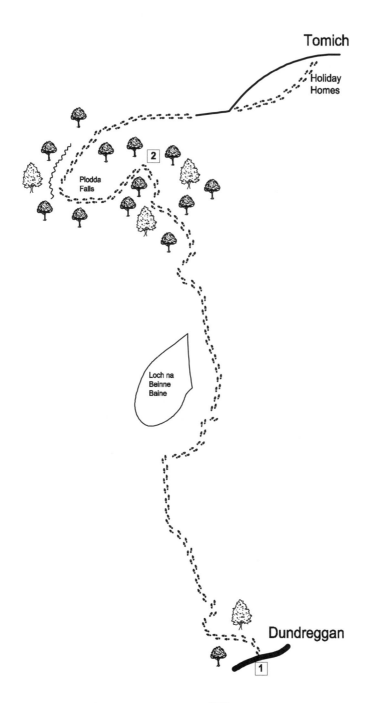

Tomich

Holiday
Homes

Plodda
Falls

2

Loch na
Beinne
Baine

Dundreggan

1

1: From the signed path turn off for 'Tomich' in Glen Moriston (NH 316 140), follow the level path to a wall corner and then follow the left wall (again level) to a path right sign and ascend on a good track. Turn left as directed and all too soon meet the Pylon Highway. Turn right and ascend on this. Ignore a track off left to stay with the main ascending track which stays close to the pylon line. The track ascends less steeply as it follows above the right side of Loch na Beinne Baine (294 193) (4.5m) rising to a height of nearly 1,800 ft. Just follow the main track beyond the loch as it gently descends towards forest. When the main track turns sharp right, go straight on, signed to 'Hilton', towards a forest gate (291 228) (7m). Take the clear track down to meet a track. Turn left and descend to a track T-junction. Turn right as signed and eventually reach a lane near Hilton Lodge (284 244) (8.3m).

2: Tomich can be reached directly by following the lane to the right, but the end-to-end route turns left for Plodda Falls, and follows the ascending lane then forest road, to the car park for the falls. Turn right through the car park and follow the main track until a branch off left, signed 'Plodda Falls 300 metres'. At the (jutting out) viewing platform, turn right and follow the path parallel to and above the allt which eventually descends to an unsurfaced track with the Abhainn Deabhag just beyond (275 240) (9.2m). Turn right and follow the main track, which turns sharp right then left, around the ruins of Guisachan House. Continue along the valley, parallel to but not close to the abhainn, and eventually the track meets a lane (297 259) (11.2m). Turn left for a third of a mile, crossing a burn and soon after passing a large barn on the left. Shortly after, fork half-right on a good unsurfaced track (300 262). Follow the track, ignoring a track off right, to holiday homes where a surfaced track is met. Turn left and descend to a lane in Tomich. Turn right and shortly reach Tomich's hotel and the end of the stage (308 274) (12.5m).

Stage 57
Tomich to Struy

VIA:	Cannich and Strathglass
DISTANCE:	11.2m [853.1m]
ASCENT:	1370ft **DESCENT:** 1500ft
EXPLORER:	415 (Glen Affric), 431 (Strathglass)
LANDRANGER:	26 (Inverness)

This is a leisurely stage following lovely Strathglass. Unfortunately, tracks and paths are thin on the ground but the lanes used are very quiet. The stage crosses to the north side of the River Glass at the first opportunity and the valley lane is followed into Cannich, passing both its small but well-stocked supermarket and a couple of places to get a cup of coffee. Paths by the river lead to the south side of the village where the river is crossed. The glen is now followed on the east side of the river and we saw both red squirrels and wild deer along this section. Close to where the route turns left to recross the river and reach the straggly tiny village of Struy, look out for a memorial stone to a standard bearer at Culloden; he did not return. There are two hotels in Struy, but otherwise no facilities.

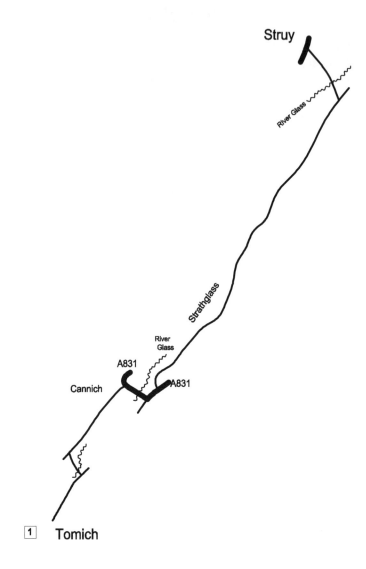

Struy

River Glass

Strathglass

River Glass

A831

Cannich

A831

1 Tomich

1: From Tomich (NH 308 274), continue along the lane to a T-junction (320 294) (1.5m). Turn left over Fasnakyle Bridge crossing the River Glass. Shortly, ignore a 'No Through Road' off left and curve right with the lane, pass a power station and continue on the lane which follows the line of the River Glass. As Cannich is approached, pass a Spar shop on the right. Shortly after, turn right at the traffic lights (3.6m) and almost immediately, turn off left through a gap in a stone wall, and use the path through woodland adjoining the road to avoid some road walking. The path re-meets the road opposite the Bog Cotton Café. Continue down the road, cross the River Glass and when the main road bends left, follow it for 250 yds and then turn off left on a lane signed 'Eskadale' (348 315) (4.4m). Follow this lovely lane for nearly 6.5 miles, then cross a cattle grid and almost immediately pass a house on the left. Immediately after the house, turn off left on a lane (404 396) (10.8m). It soon crosses the River Glass on a weight restricted bridge and continues to a T-junction meeting the A831 (400 400) (11.2m).

Stage 58

Struy to Westermoy

VIA: Hill track to Aultgowrie and quiet lanes
DISTANCE: 15.3m [868.4m]
ASCENT: 1970ft **DESCENT:** 2000ft
EXPLORER: 431 (Strathglass)
LANDRANGER: 26 (Inverness)

This is an excellent hill walk with the added attraction of largely avoiding the Pylon Highway. In fact the pylon construction is left for good early in this stage – yippee! The route taken is the access track to Orrin Reservoir which ascends northwards past Erchless Cottage into and through forest. Beyond, the track continues across open barren hillside to pass east of Loch Ballach, before twisting westwards roughly parallel with the Allt Goibhre below. After the track twists south to cross a side valley, the route leaves the track to descend to the isolated buildings of Tighachrochadair visible below. The map shows a path, but we didn't find it where shown and so made our own way down to it. However, looking back later from across the valley, a path at a different position was visible.

Tighachrochadair has an interesting history which is displayed in newspaper cuttings in the barn. Unbelievably, this tiny dwelling housed the Ross family with five children and a schoolteacher; the teacher was needed because of the dwelling's inaccessibility and remoteness. The father was a stalker for the surrounding estate and the family appear to have moved in during the 1930's. The son, Donald, who was born at Tighachrochadair, took over his father's position and continued to live there until the early 1990's. It's clear, that despite its isolation and the very basic nature of the house, where there was no electricity, drains or piped water and an open fire was used for heating and cooking, it was an extremely happy family home.

There used to be a bridge crossing of the Allt Goibhre for the family. However, this has long since disintegrated requiring the fording of the allt, which should prove no problem unless it's in spate. Beyond, the map shows an exit track but there's no trace of this or the path shown. It is therefore necessary to make one's own way through heather for half a mile to reach a track; this is the second and last time on the entire route where you have to make your own way. The track reached is then followed eastwards, above and parallel to the allt to the farm of Auchederson and out on to a lane at Aultgowrie Bridge. The lane descends to Marybank two miles north and there's very much a feeling of leaving the hills for low-lying fertile farmland. Marybank has accommodation and a pub. However, we couldn't get into the B&B here, so went beyond to a B&B at Westermoy, after crossing the River Conon on Moy Bridge.

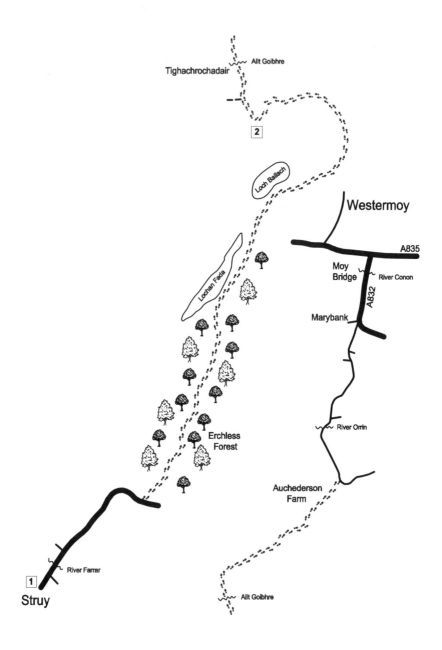

1: From the junction at Struy (NH 400 400), follow the main A831 road to the right, crossing the River Farrar by Struy Bridge. Continue on the main road, past the Cnoc Hotel on the left, to where the main road curves right and take an unsurfaced track off left along the left side of a clearing (412 409) (1.1m); the track is unsigned but there is a notice about fishing by permit only. The enclosed track ascends to pass to the left of a cottage and reach a fork. Take the left fork (no waymark) and follow the track which is now in forest. Pass under power pylon lines and continue on the track, keeping left of construction works. The track soon swings left to leave the pylon lines. Continue through the forest and towards its latter stages, there are glimpses to the left of Lochan Fada. Exit the forest by a stile (430 437) (3.3m) towards the north end of the lochan and continue on the good track, which keeps gradually ascending following the lie of the land. The track passes to the right of Loch Ballach (447 472) (5.9m) and continues to rise. Keep going on the track which turns westwards parallel to the Allt Goibhre below on the right. The track then swings left, south-southwest to negotiate a side burn of the allt and buildings by the allt can be observed; this is Tighachrochadair. The track reaches a small concrete dam at a U-bend (436 473) (7.7m).

2: Continue on the track which turns north, passing three concrete platforms on the right and turn off right to Tighachrochadair, just before the fourth. There's no discernible path, so use the burn on the right as a guide down; it's worth stopping at the barn to learn about the history of this isolated dwelling. From Tighachrochadair, ford the Allt Goibhre and ascend north-northwest for about 550 yds through heather to meet a well trodden path (432 488) (8.7m). Turn right and follow the path/track north-northeastish, parallel to the Allt Goibhre; there are good views of the Cromarty, Beauly and Moray Firths. Eventually the buildings of Auchederson (468 506) (11.5m) are reached. The track keeps right of the buildings to meet the farm's access drive. Turn right and follow Auchederson's drive out to meet a lane (478 511) (12.3m). Turn left and descend to cross the River Orrin on a bridge. Beyond, continue northwards on the lane, ignoring turn offs, to reach a cross-roads at Marybank (14.1m). Go straight on along an A-road, which crosses the River Conon by Moy Bridge, and continue beyond, to shortly meet the main A835 road. Turn left and after a quarter mile, take the first right on a rough ascending lane (478 549) which shortly passes the dwellings in Westermoy (15.3m).

Stage 59
Westermoy to Garve Station

VIA:	Contin, Rogie Falls and forest tracks
DISTANCE:	9.8m [878.2m]
ASCENT:	1160ft **DESCENT:** 1150ft
EXPLORER:	431 (Strathglass), 437 (Strathpeffer)
LANDRANGER:	26 (Inverness), 20 (Loch Broom)

If you're still feeling fit at this stage, you could contemplate a single long stage from Westermoy to the Aultguish Inn on the Ullapool to Inverness main road. However, we decided to split it into two short stages. From Westermoy, the track and field path shown on the map to Jamestown, a mile south of the town of Strathpeffer, is taken. A good and pleasant track is then taken into Contin village where there's a well-stocked store. The 1:50000 map seems to indicate a path along Black Water, but the only thing we could find was dense undergrowth, necessitating taking to the cycle track through the forest above Black Water; don't expect many views other than trees! The short detour to the Rogie Falls is worth the effort before resuming through the forest. The cycle path passes beneath the Kyle of Lochalsh railway line and then passes close to the north shore of Loch Garve; disappointingly, despite the nearness of the loch, it's difficult to view it because of the vegetation. From the loch, the public road into Garve is reached just after passing the buildings of Strathgarve Lodge. There are options for both accommodation and eating in Garve. We stayed at Birch Cottage which has a gourmet cook (recommended).

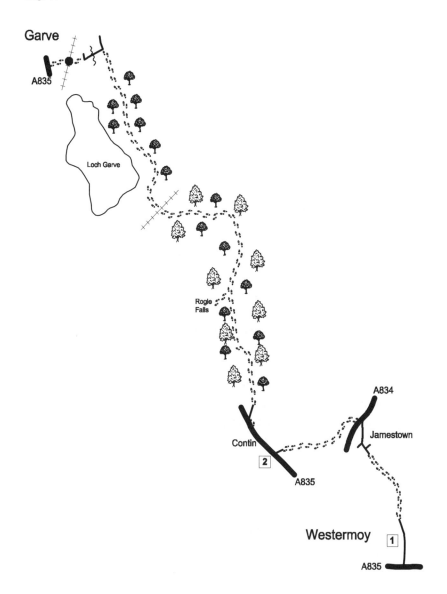

Garve

A835

Loch Garve

Rogie
Falls

Contin

2

A835

A834

Jamestown

Westermoy

1

A835

1: From Westermoy (NH 479 551), continue up the lane to Westermoy Farm where the lane continues as an enclosed track. At the end, go through the left gate and proceed a quarter-left (away from the right field boundary) to pass left of a pile of stones and reach a field turn. Continue along the right fence, curving left a short distance (parallel to the right wall) on a track to a gate on the right (482 562). Pass through, and follow the track to the right of a copse, branching off left on a track when just past the trees. The track leads into a field. Here, follow the right edge to a gate at the bottom on the right. Pass through and head half-right round marsh to a gate (aim for the right of a bungalow). Pass through the gate and in the field entered, aim for the barn, to reach a farmyard. Turn left through the yard, passing to the right of Burnside Croft Bungalow, and follow its access drive to shortly reach a lane. Follow the lane for a short distance to a lane T-junction and turn right to the main A834 road at Jamestown (477 567) (1.2m); the town of Strathpeffer lies a mile to the right along the main road. Go opposite left through black wrought iron gates on a track which meets a forest road. Turn left and shortly, when the forest road curves left, go straight on. The track soon curves right and continues to a track junction. Go straight on (left) along the main track. The track becomes a lane which is followed down to the main A835 road in Contin (459 560) (2.5m).

2: Turn right, pass the Contin Stores on the left and take a footpath a quarter-right leaving immediately after the bus stop on the right. When this footpath short-cut meets Tor View road, turn right and follow this 'No Through Road' as it curves left. The road continues as a surfaced track and beyond the last house becomes a grass path. Ignore paths off to keep on in the same direction and ascend to a forest road. Cross and take the forest track opposite. Follow this wide forest track with its signs to 'Garve' until a sign pointing left to the 'Rogie Falls, Bridge, Forest Walks' (448 585 (4.3m) Take this modest diversion to view the Falls (recommended and included in the mileage) and then retrace your steps to resume on the forest track to Garve. Follow the track through Rogie Farm and beyond, at a fork, go left (signed 'Garve 4m'). Pass under the railway line (425 593) (6.8m) and then immediately go left to meet a track. Turn left here, pass over a new bridge and at a track junction, just beyond, go half-right on an ascending track. It parallels and re-meets the new hard core construction road but is much pleasanter. After passing through a gate, the track gets close-ish to Loch Garve on the left. The track continues on beyond the loch and eventually reaches a gate. Beyond, follow the track straight on between barns, curve right (with Strathgarve Hall above on the right) and continue to meet the end of a lane (9.1m). Follow this for a short distance to a lane corner and turn left signed 'Garve'. Cross Black Water on a bridge and shortly after take a walkers' gate onto Garve railway station. Use the footbridge and the station exit to reach the main road and the end of this stage (395 613) (9.8m).

Stage 60
Garve Station to Aultguish Inn

VIA: Little Garve, Silver Bridge and drove route
DISTANCE: 9m [887.2m]
ASCENT: 1340ft DESCENT: 860ft
EXPLORER: 437 (Strathpeffer)
LANDRANGER: 20 (Loch Broom)

This is another short stage but it offers superb walking. From Garve the route starts by following the far bank of Black Water to the bridge over the water at Little Garve; Garve Bridge was built by General Wade's successor and vehicles are prevented from using it. The end-to-end route uses Garve Bridge to cross Black Water. One can leave Black Water to go directly onto the old drove route to the Aultguish Inn from Garve Bridge, but the end-to-end route keeps close to the west bank of Black Water to reach the old bridge at Silver Bridge; again, it's another bridge that cars are prevented from travelling over. The bridges and the stretch of water between them are delightful; the exposed rock with its clefts leading to the water rushing and tumbling along.

From Silver Bridge, forestry tracks lead on to the drove route over to the Aultguish Inn. The drove route initially goes through forest, but leaves the trees just before passing Lochan nam Breac and it's open hillside thereafter, as some of the forest indicated on the map has been cut down. Although shown as a path on the map, the route is there on the ground and is never in doubt! It's worth remembering here and elsewhere that drovers never lost height gained if this could possibly be avoided. The only time the path becomes indistinct is on the final approach to the inn, but by this time you are reasonably close to the inn and there's a side stream to guide you in. Furthermore the inn, which is just east of Loch Glascarnoch, will have been spotted earlier as it's the only building around. The drove inn at Aultguish must have been a most welcome sight to the drovers of old; today the inn still offers accommodation and meals to travellers on foot and to people passing on the main road.

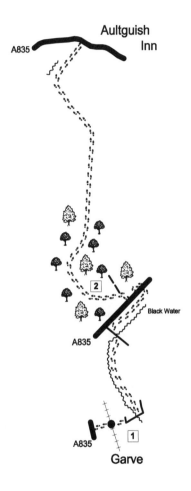

1: From Garve Station (NH 395 613) return to the bridge over Black Water, cross and take the first track off left (398 614), which after passing through a gate follows between Black Water and a right fence. When the fence turns right, go half-right to re-meet Black Water at the point where fencing along the Water starts. Follow the Water using the left or right side of the fencing (right is easiest) and at a gap, follow to the left of the fencing. Latterly, follow beside the Water for some lovely views, then pass through a gate onto the end of a lane and turn left over a delightful stone bridge (Garve Bridge) (1.4m). Immediately across, turn right and follow a good path close to Black Water to a path fork. Fork right on the more minor path which keeps close to the water. When it re-meets the more major path, turn right and almost immediately pass under the A-road then ascend steps into a car parking area. Go left for the main A835 road (after turning right for spectacular views from Silver Bridge). Turn right along the main road for 300 yds, take the first forest track off right (400 636) (2.6m) and shortly turn left on a good forest track (399 637). The gently ascending track circles the southern end of a hill clockwise to reach a track junction (389 635) (3.5m). Take the right fork signed 'Drove Road to Aultguish Inn'.

2: From the sign, the route ascends and then descends to a clearing with a wooden plank that can be used as a seat (380 651) (4.7m). Ignore the track left and take the track opposite right. This continues descending north, and after passing out of forest, becomes a path which passes to the left of Lochan nam Breac (379 664) (5.6m) to a gate. Pass through and follow the path beyond, which wends its way round features of the undulating landscape. After passing through a further gate, the path continues to come alongside a burn which is followed and then crossed. Beyond, the path ascends for a short distance to a gate with a deer stile. Continue, cross another burn and get to a stile resembling an angled trapdoor! Continue beyond on a ledge round the hillside and at the highest point (361 693) (8m), the Aultguish Inn can be clearly seen on the main road with the dam of Loch Glascarnoch to its left. Descend gently on a good track until it turns sharp right, when carry straight on, without losing significant height, towards a gate on the hillside. Pass through the gate which has a marker post and go straight ahead to shortly reach a marker post by a stream (351 700) (8.7m). Turn right, following the stream line along its top bank, to the main A835 road. The Aultguish Inn is opposite left and there is a snack bar attached to the inn (351 704) (9m).

Stage 61
Aultguish Inn to Croick Church

VIA:	Strath Vaich, Gleann Mor and Alladale
DISTANCE:	18.9m [906.1m]
ASCENT:	1710ft DESCENT: 2070ft
EXPLORER:	437 (Strathpeffer)
LANDRANGER:	20 (Loch Broom)

This is another extremely good walk, mostly well defined and easy underfoot with no significant ascents, so you can expect to make good progress. It's necessary to follow the main road to Black Bridge over Black Water to the start of the track up Strath Vaich; you will not be greatly troubled by traffic! The track up Strath Vaich keeps to the east side of the river to reach Loch Vaich. A lovely stretch along this long loch follows with wonderful views of serious mountains above. The clear track skirts the bottom of a mountain Meall a' Chaorainn and then makes for Deanich Lodge. As the lodge is approached, there seems to be no way through the steep hills behind it, but the vehicle track unerringly continues beyond into the narrow entrance to Gleann Mor. The track continues close to the river with the valley floor gradually widening. A bothy is passed but it blends in so well with its surroundings that it's easily missed. Eventually the gleann is left to cross into Glen Alladale.

From here, there's a path to Croick Church which is mainly trodden, thanks to its use by the rangers guiding guests at nearby Alladale Lodge. The path ascends the hillside on a rough track to a walkers' gate at the summit; this replaces a more interesting stile designed to be deer proof and I think also short-people proof! Beyond the gate, the path is indistinct for a very short distance and GPS readings are given to assist in picking up a reasonable track that can be followed down to Croick Church; care is needed here so as to not lose the path. The church has a sad history connected with the clearances in Sutherland. In 1845, tenant farmers and their families were evicted to make way for sheep. These were law abiding people who were punctilious in paying their rents and had been farming in Glencalvie for many generations. They took refuge temporarily in the churchyard at Croick and the messages scratched into the church windows record their desperation; it is not recorded what happened to these people on their departure from Croick, but stripped of their livelihood and home, it is unlikely to have been a happy outcome.

There is no accommodation at or near Croick so it's necessary to arrange a pick-up. Fortunately, there is a taxi firm in Ardgay, but be aware that most taxi firms in north Scotland survive from doing regular school runs and these dictate when they are able to offer a taxi service to the public. From Croick, the obvious destination is Bonar Bridge (near Ardgay) which has accommodation, eating places, a post office and general stores.

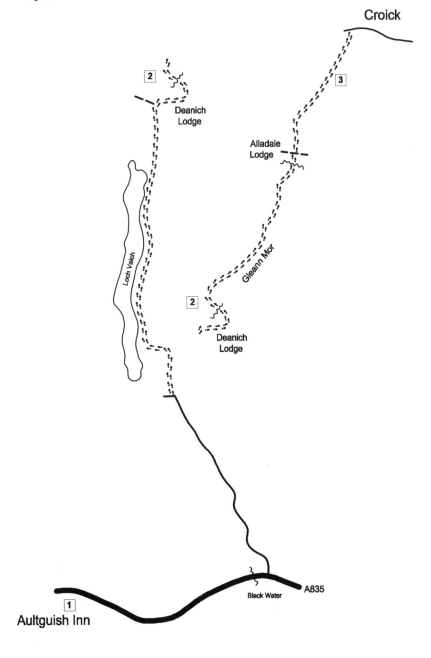

Croick

2

Deanich
Lodge

Loch Vaich

Alladale
Lodge

3

Gleann Mor

2

Deanich
Lodge

A835

Black Water

1
Aultguish Inn

1: From the Aultguish Inn (NH 351 704) follow the main road east (back towards Garve!) for 1.5 miles and having crossed Black Water on labelled Black Bridge, after a further 60 yds turn left on a surfaced estate lane (374 708) (1.6m). Follow the lane along Strath Vaich on the east side of an abhainn and reach a bridge crossing of the abhainn (355 736) (3.7m). Don't cross but turn right, northwards, on an unsurfaced track. After passing up the left side of a wood, cross a side stream on a bridge and shortly after ignore a track off right (354 747) (4.4m). Continue for a few yards towards a small concrete dam and just before it, curve left with the main track. Soon there are views of Loch Vaich to the left and the track follows the eastern shoreline along the entire length of the loch; this is a lovely section of the walk. At the end of the loch (351 799) (8m), continue on the main track as it curves right to pass between some forbidding looking hills. Eventually the track ascends round the lower slopes of the hill on the left and near the summit of the track, ignore a track off right (365 825) (9.9m) to keep straight on round the hill. The track gently descends with Deanich Lodge soon visible and a track T-junction is reached (365 834). Turn right, go through a gate and follow the descending track to the lodge. The track passes the back of the lodge and continues down the valley to a bridge crossing point of the Abhainn a' Ghlinne Mhoir (372 844) (11.2m).

2: Having crossed, the track turns right to closely follow the north bank of the abhainn down Gleann Mor. Initially the track is in a narrow pass between steep hills but the valley gradually widens out. After nearly 5.5 miles, the track ascends above the abhainn and when it descends the track does a hairpin right turn to come alongside the Alladale River on its left. This is followed for a short distance to a substantial bridge on the left over the river (441 895) (16.9m). Cross and very shortly afterwards reach a cross-track. Go straight on (signed 'Alladale Deliveries') and follow the track as it ascends, passing an animal enclosure on the left. At the highest point, reach a cross-track. Turn right here into a parking area and turn half-right again, through a gate onto a short (muddy) track, which leads through a gate to open moorland. Follow a clear, gently-ascending track which keeps almost parallel with a deer fence on the right. Eventually the fence turns right while the track continues north-of-East to a kissing gate just over the crest of the hill (NH 44764 90283) (17.8m).

3: Through the kissing gate, go north-northeast keeping left of a small tree copse to a wide small depression (NH 44816 90357). Follow the depression line still north-northeastish to the start of the visible path (NH 44865 90420). From here, drop steeply a short distance to a small pool (NH 44912 90504) and continue descending to pass between two sets of trees. Pass a fairly big stone and then pass round a lone tree (NH 45116 90735). The path turns left at NH 45270 90966 before continuing to descend in a generally north-northeast direction. After going round to the right of a small mound, the path drops to a ladder stile. Cross and follow a track to a wooden footbridge (454 912) (18.5m) over Black Water, and very shortly afterwards cross a side burn using the stones provided. Then follow between a feeder of the side burn on the left and a house boundary on the right to a walkers' gate onto the end of a public road. Croick Church is 350 yds to the right and its layby opposite makes a good place to arrange a pick-up (457 915) (18.9m).

Stage 62
Croick Church to Rosehall

VIA: Drove route to Oykel Bridge, River Oykel and quiet roads
DISTANCE: 17.8m [923.9m]
ASCENT: 1360ft   DESCENT: 1640ft
EXPLORER: 440 (Glen Oykel)
LANDRANGER: 20 (Loch Broom), 16 (Lairg)

This is another high quality walk mainly in open surroundings. The hills do not rise to the same height as those on the previous day, nevertheless this is scenery of a high order and it brings home just how empty this part of north Scotland is. From Croick, the stage follows an estate track along Strath Cuileannach. We had wanted to take the path shown on the map going north 1.25m beyond Lubachoinnich, but this is inaccessible as it is firmly fenced off by high wiring surrounding woodland. It's clearly been in this state for some time and since there's absolutely no possibility of it being used (ever again), it would be good if it were to be expunged from the map; it would save people like me from spending time looking for a path which simply cannot be done.

As a result it's necessary to continue on the track which soon afterwards leaves the strath to contour round the hills into Einig Wood where it follows above Glen Einig to reach Oykel Bridge. Here there is an old bridge to admire as well as a hotel, where, if you have made good time, you will arrive for a late lunch. A walk by track and path to Langwell Farm along the attractive River Oykel ensues. The farm's access track is then taken to the start of the public road at Brae and this very quiet lane leads to the main road. Rosehall, with its hotel, lies a mile to the north-east and has hotel accommodation. Invercassley, passed on the way in, has a small shop but this closes at 5pm so we missed it.

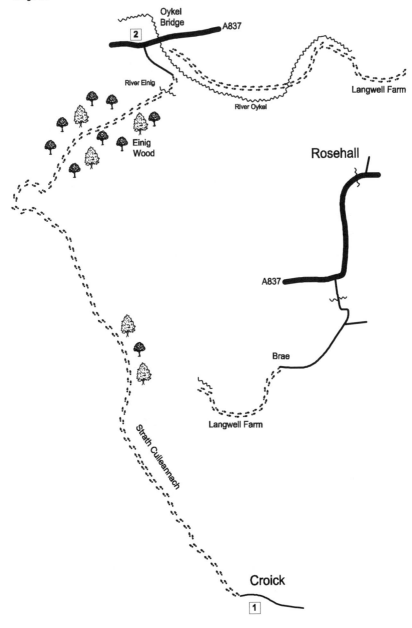

Oykel
Bridge
A837

River Einig

River Oykel

Langwell Farm

Einig
Wood

Rosehall

A837

Brae

Langwell Farm

Strath Cuilleanmach

Croick

1: From Croick Church (NH 457 915) return to the end of the lane and pass through a walkers' gate (to the left of the padlocked vehicle gate) onto a track marked as a 'Through Road to Ullapool'. Follow the very good estate track along Strath Cuileannach to eventually reach a track junction (391 963) (5.5m). Ignore the substantial track left descending to a stone building, instead curve right then shortly turn left over a wooden bridge. Continue on the main track and pass through a gate, leaving the Croick Estate. Continue on the main track to a T-junction and turn right (372 976) (7m). The track gently descends and at a sharp curve right (362 983) (7.9m), ignore a track off left, to keep descending on the main track. Pass through a deer fence to a T-junction and turn right onto a stony forest road. Continue down the interminable forestry road and eventually curve left to cross the River Einig (NC 386 002) (9.9m). Across, the forest road curves right (ignore a track coming in from the left) and passes cottages, where it becomes a lane which is followed to the main A837 road (385 009) (10.6m). The Oykel Bridge Hotel is opposite left.

2: Turn right over the bridge and turn off first right on a track which follows the north bank of the River Oykel. Follow the track to a cattle grid and continue on the track (or cut across) to a second cattle grid, where the footbridge to be used to cross the river can be clearly seen. Keep on the track to reach the suspension bridge (408 006) (12.3m). Cross and turn left on a good path which stays close to the river, keeping between the river and a right fence. Go under a second suspension footbridge and continue on the path with Langwell Farm visible on the right. When a track off right to Langwell is met, take this (416 011) to shortly meet a gravel track. Turn left along Langwell's access (right goes into Langwell). The track turns right at a barn and then reaches a track T-junction (423 007) (13.8m). Turn left, ascend steeply and then descend (ignore an ascending track off right). Cross a side burn of the river and almost immediately reach Brae Farm where the public road commences (436 010) (14.7m). Ascend on the lane past the houses of Doune and keep going to a T-junction just after a cattle grid (458 009) (16.2m). Turn left and descend to cross the River Oykel and continue to shortly meet the main A837 road (461 014) (16.7m) at Inveroykel. Turn right and follow the main road through Invercassley to a crossing of the River Cassley (472 023) (17.6m). Soon afterwards turn left on a lane to shortly reach the Achness Hotel on the right (473 024) (17.8m).

Stage 63
Rosehall to Lairg

VIA: Quiet roads and The Ord
DISTANCE: 9.2m [933.1m]
ASCENT: 870ft   DESCENT: 630ft
EXPLORER: 440 (Glen Oykel), 441 (Lairg)
LANDRANGER: 16 (Lairg)

This is a relatively short day and there's a lack of tracks so much of it is by main road. However, the main roads round here are so quiet that there's the odd sign at the side to remind you that you are on a main road. Furthermore, the main roads are largely the standard and width of minor roads in much of England! The road can be left for an approach to Lairg via a hill called The Ord. This gives a panoramic view of the area, with Lairg village and Loch Shin particularly prominent. Lairg is an interesting village, the last encountered before John O'Groats a hundred miles away. For this reason, it makes a natural stopping point and its facilities are much greater than one would expect for a village of its size. Of interest to walkers are its two small supermarkets, chemist and cash withdrawal facilities, as well as accommodation and eating places. Most accommodation in the Highlands closes over the winter so Lairg's inn is unusual in remaining open throughout.

Our stay in Lairg happily coincided with their annual music festival of traditional Scottish music. It features competitions for all age groups on accordion, piano, fiddle and for groups of five playing on these instruments; the festival culminates in an evening concert given by all the winners. The standard of playing and enthusiasm of the children on their instruments was inspiring, and I am in awe of the way the group players seamlessly changed from one tune to another. However, my favourite moment was observing the seated adjudicators for the group competition, with all three pairs of feet dancing to the music! The festival proved to be one of the outstanding memories of the walk.

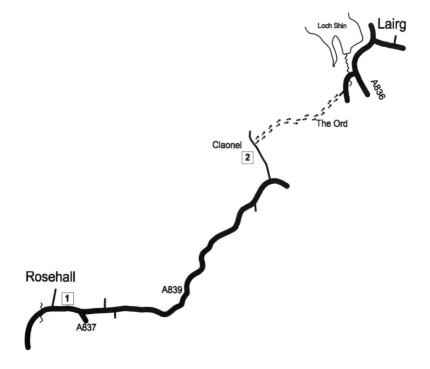

1: From the hotel at Rosehall (NC 473 024), return to the main A837 road, and turn left towards Lairg. After nearly a mile when the main road forks (483 017) (0.8m), take the left fork by the war memorial onto the A839 for Lairg. Now follows a long section on this pleasant but unremarkable A-road with easy gradients for any ups and downs. Eventually The Ord, with its wireless mast atop, can be seen directly ahead. Ignore a lane off right signed to 'Gruids' and shortly take the next lane turn off left signed to 'Sallachy' (566 045) (6.9m). After a third of a mile, turn right on a bungalow access track (564 050); it's just before the access drive to Claonel farm on the left.

2: Follow the track, which passes the front of the bungalow, to a gate to the right of the dwelling. Follow the grass track beyond, along the right side of the bungalow, before it curves right. Descend a short distance and then take a track branch off half-right to reach a field turn. The track then follows a left fence to a gate with a clear track up The Ord beyond. Ascend, branching right at a path fork to take the upper path; there are good views of Loch Shin to the left. Curve left towards the wireless mast and pass to the left of it to meet the track to the mast. Turn left to descend. Near the bottom, ignore a path off left, to stay on the main track and reach a gate with stile onto a lane. Cross the lane to take a path down the side of a house and meet the end of a residential road. Turn left and first right to re-meet the main A839 road (580 059) (8.6m). Turn left passing a small supermarket, then turn right over the bridge crossing the south-eastern arm of Loch Shin and almost immediately reach a T-junction. Turn left along the loch and after a quarter mile turn right along Lairg's Main Street, signed to 'Rogart'. The stage ends at Lairg's inn (585 063) (9.2m).

Stage 64
Lairg to Crask Inn

VIA: Saval, forest track and quiet road
DISTANCE: 13.6m [946.7m]
ASCENT: 900ft   DESCENT: 460ft
EXPLORER: 441 (Lairg), 443 (Ben Klibreck)
LANDRANGER: 16 (Lairg)

Today's destination is the old droving inn at Crask. This isolated dwelling stands on its own in a highly remote area of Sutherland. It must have been like an oasis in the desert to drovers and there's a similar feeling for today's travellers. It's unpretentious, comfortable and very welcoming with delicious home cooked food, much of it produced by the owners who work the surrounding land. Electricity comes from their own generator, which is turned off overnight, and they have their own water supply. In short, it's a unique experience but is not for those who are unable to do without four-star luxury! It is much loved by the walkers and cyclists who stay there and the owners take a genuine interest in their visitors. On this stage we met a large flock of cyclists on their way to John O'Groats who managed to get fed at the inn, even though they descended on the Crask without warning.

There's extensive forest shown between Lairg and the Crask Inn and the route taken is designed to miss this as much as possible. Minor lanes northwards are therefore taken to the end of the public road at Saval, from where a track is taken which heads north-westwards into the forest. The interesting track continues in this direction into and through forest emerging onto the main road from Lairg. The route continues along the quiet main road, with more open views than might be expected, due to areas being felled and some areas adjacent to the road being left clear.

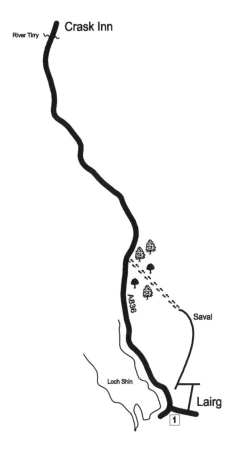

1: From Lairg's inn (NC 585 063) continue along Main Street for a short distance and after 150 yds take the first lane off left (Laundry Road), opposite the caravan site (and Crofters Restaurant). The lane soon bends right through a yard, shortly afterwards crosses a stream, then ascends as a gated road to reach a T-junction (590 068) (0.5m). Turn left for 330 yds to a T-junction and turn right, signed 'Saval'. Just as the lane ends at the final farm, turn right through a gate (587 085) (2m), pass to the right of a barn and through a gate onto an enclosed track. Follow the track to reach open ground and then continue to follow a clear track towards the forest. The track reaches a gate into the forest (581 092) (2.7m) and beyond, follow the track on the ground through a wide break between trees. Exit the forest via a gate onto the main A836 road (574 103) (3.5m). Turn right and follow the road northwards along Strath Tirry; the road stays to the right of the River Tirry. The water of Feith Osdail (which flows into the river) is bridged at (575 140) (5.9m) and the Abhainn Sgeamhaidh (which also flows into the River Tirry) is crossed by Rhian Bridge (563 166) (7.7m). Continue on the road and eventually cross the River Tirry (524 246) (13.5m). The Crask Inn is a short distance beyond on the right (524 247) (13.6m).

Stage 65
Crask Inn to Badanloch Lodge

VIA: Bealach Easach, Loch Choire and estate track
DISTANCE: 21m [967.7m]
ASCENT: 1470ft   DESCENT: 1780ft
EXPLORER: 443 (Ben Klibreck), 448 (Strath Naver)
LANDRANGER: 16 (Lairg), 17 (Helmsdale)

This is a wonderful day's walking and although quite long, it is easy going underfoot. It was a pleasant, sunny day and the scenery to the end of Loch Choire is lovely so we took our time over this. Despite this, it took us only eight hours to complete this stage. The path from the Crask Inn follows the level moorland of Srath a' Chraisg and there's a clear path, sufficiently good for yesterday's cyclists to use. The path then contours around the hillside, without losing height, to the top of a pass called the Bealach Easach, meaning pass of the (small) waterfalls.

From here, the descending track down to Loch a' Bhealach and beyond to Loch Choire is visible. On reaching the west end of Loch Choire, there is a choice of following its north or south side. We chose the south side which, while slightly longer, is the more scenically interesting route. To reach the south side, there's a bridge that needs to be crossed with a large gap between the two sides, definitely a place to 'tread on the nails'! On reaching the south side, there's a very well kept bothy. The track that follows along Loch Choire is a delight as it undulates, keeping close to the water, with good views across and along the loch. The track continues beyond the buildings of Loch Choire Lodge (at the east end of the loch) as a sandy access track. However, after passing a small green hut with a corrugated iron roof, which in past days served as a schoolroom to the children from the lodge dwellings, the access track is left for a much more interesting hillside track.

After the track re-emerges on the access track, the scenery and walk are less interesting from this point onwards. The vista is now of flat moorland broken up by large lochs and views of distant hills. The track meets a public road at Badanloch Lodge which is the first road encountered since leaving the Crask Inn. The lodge is spotted from a great distance away, but it seems to take forever to reach it! Accommodation is scarce in this area, with the only feasible public transport being a very infrequent train service from Kinbrace more than four miles away. As a consequence, we decided to base ourselves for three nights at the Forsinard Hotel (seven miles north of Kinbrace) and use the train service on the subsequent stages. The hotel is over eleven miles away from Badenloch and we arranged with the hotel to be picked up here (and dropped back the following day).

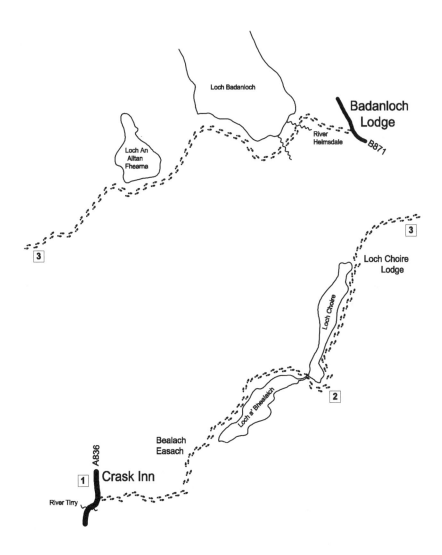

1: From the Crask Inn (NC 524 247), retrace the route along the main road to the River Tirry but don't cross it. Instead turn left through a walkers' gate (524 246) and follow a good path (sometimes a track) which keeps to the north side of the river. The path heads for and then follows parallel to the forest on the right. The path curves left and appears to finish, but keep contouring left round the hill without losing or gaining height to quickly pick up the trodden path again. From the summit of the pass (575 252) (3.5m), the view suddenly opens up and there are breathtaking views ahead of Loch a' Bhealaich below with Loch Choire beyond. Follow the clear track down to and along Loch a' Bhealaich. The track continues beyond the loch to a track T-junction at Loch Choire (6.4m) (613 274). Turn right to take the track on the southern side. The path keeps close to the shore, using two suspension 'bridges' to pass over side streams. Near a bothy at the south-east end of the loch, a track is met (619 269) (7m).

2: Turn left on a good track that follows the southern shore line of the loch. Eventually the track reaches the front of Loch Choire Lodge (651 303) (10.2m). Follow the track along the right side of the house and into its back yard. Pass down the yard and descend to a track junction (left goes via the north side of Loch Choire to the Crask Inn). Go straight on, north-northeast, along the unsurfaced sandy access track and after 340 yds pass a green tin hut on the right (653 307). Continue for another 160 yds and pass a track off left then very shortly afterwards take the next (grass) track off right (654 308). Follow the main track eastwards, keeping left at any forks. Follow the track through two (new) high deer gates and shortly beyond the second, the track re-meets the access drive (685 311) (12.5m).

3: Turn right on this sandy track and follow it eastwards then north-eastwards to a bridge crossing of Gearnsary Burn (731 321) (15.6m). Beyond, the track continues to the south-west end of Loch an Alltan Fhearna (745 331) (16.7m) before making its way to Loch Badanloch (763 335) (18m). The track now follows Loch Badanloch's shoreline. Ignore a track off right (780 326) (19.3m) and continue to the loch's eastern end where the River Helmsdale is crossed (789 332) (20.1m). Beyond, the track turns right, away from the loch, and is followed out south-of-East to join the single track B871 road to Kinbrace (801 330) (21m); this is the first public road since the start of the day and is a good place to arrange a pick-up.

Stage 66
Badanloch Lodge to Forsinard

VIA: Quiet roads through Kinbrace
DISTANCE: 11.6m [979.3m]
ASCENT: 590ft   DESCENT: 530ft
EXPLORER: 449 (Strath Halladale)
LANDRANGER: 17 (Helmsdale), 10 (Strathnaver)

This is a very straightforward road walk starting from where the drove route from the Crask Inn emerges on the single track B-road. We had planned to do some of this cross-country, but it was raining sporadically, the grass looked uneven and very wet, so there was a unanimous vote for legging it along the very quiet roads to arrive back in Forsinard for a late lunch at the hotel. The route follows the uneventful B-road, where deer were much in evidence. After 4.4 miles, the tiny village of Kinbrace is reached after passing its railway station; some of the houses are gaily painted as if to combat the harsh environment. The main road is met at Kinbrace and it's then just a question of following it northwards. Flow country, a huge area of blanket bog, is entered just north of the village. The road runs parallel to the railway line, with its snow fences, for just over seven miles to the hotel in Forsinard.

Forsinard is a tiny community in the flow country. However, the hamlet does have a hotel, which also houses a limited-hours Post Office service. There's a warm welcome for guests at the hotel and the owners are both helpful and informative. Forsinard has a railway station and all the trains (such as they are) stop there. The railway building houses a RSPB Visitor Centre which is well worth a visit, even if you feel you don't need to go out and view the flow country from their nature trails! After our visit to the RSPB centre, we encountered a gentleman walking to Dover, by road, complete with a harness to attach him to his small cart of belongings. He set off from Forsinard to camp, provisioned with all he reckoned he needed for his journey, namely a loaf of bread, an uncooked egg and a bottle of whisky. The whisky was evidently insufficient for the trials ahead as he turned up the next morning to acquire another bottle; after his second exit, we were amused to hear him described as being 'as mad as a box of frogs'!

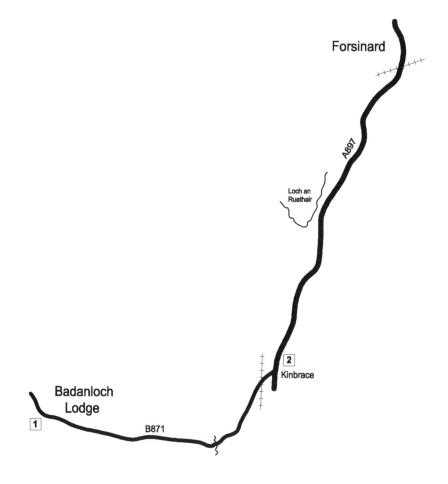

Forsinard

A897

Loch an
Ruathair

Badanloch
Lodge

1

B871

2
Kinbrace

1: From the junction at Badanloch Lodge, where the drove route emerges on the B-road (NC 801 330), follow the road south-of-East towards Kinbrace; it's very quiet and there are plenty of verges to get off the tarmac. Having crossed a burn, the road starts turning northwards, crosses the railway on the level crossing at Kinbrace and ascends to meet the main road (863 319) (4.4m).

2: Turn left on the quiet main road, following it northwards. Generally, there are good views across the valley to the left and again there's ample opportunity to get off the tarmac by using the verges. Eventually, a wireless mast can be spotted on a hill and after going right around its base, the road drops down to cross the railway line in Forsinard and the hotel is a short distance beyond on the left (891 426) (11.6m).

Stage 67
Forsinard to Alnabreac Station

VIA:	Quiet road to Forsinain and forestry tracks
DISTANCE:	14.1m [993.4m]
ASCENT:	920ft
EXPLORER:	449 (Strath Halladale)

ASCENT: 920ft   DESCENT: 910ft

LANDRANGER: 10 (Strathnaver), 11 (Thurso and Wick)

This is a lovely day's walk through the flow country to Altnabreac railway station in the middle of nowhere. We set off from our base at the Forsinard Hotel with an appetising packed lunch designed for hungry people; however, the best treat of all was to be given a flask of coffee! We had not taken flasks because of the weight. The main road is taken northwards to Forsinain along Strath Halladale. Here a signed track is followed which crosses the Halladale River and heads south-eastwards towards an entry into the forest. The forest road to be taken is both obvious and signed. It is used by fishermen for vehicle access to lochs and by ScotRail to reach Altnabreac station, so the route is never in doubt. The map shows the area as mainly forested, but many of the plantations have been removed so as to return the area to its original wetland state, although this will take time. The removal of many of the trees means that it is possible to appreciate the vastness, bleakness and stillness of this boggy area. It's therefore a surprise to see a train a couple of miles away trundling across this territory without sinking, but this is the line from Wick and Thurso to Forsinard. Eventually, the road descends through forest to cross the railway line and then follows it to reach the request stop at Altnabreac station.

There's a seat and also a shelter with a telephone which connects to a person at an information point. It was a pleasure to sit outside and wait for the train. The last train of the day to Forsinard is just before 5pm and was sufficiently late for us to phone through to enquire where it was. There was much relief that it was running late and it appeared a few minutes later. There's a bend coming in to the station and the train is doing quite a speed on its approach, so clear signalling from intending passengers is required. It's possible to view much of the day's walk from the train and the journey back to Forsinard only takes 10 minutes!

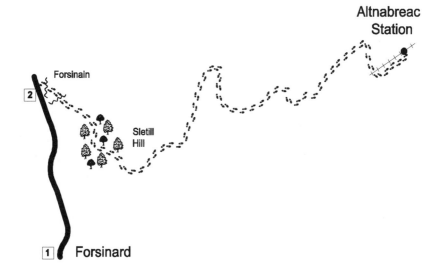

Altnabreac
Station

Forsinain

2

Sletill
Hill

1 Forsinard

1: From the Forsinard Hotel (NC 891 426) follow the main A897 road north. This quiet road runs parallel to the Halladale River on the right. After four miles take the signed track (to Halkirk) off right at Forsinain (903 486); the route required has blue colour coded signs.

2: Cross the river on a substantial bridge, then immediately turn right (waymarked) on an excellent, unsurfaced, wide sandy track. The track follows the river for a short distance then turns off right (waymarked), crosses a side stream by a bridge and continues towards the forest. The track ascends to the forest, follows the side of the forest and then enters the forest. Thereafter, just follow the main sandy track; it's easy walking with a good surface and no navigational problems so you should make good time. The forest is left by a cattle grid to go around Sletill Hill. On the track around the hill, ignore a RSPB track off right and keep left as waymarked. Go through a gate marking the entry to the next area of plantation (937 460) (7.2m), but much has been felled, enhancing the enjoyment of the walk. Cross a burn and very shortly beyond, ignore a track off left (signed 'Taleheel') to follow a waymark indicating straight on. Continue on the main track, obtaining a view of Loch Leir on the right just before going through a gate. Ascend gently through open territory and at a 'summit', ignore a track off left, to curve right as signed. Further on, ignore a descending track off right to keep with the main track curving left (waymarked). Ignore a track off left signed 'Raphan' to keep straight on (waymarked) and shortly pass through a gate. Continue on the main track. Ignore a left turn off signed to 'Catanach' (follow the waymark straight on) before the track plunges into trees on the final gradual descent to a level crossing across the railway line (ND 000 452) (13.6m); the final square on the end-to-end has been entered. The track then turns left to follow the line. Ignore a track off left and continue to a sign at a track T-junction. Turn left for Loch More and soon branch left to very shortly pass to the right of a house, cross a cattle grid and pass to the right of a bungalow onto the platform of Altnabreac Station (004 457) (14.1m).

Stage 68
Altnabreac Station to Watten

VIA: Forestry tracks, Westerdale and Mybster
DISTANCE: 19.3m [1012.7m]
ASCENT: 550ft   DESCENT: 970ft
EXPLORER: 450 (Flow Country), 451 (John O'Groats)
LANDRANGER: 12 (John O'Groats)

Returning by train to Altnabreac, the route continues along the signed route through forestry, with a gate that prevents general access to cars. Initially it follows close to the railway line before plunging through forest, generally eastwards, to eventually reach the northern shore of Loch More where the track used for postal deliveries is met. The postal track is then followed through and out of the forest to meet a public road. And what a windswept, flat, barren landscape greets the eye at this point!

There is still much mileage to do in reaching Watten, the nearest point of accommodation. It's all on roads and compared to the previous walking in Scotland is somewhat dull. A lane eastwards following the River Thurso and then northwards leads to a B-road at the hamlet of Westerdale. Soon afterwards the River Thurso is re-met, and if you want a pleasant place for a rest before continuing, then there are steps down to the river bank on the left with good views of an old mill opposite. The stage continues eastwards on the quiet B-road up to the hamlet of Mybster where the A9 (now much quieter) is met. The route takes the B-road opposite going north-eastwards before turning eastwards. Despite the dwellings seen since reaching the roads, this is still an area of wild openness and it is only on the final approach to Watten that hedges start appearing and the farmland appears worked. The B-road meets a main road in the centre of Watten. The Brown Trout Hotel opposite offers excellent accommodation and on the evening we were there we were able to have fish caught from the local loch.

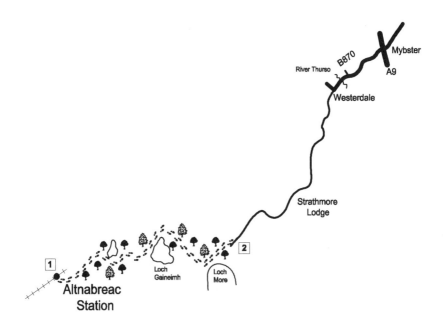

1: From Altnabreac Station (ND 004 457), return to the track junction, turning left through a barrier on a wide sandy track. Initially the track follows the railway line but then curves right to pass to the right of Loch Caise (024 464) (1.5m). Beyond, the track passes through forest. Just after Garbh Loch, ignore a track off to follow the waymark and stay on the main sandy track. Temporarily leave the forest to pass round to the north of Loch Gaineimh (051 475) (3.7m) and beyond, continue through forest on the main track. Exit the forest at a small barrier gate and immediately reach a track T-junction (073 464) (5.3m). Turn left, joining the postal route along the north end of bleak Loch More. The track passes through forest for the final time and on exiting the forest follow the track to meet a lane (091 472) (6.6m).

2: Turn left on the lane (signed for 'Halkirk') and soon pass Strathmore Lodge on the right. Continue to follow the lane to Westerdale where a B-road is met (128 516) (10.9m). Ignore the left turn signed 'Scotscalder' and continue straight on along the B870 signed for 'Inverness'(!). Ignore a left turn off to Halkirk to continue on the B-road and meet the A9 at Mybster (169 529) (13.7m). Go straight across (signed 'Watten') to continue on the B870 road. Ignore turn-offs left and right to stay on the B-road as it twists its way to Watten, and continue until the main A882 road is met in the centre of Watten village (242 544) (19.3m).

Stage 69
Watten to Gills

VIA: Mains of Watten, Lyth and Slickly
DISTANCE: 13.8m [1026.5m]
ASCENT: 610ft   DESCENT: 610ft
EXPLORER: 450 (Flow Country), 451 (John O'Groats)
LANDRANGER: 12 (Thurso & Wick)

Most end-to-enders' routes take a single day to walk into John O'Groats from Watten. However, after doing over 19 miles to get to Watten in the previous stage, we didn't want to arrive shattered at John O'Groats. Moreover, as the true north-eastern point is beyond John O'Groats then as far as I was concerned, the walk had to incorporate Duncansby Head. Hence the decision evolved to spread the finish of the walk over two stages rather than one. It's a relatively easy day to Gills, mainly on very straight and long roads.

It was raining hard when we left Watten and even when the rain stopped, it was a cold and windy day with poor visibility, and an open bleak landscape with no shelter from the elements. The day started badly with a visit to Watten's general stores, which offered such a poor selection of goods for a decent 'picnic' lunch, that we quickly retreated to the local hotel where we were well provisioned. From Watten, B-roads are taken north-eastwards to meet a more major B-road from Castletown. There's an opportunity here to take a track through the hamlet of Stanstill onto the lane running north-eastwards through Lyth and Slickly, where there's barely a building to be seen. Just after Slickly, there's a trig point just off the road on the left perched on some inhospitable moorland; it marks 215ft above sea level.

After this, there's nearly another 4 miles to get to the T-junction at Upper Gills and although we could sense that the sea was nearby, in the murky conditions we couldn't see it! However, a track leads down onto the road down to Gills Bay, where the car ferry over to Orkney leaves. It was sobering to see the sea of northern Scotland after nearly 10 weeks of walking. There are a couple of B&Bs near the bay and we also found that the ferry terminal has a nice warm café where we were able to get a snack, having arrived before the last sailing of the day.

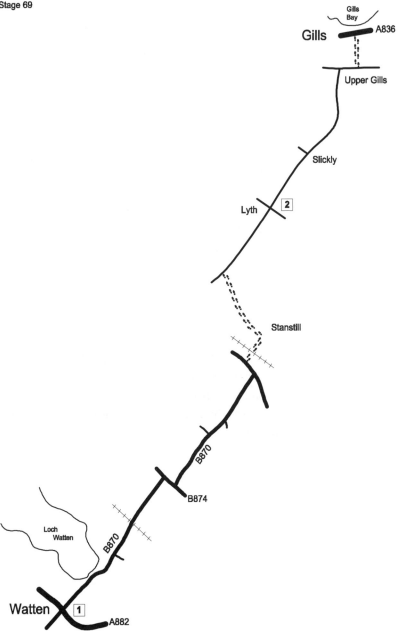

1: Go straight across the main road A882 road in Watten (ND 242 544) to continue along the B870 road, pass to the right of the east end of Loch Watten and cross the railway line from Wick. On reaching a B-road T-junction (252 562) (1.3m), turn right for 250 yds (signed 'Stanstill') and then turn off left on the continuation of the B870 (254 561), also signed for 'Stanstill'. Follow the B870 north-northeast to a B-road T-junction (276 598) (4.2m). Turn left on the B876 (signed 'Castletown') for 240 yds and then turn right (275 600) on an unsurfaced track to the houses of Stanstill. Cross an ungated level crossing with care and continue on the farm track. Having passed a house on the left, turn off left and very shortly reach a track branch. Take the left branch passing around Stanshill Farm to the left and shortly reach a track T-junction (278 609). Here, turn left on a surfaced access drive to emerge on a lane (271 614) (5.6m). Turn right and follow the lane in a north-northeast direction to the cross-roads in the hamlet of Lyth (281 634) (7m), with its war memorial on the corner.

2: Take the lane opposite (signed 'Gills') and continue north-northeast through even smaller Slickly (300 668) (9.4m). The lane eventually turns north, just after a wireless mast, (325 703) (12m) and reaches a lane T-junction at Upper Gills (326 720) (13.1m). Turn right signed 'Canisbay' and after 280 yds, take the unsurfaced track which is the second left off this road (the first left is an access drive to a house). Follow the track down to meet the main A836 road from Thurso to John O'Groats at Gills Bay (329 727) (13.8m); the ferry terminal is to the left.

Stage 70
Gills to John O'Groats & Duncansby Head

VIA: Huna, John O'Groats pier and coastal path
DISTANCE: 8m [1034.5m]
ASCENT: 590ft   **DESCENT:** 680ft
EXPLORER: 451 (John O'Groats)
LANDRANGER: 12 (Thurso & Wick)

On this of all days you are entitled to ask if you are nearly there. And the answer is a resounding YES! On our visit to Gills Bay on the previous day, we had looked carefully to see if there was any sort of coastal path that could be taken. There wasn't and as a result we took to the coastal road through Kirkstyle and on through Huna, where again dwellings are thin on the ground. When fairly close to John O'Groats, a track is taken down to the coast and it's then a short distance to the pier at John O'Groats.

John O'Groats is horribly tacky, but you can get a signpost photograph to show your nearest and dearest that you have completed the walk! And if the walk ended here then it would be a real let-down. However, the best bit of this stage is still to come and it's a truly magnificent walk along the coastal path, ascending to the true north-eastern point of the lighthouse at Duncansby Head. It's possible to follow the coast closely and view coastal ravines with birds nesting down the cliff sides, a blow-hole and a natural arch, all from the safety of a good fence. While all this is good, even better awaits! The coastal path continues beyond the lighthouse, and from the comfort of the fencing, you can view the sea-stacks of The Knee and the Stacks of Duncansby as well as the natural arch of Thirle Door and another coastal ravine. This is a truly fitting end to the journey of a lifetime and it's worth lingering over.

It's a simple matter, after the exhilarating coastal walk, to take a path back to the lane from the lighthouse and follow this to John O'Groats village. The village is about half a mile from the pier and there's plenty of accommodation to be had. However, the only place to eat in the evening appears to be the Seaview Hotel and from its dining room, you will be able to observe flocks of happy cyclists cycling down to the pier to complete their end-to-end ride.

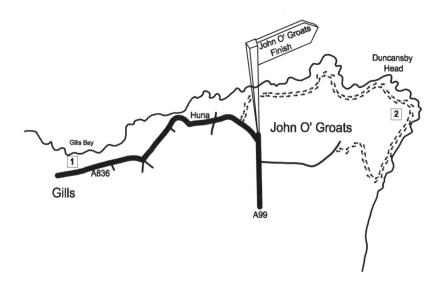

1: The main road from Gills to John O'Groats runs close to the coast and there's a definite feeling of being close to the sea and to the end of the journey. Turn right (ND 329 727), eastwards, and proceed along the fairly quiet main road; there are good views of the coast and the island of Stroma with Orkney beyond. Pass Canisbay's church (1m) and the scattered buildings of Huna. Continue on past the derelict Mill on the left (2.9m) and immediately after the entry to Windy Ha B&B (376 730), turn left on a good track which is followed to meet a gravel path along the coast. Turn right on this to John O'Groats pier (380 734) (3.7m). From the signpost at the pier (identical to the one at Land's End), continue to the nearby 'Last House in Scotland' and to its left, pass through two stone pillars with a sign to the 'Ness of Duncansby'. Follow the gravel path, which is initially along the sea shore but then rises onto and follows open headland, with a gentle slope down to the sea. Keep to the coastline as the Burn of Sannick is crossed to reach a stile above it. Now follow a left fence as it twists round the natural features of the coast, to eventually arrive at the lighthouse at Duncansby Head (405 733) (5.6m).

2: From the lighthouse, take the signed path to Duncansby Stacks, after bagging the trig point just beyond the lighthouse. Again, there's the safety of a left fence all the way to view the Knee, the Stacks and Thirle Door, which are relatively close together and a short distance down the coast. When a kissing gate is reached, the fencing along the cliff edge finishes. Don't go through but turn right along the left fence away from the coast. When the fencing turns left, turn left and continue to follow it onto a lane at a cattle grid (396 729). Turn left along the lane ignoring any right turn-offs, follow the lane westwards to meet the main road to Wick (380 726) (8m). The John O'Groat's Store/Post Office is opposite and the Sea View Hotel is a short distance to the right. The pier is just over half a mile from the road junction.

Summary of End-to-End Route

	Stage	Miles	Ascent ft	Descent ft	Total Miles
0	Land's End to St Just	6	960	720	6
1	St Just to St Erth	15.9	1480	1850	21.9
2	St Erth to Nance (Illogan)	12.4	1110	910	34.3
3	Nance to St Newlyn East	15.9	1290	1240	50.2
4	St Newlyn East to St Wenn	13.4	1350	1280	63.6
5	St Wenn to Cardinham	11.3	1470	1310	74.9
6	Cardinham to Minions	13.5	2060	1430	88.4
7	Minions to (near) Lamerton	14.9	1590	2000	103.3
8	(near) Lamerton to Okehampton	17.4	1840	1870	120.7
9	Okehampton to Clannaborough Barton	15.3	1380	1560	136
10	Clannaborough Barton to Bickleigh	16.3	1600	1930	152.3
11	Bickleigh to Hagley Bridge	16.1	1950	1700	168.4
12	Hagley Bridge to Waterpits	15	2240	1980	183.4
13	Waterpits to Cossington	14.6	670	1210	198
14	Cossington to Cheddar	14	420	460	212
15	Cheddar to Long Ashton	15.2	1960	1960	227.2
16	Long Ashton to Northwick	13.9	930	1010	241.1
17	Northwick to St Briavels	15.5	2270	1610	256.6
18	St Briavels to Ross-on-Wye	16.4	2780	3280	273
19	Ross-on-Wye to Hereford	16	1490	1470	289
20	Hereford to Leominster	16.3	900	860	305.3
21	Leominster to Onibury	18	1550	1450	323.3
22	Onibury to Bridges	16.4	2610	2100	339.7
23	Bridges to Shrewsbury (Coton Hill)	16.1	1000	1670	355.8
24	Shrewsbury (Coton Hill) to Wem	12.8	690	620	368.6
25	Wem to Bell o' th' Hill	12.8	460	390	381.4
26	Bell o' th' Hill to Tarporley	14.9	1420	1450	396.3
27	Tarporley to Barnton	12.9	530	790	409.2
28	Barnton to Glazebrook	14.9	570	550	424.1
29	Glazebrook to Horwich	14.4	630	350	438.5
30	Horwich to Billinge	15.4	2330	2070	453.9
31	Billinge to Dunsop Bridge	16.4	1880	1960	470.3
32	Dunsop Bridge to Wray	14.2	1520	1720	484.5
33	Wray to Barbon	15.7	1680	1490	500.2
34	Barbon to Carlingill Bridge	16.1	2640	2370	516.3
35	Carlingill Bridge to Bolton (on Eden)	18.1	1980	2180	534.4

	Stage	Miles	Ascent ft	Descent ft	Total Miles
36	Bolton (on Eden) to Melmerby	11.5	700	560	545.9
37	Melmerby to Castle Carrock	14.9	1620	1700	560.8
38	Castle Carrock to Roweltown	16.5	890	1090	577.3
39	Roweltown to Newcastleton	11.9	1100	1040	589.2
40	Newcastleton to Hawick	20.3	1830	1800	609.5
41	Hawick to Yarrowford	13.8	1720	1520	623.3
42	Yarrowford to Peebles	15.8	2710	2730	639.1
43	Peebles to Carlops	15.7	2070	1680	654.8
44	Carlops to Kirkliston	15.7	940	1890	670.5
45	Kirkliston to Carnock	14.5	1200	1000	685
46	Carnock to Dollar	12.5	1100	1280	697.5
47	Dollar to Auchterarder	11.8	2020	1880	709.3
48	Auchterarder to Crieff	12.1	530	610	721.4
49	Crieff to Amulree	12.6	1880	1720	734
50	Amulree to Keltneyburn	15.3	1430	1950	749.3
51	Keltneyburn to Kinloch Rannoch	13.7	2600	2270	763
52	Kinloch Rannoch to Dalwhinnie	20.3	1550	1040	783.3
53	Dalwhinnie to Garva Bridge	20.9	1560	1790	804.2
54	Garva Bridge to Fort Augustus	17.2	2200	3110	821.4
55	Fort Augustus to Dundreggan	8	1360	1170	829.4
56	Dundreggan to Tomich	12.5	2120	2140	841.9
57	Tomich to Struy	11.2	1370	1500	853.1
58	Struy to Westermoy	15.3	1970	2000	868.4
59	Westermoy to Garve	9.8	1160	1150	878.2
60	Garve to Aultguish Inn	9	1340	860	887.2
61	Aultguish Inn to Croick Church	18.9	1710	2070	906.1
62	Croick Church to Rosehall	17.8	1360	1640	923.9
63	Rosehall to Lairg	9.2	870	630	933.1
64	Lairg to Crask Inn	13.6	900	460	946.7
65	Crask Inn to Badanloch Lodge	21	1470	1780	967.7
66	Badanloch Lodge to Forsinard	11.6	590	530	979.3
67	Forsinard to Altnabreac Station	14.1	920	910	993.4
68	Altnabreac Station to Watten	19.3	550	970	1012.7
69	Watten to Gills	13.8	610	610	1026.5
70	Gills to John O'Groats & Duncansby Head	8	590	680	1034.5

Accommodation

In planning a walk of over a thousand miles requiring bed & breakfast accommodation, the finding and booking of accommodation is a significant and time-consuming task. Occasionally, where there was no B&B, we stayed in a hostel and even more rarely had to self-cater. Thus we always had a roof over our heads and a comfortable bed to clamber into, which to my mind greatly added to the enjoyment of the walk. In addition I asked some of the B&Bs if I could send them a parcel of maps for the next stages of our walk, to await our arrival. Having staging posts at roughly ten day intervals meant we never had to carry more than eight Explorer maps.

I have always found it frustrating to have route guides that provide no information about accommodation, other than a list of Tourist Information Centre (TIC) telephone numbers. While I'm sure these centres are very good, there's an assumption that one has a car, so distance is no object and the rating system seems to depend on a lot of features of no interest to your average walker – being able to dry out your wet stuff is of far more importance than the number of cushions provided! Furthermore, there's quite a bit more accommodation out there than register with TICs.

So in planning the end to end walk, I searched the internet and used booklets that we had acquired over the years to devise my own accommodation list in the places I thought would be stage end points. This 2012 list is given as a *starting point* for finding accommodation. The listing given also includes some accommodation noted as we passed by. It is by no means a comprehensive list and things do alter; a B&B may change to self-catering or the owners may retire. In particular, in the current climate many hotels and inns are closing; moreover, information on the internet about these places is quite often out of date and there is no accommodation to be had. If stuck, it's worth looking on Google Maps for new accommodation. On the end-to-end walk, most places only had one or two rooms so we booked the accommodation six months in advance in order to make sure we had somewhere to stay in a location we wanted. Overall, we were very pleased by our choice of accommodation and these places have a star by them. Places that we found exceptionally good have been given two stars and we each chose just one place that we thought was in a class on its own so is awarded three stars; my three star B&B was at Newcastleton while my companion chose the Crask Inn. Finally and obviously, we have not investigated places we haven't stayed at!

St Just, Penzance, Cornwall
1. Old Fire Station, Nancherrow Terrace, TR19 7LA. Tel. 01736 786 463.
2. St Just B&B, 2 Fore St, TR19 7LL. Tel. 01736 787 784.
3. *YHA, Letcha Vean, TR19 7NT. Tel. 0845 371 9643.

St Erth, Hayle, Cornwall
Blanche Cottage, Fore St, TR27 6HT. Tel. 01736 756 623.

Illogan, Redruth, Cornwall
1. *Nance Farm B&B, TR16 4QX. Tel. 01209 842 244.
2. Aviary Court Hotel, Mary's Well, TR16 4QZ. Tel. 01209 842 256.

Cambrose, Nr Portreath, Cornwall
Elm Farm, TR16 5UF. Tel. 01209 891 498. Mob. 07711 808 595.

St Newlyn East, Cornwall
1. **Chy-an-Eglos B&B, 5 Churchtown, TR8 5LQ. Tel. 01872 519 270.
2. Degrembis Farmhouse B&B, TR8 5HY. Tel. 01872 510 555.

St Columb Major, Cornwall
Lowena B&B, Tregonetha, TR9 6EL. Tel. 01637 881 800. Mob. 0797 974 2220.

St Wenn, Nr. Bodmin, Cornwall
1. *Mrs Tucker, Treliver Farm, PL30 5PQ. Tel. 01726 890 286.
2. Mrs Hawkey, Tregolls Farm B&B, PL30 5PG. Tel. 01208 812 154.

Bodmin, Cornwall
The White Hart Inn, Pool St, PL31 2HA. Tel. 01208 72597.

Cardinham, Bodmin, Cornwall
1. **Mrs Pidcock, Old School House, PL30 4EA. Tel. 01208 821 303. Mob. 07977 106 963.
2. Mrs Dell'Erba, The Stables at Welltown, PL30 4EG. Tel. 01208 821 316.

Mount, Nr Bodmin, Cornwall
Mount Pleasant Farm, PL30 4EX. Tel. 01208 821 342.

St Neot, Liskeard, Cornwall
London Inn, School Hill, PL14 6NG. Tel. 01579 326 756.

Common Moor, Liskeard, Cornwall
Gimble Mill Farmhouse B&B, PL14 6EH. Tel. 01579 346 164.

Minions, Liskeard, Cornwall
1. *Cheesewring Hotel, PL14 5LE. Tel. 01579 362 321.
2. Te Chy, Post Office House, PL14 5LE. Tel. 01579 363 386.

Pensilva, Liskeard, Cornwall
1. Wheal Tor Hotel, Caradon Hill, PL14 5PJ. Tel. 01579 363 401.
2. Moor Gate B&B, Higher Rd, PL14 5NJ. Tel. 01579 362 386.
3. Mrs Tucker, Penharget Farm, PL14 5RJ. Tel. 01579 363 221.

Golberdon, Callington, Cornwall
Mrs Parkyn, Keadeen B&B, PL17 7LT. Tel. 01579 384 197. Mob. 07749 866 254.

Callington, Cornwall
Mrs Barriball, Polhilsa Farm, PL17 8PP. Tel. 01579 370 784.

Lamerton, Nr Tavistock, Devon
*Appledown House B&B, PL19 8SD. Tel. 01822 610 478.

Okehampton, Devon
1. *Mrs Goodwin, Capella, 31 Station Road, EX20 1EA. Tel.01837 53607.
2. Meadowlea, 65 Station Road, EX20 1EA. Tel. 01837 53200.

Morchard Road, Copplestone, Devon
1.Devonshire Dumpling, EX17 5LP. Tel. 01363 85102.
2. Woolsgrove Court, EX17 5LQ. Tel. 01363 84226.

Crediton, Devon
Great Park Farm, EX17 3PR. Tel. 01363 772 050.

Bickleigh, Tiverton, Devon
Fisherman's Cot, EX16 8RW. Tel. 01884 855 237.

Hagley Bridge, Waterrow, Nr Taunton, Somerset
*Mrs Gibbs, Hagley Bridge Farm, TA4 2BQ. Tel. 01984 629 026.

Waterrow, Nr Taunton, Somerset
Rock Inn, TA4 2AX. Tel. 01984 623 293.

Bishops Lydeard, Taunton, Somerset
1. Sully's Farm B&B, 20 High St, TA4 3AX. Tel. 01823 433 531.
2. Pound Farm, TA4 3DN. Tel. 01823 433 443.
3. Mrs Pattemore, West View, Minehead Road, TA4 3BS. Tel. 01823 432 223.

Cothelstone, Nr Taunton, Sonerset
Mrs Muers-Raby, Cothelstone Manor, TA4 3DS. Tel. 01823 433 480.

Waterpits, Broomfield, Bridgwater, Somerset
*Mrs Honeyball, Manor Farm, TA5 1AT. Tel. 01823 451 266.

Bridgwater, Somerset
1. Admirals Rest, 5 Taunton Road, TA6 3LW. Tel. 01278 458 580.
2. Brookland Hotel, 56 North St, TA6 3PN. Tel. 01278 423 263.

Chedzoy, Bridgwater, Somerset
Mrs Denning, Apple View B&B, Temple Farm, TA7 8QR. Tel. 01278 423 201.
Mob. 07709 253 366.

Cossington, Bridgwater, Somerset
*Mrs Bell, Brookhayes Farm, Bell Lane, TA7 8LR. Tel. 01278 722 559.

Cheddar, Somerset
1. *Bramblewood, Upper North St, BS27 3HX. Tel. 01934 744 310. Mob. 07787 548 455.
2. Mrs Agar, Old Police House, Norville Lane, BS27 3HJ. Tel. 01934 744 430. Mob. 07813 311 401.
3. Chedwell Cottage, 59 Redcliffe St, BS27 3PF. Tel. 01934 743 268.
4. The Gordons Hotel, Cliff St, BS27 3PT. Tel. 01934 742 497.
5. Cheddar YHA, Hillfield, BS27 3HN. Tel. 0845 371 9730.

Dundry, Bristol
Greenditch Farm, Dundry Lane, BS41 8JQ. Tel. 01275 472 854. Mob. 07557 681 438.

Long Ashton, Bristol
*Angel Inn, 172 Long Ashton Road, BS41 9LT. Tel. 01275 392 244.

Northwick, Pilning, Bristol, Avon
**The Old Piggery, Northwick Pig Farm, Aust Road, BS35 4HG. Tel. 01454 632 504.

St Briavels, Lydney, Gloucestershire
1. **St Briavels B&B, Church St, GL15 6RG. Tel. 01594 531 280; Mob. 07860 279 194.
2. St Briavels YHA, GL15 6RG. Tel. 0845 371 9042.

Ross-on-Wye, Herefordshire
1. *White House, 13 Wye St, HR9 7BX. Tel. 01989 763 572.
2. Linden Guest House, 14 Church St, HR9 5HN. Tel. 01989 565 373.
3. Sunnymount Hotel, Ryefield Road, HR9 5LS. Tel. 01989 563 880.
4. Broadlands B&B, Ledbury Road, HR9 7AU. Tel. 01989 563 663.

Hereford, Herefordshire
No. 21, Guest House, Aylestone Hill, HR1 1HR. Tel. 01432 279 897.

Leominster, Herefordshire
1. *Leominster YHA, Old Priory, HR6 8EQ. Tel. 01629 592 700 or 0845 371 9127. Self-catering.
2. Mrs Crick, Copper Hall, South St, HR6 8JN. Tel. 01568 611 622. Mob. 07811 417 669.
3. Highgate House, 29 Hereford Road, HR6 8JS. Tel. 01568 614 562.

Ludlow, Shropshire
1. *The Mount Guest House, 61 Gravel Hill, SY8 1QS. Tel. 01584 874 084.
2. Henwick House, Gravel Hill, SY8 1QU. Tel. 01584 873 338.
3. Number Twenty Eight, 28 Lower Broad St, SY8 1PQ. Tel. 01584 875 466.
4. Branlea, Brand Lane, SY8 1NN. Tel. 01584 876 093.

Bridges, Ratlinghope, Shrewsbury, Shropshire
*Bridges YHA, SY5 0SP. Tel. 01588 650 656.

Coton Hill, Shrewsbury, Shropshire
1. *Sydney House Hotel, Coton Crescent, SY1 2LJ. Tel. 01743 354 681.
2. Royal Oak, Ellesmere Road, SY1 2DZ. Tel. 01743 344 338. Mob. 07969 811 060.

Wem, Shropshire
1. *Mrs Dulson, Aston Lodge, Soulton Rd, SY4 5BG. Tel. 01939 232 577.
2. The Rowans, Mill St, SY4 5EX. Tel. 01939 234 708.
3. Old Rectory Hotel, Lowe Hill Road, SY4 5UA. Tel. 01939 233 233.

Tushingham, Nr Whitchurch
1. Mrs Stafford, Bell Farm, Bell o' th' Hill, SY13 4QS. Tel. 01948 662 074.
2. Mrs Kay, Tushingham House Farm, SY13 4QR. Tel. 01948 666 884.

Tarporley, Cheshire
1. Foresters Arms, 92 High Street, CW6 0AX. Tel. 01829 733 151.
2. Crown Hotel, 78 High Street, CW6 0AT. Tel. 01829 732 416.

Barnton, Northwich, Cheshire
The Beech Tree, 174 Runcorn Road, CW8 4HS. Tel. 01606 786 678.

Glazebrook, Warrington, Cheshire
Rhinewood Country House Hotel, Glazebrook Lane, WA3 5BB. Tel.0161 775 5555.

Hindley Green, Wigan, Lancashire
Alexandra Hotel, 619-621 Hindley Road. WN2 4EX. Tel. 01942 255 219.

Horwich, Bolton, Lancashire
1. Wendover Guest House, 603 Chorley Road, BL6 6LA. Tel. 01204 468 400.
2. Premier Inn (Reebok), Arena Approach 3, BL6 6LB. Tel. 0871 527 8116.
3. Archangelos, 82 Pennine Road, BL6 7HW. Tel. 01204 692 303.

Blackburn, Lancashire
1. Woodlands Hotel, 361-363 Preston New Road, BB2 7AA. Tel. 01254 681 368. May have closed.
2. Chimneys, Guest House, 139 Preston New Road, BB2 6BJ. Tel. 01254 665 026.
3. Oaklands Hotel, 102 Preston New Road, BB2 6BH. Tel. 01254 533 09.
4. Hillview Hotel, 90 Preston New Road, BB2 6BH. Tel. 01254 662 242.

Mellor, Blackburn, Lancashire
1. Old Dad's Barn, Mellor Lane, BB2 7EN. Tel. 01254 812 434.
2. The Millstone at Mellor, Church Lane, BB2 7JR. Tel. 01254 813 333.

Clayton-le-Dale, Blackburn, Lancashire
Myre Edge Farm, Showley Road, BB1 9DR. Tel. 01254 814 140.

Dunsop Bridge, Clitheroe, Lancashire
1. Wood End Farm, BB7 3BE. Tel. 01200 448 223.
2. Root Farmhouse B&B, BB7 3BB. Tel. 01200 448 214.

Wray, Lancashire
George & Dragon, Main St, LA2 8QG. Tel. 01524 221 403.

Barbon, Kirkby Lonsdale, Cumbria
1. Barbon Inn, LA6 2LJ. Tel. 015242 76233.
2. Mrs Groves, Kemps Hill B&B, Moorthwaite Lane, LA6 2LP. Tel. 015242 76322.

Howgill, Nr Sedbergh, Cumbria
1. Mrs D M Parker, Thwaite, LA10 5JD. Tel. 01539 620 493.
2. Mrs J Postlethwaite, Bramaskew, LA10 5HX. Tel. 01539 621 529.
3. Mr J W Mattinson, Ash-Hining Farm, LA10 5HU. Tel. 0153 962 0957. Mob. 07774 281 767.

Tebay, Penrith, Cumbria
1. The Old School, CA10 3TP. Tel. 01539 624 286.
2. Primrose Cottage, CA10 3TL. Tel. 01539 624 791.
3. Cross Keys Inn, Main Street, CA10 3UY. Tel. 01539 624 240.

Crosby Ravensworth, Penrith, Cumbria
Mrs Brass, Low Row Farm, CA10 3JJ. Tel. 01931 715 238.

Maulds Meaburn, Penrith, Cumbria
1. Mrs Tuer, Crake Trees Manor, CA10 3JG. Tel. 01931 715 205.
2. Mrs Bousfield, Trainlands, CA10 3HX. Tel. 01768 351 249.

Bolton (on Eden), Appleby-in-Westmorland, Cumbria
1. Mrs Gill, North End Farmhouse, CA16 6AX. Tel. 017683 61959.
2. Mrs Neilson, Tarka House, CA16 6AW. Tel. 017683 61422.

Gullom Holme, Milburn, Penrith, Cumbria
Low Howgill B&B, CA10 1TL. Tel. 01768 361 595. Mob. 07801 868 740.

Melmerby, Penrith, Cumbria
1. *Mrs James, Greenholme, CA10 1HB. Tel. 01768 881 436.
2. Gale Hall Farm, CA10 1HN. Tel. 01768 881 254.
3. Mrs Morton, Meadowbank, CA10 1HF. Tel. 01768 881 652.

Castle Carrock, Carlisle, Cumbria
*Mrs Robinson, Gelt Hall Farm, CA8 9LT. Tel. 0122 867 0260.

Talkin, Brampton, Cumria
1. Blacksmiths Arms, CA8 1LE. Tel. 016977 3452.
2. Hullerbank Farmhouse, CA8 1LB. Tel. 016977 46668.

Walton, Nr Brampton, Cumbria
Sandysike House, CA8 2DU. Tel. 0169 772 330. (Bunkhouse, B&B, camping)

Roweltown, Carlisle, Cumbria
*Low Luckens Organic Resource Centre, CA6 6LJ. Tel. 01697 748 331. Self-catering.

Newcastleton, Roxburghshire
1. ***Mrs Bogg, Woodside, North Hermitage St, TD9 0RZ. Tel. 013873 75431.
2. Grapes Hotel, 16 Douglas Square, TD9 0QD. Tel. 013873 75245.
3. Liddesdale Hotel, 17 Douglas Square, TD9 0QD. Tel. 013873 75255.

Hawick, Scottish Borders
1. **Mrs M. Richards, Oakwood House, Buccleuch Rd, TD9 0EH. Tel. 01450 372 814.
2. North Bridge Guest House, 28 North Bridge St, TD9 9QS. Tel. 01450 376 200.
3. Mrs Redpath, Elm House Hotel, 17 North Bridge St, TD9 9BD. Tel. 01450 372 866.
4. Bank Guest House No. 12 High St, TD9 9EH. Tel. 01450 363760.
5. The Laurels Guest House, 8 Princes St, TD9 7AY. Tel. 01450 370 002.
6. Weensland Guest House, 6 Weensland Rd, TD9 9NP. Tel. 01450 373 506.

Yarrowford, Selkirk, Scottish Borders
*Broadmeadows YH, Old Broadmeadows, Yarrowford, TD7 5LZ. Tel. 01750 76372. Self-catering.

Selkirk, Scottish Borders
1. Ivy Bank, Hillside Terrace, TD7 4LT. Tel. 01750 212 270.
2. Mrs Chalmers, Sunnybrae House, 75 Tower St, TD7 4LS. Tel. 01750 21156.
3. The Firs, Manorhill Rd, TD7 5LS. Tel. 01750 20409.

Traquair, Innerleithen, Scottish Borders
Mrs Hudson, Quair View, EH44 6PL. Tel. 01896 830 506.

Peebles, Scottish Borders
1. Mrs Henderson, Lindores Guesthouse, 60 Old Town, EH45 8JE. Tel. 01721 722 072.
2. Whities B&B, 69 High St, EH45 8AN. Tel. 01721 721 605.
3. Mrs Mitchell, Viewfield, 1 Roseta Road, EH45 8JU. Tel. 01721 721 232.
4. Crown Hotel, 54 High St, EH45 8SW. Tel. 01721 720 239.

West Linton, Scottish Borders
1. The Meadows B&B, 4 Robinsland Drive, EH46 7JD. Tel. 01968 661 798.
2. Mrs Drummond, West Lynn Grove B&B, 6 West Lynn Grove, EH46 7HX. Tel. 01968 660 321.
3. Mrs J Muir, Jerviswood, Lintonbank Drive, EH46 7DT. Tel. 01968 660 429.

Nr West Linton, Scottish Borders
Mrs Simpson, Fairslack Farm, EH46 7AS. Tel: 01968 661303.

Carlops, Nr Penicuik, Midlothian, Scotland
1. *Mrs Burke, Patieshill Farmhouse B&B, EH26 9NB. Tel. 01968 660 551.
2. Allan Ramsay Hotel, EH26 9NF. Tel. 01968 660 258.

Balerno, Edinburgh
Haughead Farm, EH14 7JH. Tel. 01314 493 875.

Kirkliston, West Lothian
1. **Mrs P. Hull, 7 Almondhill Cottages, EH29 9EQ. Tel. 0131 333 1570.
2. Mrs Westacott, Craigbrae Farm, EH29 9EL. Tel. 0131 331 1205.

Dunfermline, Fife
Grange Farmhouse B&B, Grange Road, KY11 3DG. Tel. 01383 733 125.

Carnock, by Dunfermline, Fife
*Mrs K. Craig, Carneil Farmhouse B&B, Carneil Rd, KY12 9JJ. Tel. 01383 850 285.

Dollar, Clackmannanshire
1. *Tigh Ur, 4 Hillfoots Road, FK14 7BB. Tel. 01259 742 786.
2. Castle Campbell Hotel, 11-13 Bridge St, FK14 7DE. Tel. 01259 742 519.

Glendevon, Perthshire
Tormaukin Inn, FK14 7JZ. Tel. 01259 781 252.

Auchterarder, Perthshire
1. Allandale House, 17 High St, PH3 1DB. Tel. 01764 663 329.
2. Craigpark B&B, Craigpark, Townhead, PH3 1JG. Tel. 01764 662 564.
3. Basset Cottage B&B, 20 Townhead, PH3 1AH. Tel. 01764 662 237.
4. Alma Guest House, Hunter St, PH3 1PA. Tel. 01764 662 894.

Crieff, Perthshire
1. **Galvelmore House B&B, 5 Galvelmore St, PH7 4BY. Tel 01764 655 721.
2. Comely Bank Guest House, 32 Burrell St, PH7 4DT. Tel 01764 653 409.
3. Crieff Hotel, 43-49 East High St, PH7 3HY. Tel. 01764 652 632.
4. James Cottage Guest House, 77 Burrell St, PH7 4DG. Tel. 01764 655 814.
5. Mrs Clifford, Merlindale, Perth Road, PH7 3EQ. Tel. 01764 655 205.

Sma' Glen, Crieff, Perthshire
1. *Mr Devaney, Corrymuckloch B&B, PH8 0EG. Tel. 01350 725 206. Mob.
0782 527 9671.
2. Mrs Waugh, Fendoch Guest House, PH7 3LW. Tel. 01764 655 619 or Tel.
01764 653 446.

Keltneyburn, Perthshire
1. **Mrs E. Matheson, Blairmason, Donafuil, PH15 2LE. Tel. 01887 830 321.
2. Coshieville House, PH15 2NE. Tel. 01887 830 319.

Kinloch Rannoch, Perthshire
The Macdonald Loch Rannoch Hotel, PH16 5PS. Tel. 0844 879 9059.

Dunalastair, Kinloch Rannoch, Perthshire
Mrs Wilson, The Gardens, PH16 5PB. Tel. 01882 632 434. Need transport to
get there.

Drumochter Pass, Dalwhinnie, Inverness-shire
Balsporran Cottage B&B, PH19 1AF. Tel. 01528 522 389.

Laggan, Inverness-shire
**Mrs Dodds, The Rumblie, Gergask Avenue, PH20 1AH. Tel. 01528 544
766.

Fort Augustus, Inverness-shire
1. *Mrs S. Johnson, Caledonian Cottage, Station Rd, PH32 4AY. Tel. 01320 366 305.
2. Oaklands B&B, Fort William Rd, PH32 4BQ. Tel. 01320 366 487.
3. Mrs Pell, Beaufort House, Station Rd, PH32 4AY. Tel. 01320 366 208.
4. Nia Roo Lodge, Fort William Rd, PH32 4BQ. Tel. 01320 366 783.
5. Lorien House, Station Rd, PH32 4AY. Tel. 01320 366 736.
6. Mrs Paterson, Cartref B&B, Fort William Rd, PH32 4BH. Tel. 01320 366 255.
7. Bank House, Station Road, PH32 4AY. Tel. 01320 366 755.
8. Fort Augustus Youth Hostel, Morag's Lodge, Bunoich Brae, PH32 4ND. Tel. 0845 293 7373.
9. Stravaigers Lodge (Independent Hostel), PH32 4BG. Tel. 01320 366 257.

Dundreggan, Glenmoriston, Highlands
1. **Mrs B. Taylor, Graineag B&B, Redburn, IV63 7YJ. Tel. 01320 340 295.
2. Serendipity, Dalchreichart, IV63 7YJ. Tel. 01320 340 356.

Tomich, Cannich, by Beauly, Inverness-shire
*Tomich Hotel, IV4 7LY. Tel. 01456 415 399.

Cannich, by Beauly, Inverness-shire
1. Mrs Mann, Westward B&B, IV4 7LT. Tel. 01456 415 708.
2. Kerrow House, IV4 7NA. Tel. 01456 415 243.

Struy, by Beauly, Inverness-shire
1. *Cnoc Hotel, IV4 7JU. Tel. 01463 761 264.
2. Drumbae Guest House, IV4 7JS. Tel. 01463 761 378.
3. Struy Inn, IV4 7JS. Tel. 01463 761 308.

Marybank, by Muir of Ord, Ross-shire
Balloan House, IV6 7UW. Tel. 01997 433 696.

Westermoy, Urray, Muir of Ord, Ross-shire
*Mrs Coli, Tiree House, IV6 7UX. Tel. 01997 433 410.

Contin, by Strathpeffer, Ross-shire
1. Achilty House B&B, IV14 9EG. Tel. 01997 421 355.
2. An Darach Guest House, Craigdarroch Drive, IV14 9EL. Tel. 01997 421 408.
3. Coul House Hotel, IV14 9ES. Tel. 01997 421 487.

Garve, Ross-shire
1. **Mrs L. Turner, Birch Cottage, 7 Station Rd, IV23 2PS. Tel. 01997 414237.
2. Mrs Frost, Hazelbrae House, IV23 2PX. Tel. 01997 414382.

By Garve, Ross-shire
1. *Aultguish Inn, Main Road, IV23 2PQ. Tel. 01997 455 254.
2. Inchbae Lodge, IV23 2PH. Tel. 01997 455 269.

Bonar Bridge, Sutherland
1. **Mrs S. Thomson, Kyle House, Dornoch Road, IV24 3EB. Tel. 01863 766 360.
2. Monarch House, Dornoch Road, IV24 3EB. Tel. 01863 766 147.
3. Dunroamin Hotel, Lairg Road, IV24 3EA. Tel. 01863 766 236.
4. Bridge Hotel, Dornoch Road, IV24 3EB. Tel. 01863 760 030.

Oykel Bridge, Rosehall, by Lairg, Sutherland
Oykel Bridge Hotel, IV27 4HE. Tel. 01549 441 218.

Rosehall, by Lairg, Sutherland)
*Achness Hotel, IV27 4BD. Tel. 01549 441 239.

Lairg, Highlands
1. *Nip Inn, Main Street, IV27 4DB. Tel. 01549 402 243.
2. Mrs Morgan, Lochview, Lochside, IV27 4EH. Tel. 01549 402 578.
3. Tordarroch, Builnatobrach, IV27 4DB. Tel. 01549 402 282.
4. Park House, Station Rd, IV27 4AU. Tel.01549 402 208.

Crask, By Lairg, Highland
***Crask Inn, IV27 4AB. Tel. 01549 411 241.

Garvault, by Kinbrace, Sutherland
Garvault Hotel, KW11 6UF. Tel. 01431 831 224.

Forsinard, Sutherland
*Forsinard Hotel, KW13 6YT. Tel. 01641 571 221.

Watten, By Wick, Caithness
1. **Brown Trout Hotel, Station Road, KW1 5YN. Tel. 01955 621 354.
2. Corrigall B&B, Thurso Road, KW1 5XG. Tel. 01955 621 955.

Upper Gills, Canisbay, By John O'Groats, Caithness
*Mrs Barton, Bencorragh House, Upper Gills, KW1 4YD. Tel. 01955 611 449.

Gills, Canisbay, By John O'Groats, Caithness
Teuchters, KW1 4YB. Mob. 0756 370 2970 or 0779 389 1167.

John O'Groats, Caithness
1. *Mr Asher, Hamnavoe, KW1 4YR. Tel. 01955 611 776. Mob. 0787 678 4847.
2. Mrs Cowe, Windy Ha B&B, KW1 4YR. Tel. 01955 611 470.
3. Mr Grant, John O'Groats Guest House, The Broo, KW1 4YR. Tel. 01955 611 251.
4. Mrs Simpson, Anchorage B&B, KW1 4YS. Tel. 01955 611 384.
5. Seaview Hotel, County Road, KW1 4YR. Tel. 01955 611 220.

Transport

On the whole, the walk is designed so that stage ends are in places where B&B or hostel accommodation is available. However, there are some places, particularly in north Scotland where a pick-up of some description is required. This section also has some comments about getting to Land's End and leaving John O'Groats by public transport. Note that transport times do alter, so you should check for the latest information. If you need picking up or bags carrying, it's always worth asking your B&B host. Failing that, the local taxi firm can usually help. In addition, Brigantes Baggage Carriers, Tel. 01729 830 463, cover much of the north of England.

Reaching Land's End

There is a good train service from most parts of the country to Penzance. This takes around 8 hours from the Manchester area. Penzance bus station is adjacent to its railway station.

Bus: Service 1/1A is a two-hourly service to Land's End running Monday to Saturday at 09:40, 11:40, 13:40, 16:40 and 17:45; the journey takes about an hour. There is no Sunday service.

Clannaborough Barton

Taxis: 1. White Swan Taxi Service, Crediton. Tel. 01363 777 786.

2. Crediton Taxis. Tel. 01363 777 714

3. Express Cars of Crediton. Tel. 01363 777 177.

Bus: There's a two hourly 315 bus service Monday to Saturday through Bow and Copplestone to Crediton and Exeter. From April 2011, it leaves the Spar shop in Bow at 16:27 and 18:17, Copplestone Stone at 16:36 and 18:25 and arrives in Crediton 16:45 and 18:32. For the Crediton B&B, alight as near the railway station as possible.

From April 2011 the 315 bus is two hourly Monday to Saturday from Exeter to Copplestone and Bow via Crediton. It leaves Crediton at 08:37 and 10:42.

Onibury

Bus: The 435 bus Service between Shrewsbury and Ludlow is hourly Monday to Saturday. It goes from Onibury Level Crossing to Ludlow at 16:36 and 17:31; there is a request stop only bus at 18:46. The journey to Corve Street in Ludlow takes 10 minutes.

Service 435 from Ludlow to Shrewsbury is roughly hourly Monday to Saturday. It takes 10mins to Onibury and leaves Corve St in Ludlow at 09:10 and 10:20.

Taxis: 1. Annette's Tel. 01584 878 787

2. Trev's Tel. 01584 873 939

3. O'Grady's Tel. 01584 877 996

4. Price's Tel. 01584 872 941

5. Mear's Tel. 01584 879 090. Mob. 07970 031 422

Carlingill Bridge

Taxis: 1. Grab-a-Cab, Old Tebay. Tel. 07765 575 828.

2. Atlantis Taxis, Maulds Meaburn. Tel. 07738 151 078.

3. Easter Bunny's Taxi Company, Selside. Tel. 07570 844 952.

Roweltown

1. Brampton Cars, Brampton. Tel. 0169 773 386 or 0169 774 2851

2. Airbus 2000, Brampton. Tel. 0169 773 735.

Kinloch Rannoch

Broons Taxis, Kinloch Rannoch. Tel. 01882 632 331.

Dalwhinnie and Garva Bridge

For these stages we stayed two nights at The Rumblie in Laggan and if we had not had family members doing pick-up, we would have asked our B&B hosts to do the transporting. There is also Kingussie Taxis. Tel. 01540 661 343.

Croick Church

Taxis: Ronnie's Taxis (Ardgay) Tel. 01863 766 422. Mob. 07778 181 208. This is the nearest taxi service to the church and is what we used to get to and from Bonar Bridge.

Lairg

Northern Sights Taxis, Lairg. Tel. 01549 402 399.

Badanloch Lodge

There are no taxi services nearby and we arranged to be picked-up here by the Forsinard Hotel.

Leaving John O'Groats

Bus: From Jan 2012 Stagecoach Highland X97 bus leaves John O'Groats Road End (by the Seaview Hotel) at 09:21 to Dunbeath War Memorial at 10:26 where there is a connecting X99 bus to Inverness Bus Station arriving at 12:43. Trains: Inverness 14:48 to Perth 16:51; Perth 17:00 to Edinburgh 18:25; Edinburgh 18:52 to Crewe 21:59; Crewe 22:13 to Stockport 22:38.

Unbelievably, this all worked exactly as stated, taking us only a single day to return to Stockport. From the bus, we spotted the end-to-end lady we had met in West Linton; she was scrabbling up the bank to avoid the traffic hurtling down the A9! In Inverness we had time for lunch and a look round the Victorian Market, full of interesting independent shops, before catching the train. It was on the journey from John O'Groats, as the train raced along, that the large amount of distance we had walked started to sink in....

Good Reads

There are many publications but most tend to be overviews of the end-to-end route taken, rather than detailed route descriptions down to field level. Personally, I prefer those that concentrate on the route details. So, I think that the following are particularly well worth looking at if you are planning to undertake an end to end walk.

1: Andrew McCloy *Land's End to John O'Groats*. Coronet Books 1994. This gives an overview of a west, central and eastern route, using trails known at that time. This would be a recommended starting point for planning your own route, although many more trails are now available.

2: Mike Salter *Land's End to John O'Groats*. Folly Publications 2006. The author's interests of visiting historic monuments, churches and castles are evident in this description, which is claimed to be a thousand miles. It avoids the national trails more than other routes. Two alternative routes through north Scotland are described. One is through Inverness, where the A9 features heavily, and the other is through Fort William and Fort Augustus. Beyond Fort Augustus, use is made of old drove and military tracks where possible.

3: Andy Robinson *The End to End Trail*. Cicerone 2007. This is the most detailed and challenging of all the routes described, with a daily average mileage of nearly 20 miles. It provides a comprehensive description with detailed maps (down to field level) to link the most strenuous of the national trails in England and it connects to the West Highland Way in Scotland. Beyond Fort William, the route looks very tough in terms of the landscape traversed and the underlying terrain.

4: John Butler's web site *An End To End Walk* at http://www.jbutler.org.uk/e2e/ is also recommended. The walk has clearly been a labour of love undertaken over many years and there is a stunningly good photographic record of the journey. Unusually, the walk starts with the south coast of Cornwall. Good use is made of available national trails and other semi-official routes to reach Fort Augustus. Thereafter available tracks are linked to reach John O'Groats.

5: Scottish Rights of Way & Access Society *Scottish Hill Tracks* Fifth Edition 2012. If you're planning your own route across Scotland then this is a must read, although I personally find the details of the routes a bit sparse. I used the 1995 third edition in planning the route we undertook.

6: The Long Distance Walkers Association web site at www.ldwa.org.uk has a searchable database of trails and is an excellent resource.